READING THE FIGURAL,

or, Philosophy after the New Media

Post-Contemporary Interventions

Series Editors: Stanley Fish & Fredric Jameson

READING THE FIGURAL,

or, Philosophy after the New Media   *D. N. Rodowick*

DUKE UNIVERSITY PRESS   DURHAM & LONDON 2001

© 2001 Duke University Press   All rights reserved
Printed in the United States of America on acid-free paper ∞
Designed by Rebecca M. Giménez   Typeset in Minion with
Franklin Gothic display by Tseng Information Systems, Inc.
Library of Congress Cataloging-in-Publication Data
appear on the last printed page of this book.

For **DOMINIQUE** and **SARAH**

CONTENTS

PREFACE

"A good book," writes Jean-François Lyotard in *Discours, figure,* "would be one where linguistic time (the time of signification and of reading) would itself be deconstructed: that the reader could start wherever s/he wishes and in whatever order, a book for grazing" (18; my translation). Like Lyotard's *Discours, figure,* this is not a good book, an artist's book, but rather a book of philosophy that still dreams of signification. But perhaps philosophy can operate its own figural discourse: that of the rhizome. In this book, the figural functions as a nomadic concept circulating by knight's moves among seven essays while mutating in its forms and dimensions through its encounters with diverse philosophers. Most of the essays included here have appeared in some published form, though all have been rewritten and most expanded to bring forward their conceptual links. These links are detachable, however. The organization of the book is somewhat nonlinear, and the ordering of chapters is nonchronological, though not random. A rhizome, then, and not a book; each chapter may be read out of order, and perhaps readers will want to find their own paths. Consider the following, then, as one map for reading the figural.

Although these essays were written over a period of seventeen years, they emerged from a common research project responding to what was, for me, a fundamental intuition. Although I am a child of the seventies, and thus of a visual semiology inspired by the linguistics of Ferdinand de Saussure, a form of structural analysis inspired by Claude Lévi-Strauss, and a theory of ideology forwarded by *Screen,* my encounters with deconstruction and its critique of logocentrism convinced me early on that a linguistically inspired semiology was inadequate for the study of visual culture. Moreover, with the explosive

appearance of Music Television in 1980, and the increasing proliferation of digital technologies and digital imaging throughout the mass
media thereafter, I also came to the following conclusions. Contemporary electronic media were giving rise to hybrid and mutant forms that
semiology was ill equipped to understand. Moreover, the creation of a
social theory and mode of philosophical analysis adequate for understanding the new images also seemed to require a deconstruction of
the aesthetic philosophy, ingrained for more than two hundred years,
that was inhibiting cultural studies from understanding this phenomenon in its depth and complexity. New media were emerging from a
new logic of sense—the figural—and they could not be understood
within the reigning norms of a linguistic or aesthetic philosophy. For
these reasons, mass culture has always posed a problem for the idea
of the aesthetic. (This is nowhere more clear than in the philosophy
of Lyotard, as I will discuss in chapter 1.) The new media have exac-
erbated this situation. Philosophy traditionally considers the aesthetic
as a separate domain of experience whose unity is preserved in two
ways. First, it defines the self-identity of the arts through the opposition of linguistic to plastic expression and then produces a hierarchy of
value based on this opposition that renders thought equivalent to linguistic sense. Second, the aesthetic is distinguished from the social and
from everyday life as a separate philosophical domain. Paradoxically,
the modern idea of the aesthetic was invented at a point when the value
and meaning of artistic work became increasingly deracinated from its
prior religious and political contexts, instead circulating in the paths
of commodity exchange. In other words, there is an inverse ratio between philosophy's assertion of the "disinterestedness" of art and the
historical transformation of aesthetic value by the forms of commodity
exchange.

Therefore, as a philosophical problem, the concept of the figural as
presented in this book is meant to intervene in three areas: as a semiotic
theory that comprehends what the image becomes when freed from the
opposition of word to image; as a social theory that contests, through
a deconstruction of the aesthetic, the dominance of art and social life
by the commodity form; and finally as a theory of power that unlocks
the figural as a historical image or social hieroglyph wherein the spatial
and temporal parameters of contemporary collective life can be read

as they are reorganized by the new images and new communications technologies.

The figural, then, describes a general transformation of the discursive field, both in the history of philosophy and in the visual history of the twentieth century, which has been dominated by photography, cinema, and electronic as well as digital media. Chapter 1 introduces the figural in its variegated forms. I begin by discussing Lyotard's radical transformation of the concept of discourse in *Discours, figure* as well as his aesthetic essays of the seventies and eighties. Here discourse becomes figural when its proper forms are disordered by spacing and desire. In his later discussions of postmodernism and the sublime, Lyotard raises the political stakes of the figural while introducing to it a temporal and historical dimension, though not without entertaining certain contradictions involving aesthetic judgment and the ontological status of art. Where this chapter begins by exploring how a concept of *discourse* is disordered by the figural, I conclude by discussing how *visuality* is rendered as a paradoxical concept in its encounters with the figural, and in the technological transformations of space and perception that are the hallmarks of the "new" media. Here reading the figural requires not only a critical genealogy of the aesthetic but also an analysis of the spatial and temporal architectures of power produced by audiovisual regimes.

Chapter 2 continues laying out the philosophical stakes of the book. While wishing to maintain the "figural" as a heuristic and mobile concept, here I make my most direct case for defining it. The figural is treated not only as a transformation of discourse but more importantly as a means for understanding the functioning of power in given societies. My point of departure is Gilles Deleuze's reading of the work of Michel Foucault. Two concepts are especially important here. First is the *diagram* as a cartography of strategies of power. In many respects, this concept resembles the historical image as discussed in chapter 5: it shares with Walter Benjamin's thought the quality of immanence, and with Siegfried Kracauer's a sense of the abstraction of social space by capitalist relations of force. Second is that of the *audiovisual archive*. In Deleuze's reading, every epoch is defined by its own practices of knowledge and strategies of power, which are composed from regimes of visibility and procedures of expression. The example of the audiovisual archive demonstrates with philosophical precision how the figural operates as intercalations of the expressive and the visible in different dimensions of space: *correlative space,* which associates what can be said with what can be seen or observed; *complementary space,* which establishes relations between discursive and nondiscursive spaces as the institutional basis of power; and *collateral space,* where enunciation is defined by specific mutations of plastic space and linguistic reference, figure and text. The Modern era required a strict separation between plastic space, which organizes representation, and linguistic reference, which excludes it. But in the era of electronic and digital communication, the figural is increasingly defined as a semiotic regime where the world of things is penetrated by discourse, with its ambiguous power to negate and divide or differ, and the independent weight of things congeals into signs that proliferate anonymously in everyday life. This is a condition that Foucault characterized as *similitude.* Here the figural disturbs the collateral relation that divides figure and text into two separate streams, one characterized by simultaneity (repetition-resemblance), the other by succession (difference-affirmation). Lessing divided the linguistic from the plastic arts by opposing succession to simultaneity. Now the temporality of "discourse" has thoroughly permeated plastic space, and this is one way of reading the figural.

Chapter 3 returns implicitly to Lyotard in taking up problems of figure and text as a general transformation of discourse, though here in the domain of film theory. This chapter examines the contributions of contemporary film theory to the figural by looking at two approaches to "filmic writing"—Thierry Kuntzel's concept of figuration, or semiotic "constellations" in the film-work, and Marie-Claire Ropars-Wuilleumier's theory of *cinécriture.* In both cases, deconstruction is invoked to think the figural as that which eludes the opposition between the linguistic and the plastic arts. Kuntzel's approach is modeled on Freud's notion of the dream-work as read through Derrida's essay "Freud and the Scene of Writing." Here film's logic of signification reprises the plastic and mutable qualities of dreaming and fantasy life in that the logical relations (conscious and/or unconscious) that bind images into a discourse are intelligible only in the degree in which the presence of the visual field is broken and the text of the film is understood as a figural script. Alternatively, Ropars focuses on modernist film practice for her theory of filmic writing. Looking at modernist montage strategies, she proposes to replace a theory of the sign with the model of the *hieroglyph*—a hybrid written and imaged form of figural activity that confounds the phonocentric model of signification. However, her theory assumes oppositions based on aesthetic value, as well as a model of enunciation and textual system, which nonetheless re-invoke many of the semiological and aesthetic concepts she wishes to deconstruct.

Chapter 4 takes a closer look at the philosophical paradoxes of the aesthetic as introduced in chapter 1 through a critical reading of Kant's *Critique of Judgment* as played out in Jacques Derrida's book *Truth in Painting,* and his essay "Economimesis." I trace a genealogy of the aesthetic as a concept of modern philosophy that emerges slowly throughout the eighteenth century in the work of Christian Wolff, Alexander Baumgarten, and Gotthold Lessing, passing through Kant's Third Critique, and finally culminating in Hegel's *Lectures on Aesthetics.* Here Derrida's concepts of the *parergon, economimesis* and *exemplorality* demonstrate how the idea of the aesthetic supposed a systematic retreat from the social and historical forces informing representational practices that were, and continue to be, concomitant with the increasing commodification of art. In asserting the value and self-identity of autonomous art as free of monetary value, and by proclaiming the autonomy of the aesthetic as an interior and subjective activity as opposed to social and collective ones, idealist philosophy creates an inverse ratio between the ontological and the historical. Here the idealist elaboration of the aesthetic as an ontological question increasingly excludes consideration of the (capitalist) material and historical forces continually transforming representational practices and aesthetic experience. Assertions of the autonomy and universality of the aesthetic become ever more shrill in direct relation to the dominance of representational practices by the logic of commodities and the emergence of a mass public, a process that has been reconfirmed by the controversies involving the defunding of the National Endowment for the Arts and National Endowment for the Humanities by cultural conservatives. By demonstrating the ontological insecurity of the aesthetic, deconstructive philosophy helps produce a critical genealogy that may liberate new concepts for critiquing the permeation of capital into all areas of cultural experience, and for understanding critically the social function of new media as a figural discourse.

Chapter 3 examines the figural as a semiotic concept where the model of the linguistic sign is replaced by that of the constellation and dream-work in Kuntzel, and the hieroglyph and filmic writing in Ropars. In Chapter 4 the figural is treated as a philosophical concept whose force demonstrates the ontological insecurity of the aesthetic. Chapter 5 examines the figural as a historical concept in the idea of "historical images" elaborated in Walter Benjamin's and Siegfried Kracauer's studies of film and photography. "Spatial images are the dreams of society," wrote Kracauer in the 1920s. "Wherever the hieroglyphics of these images can be deciphered, one finds the basis of social reality." Through the concept of the *social hieroglyph,* or the spatial forms of an emergent mass culture, the role of critical theory is to decipher social tendencies revealed in ephemeral cultural phenomena while unlocking the specific forms of historical knowledge they communicate. The culture of the mass, despised by traditional aesthetics, contains a measure of reality in the form of social knowledge no longer accessible through Art or Philosophy. This is why history is important as a form of intermediate knowledge, as Kracauer's final book, *History: The Last Things before the Last,* makes clear. Both Kracauer and Benjamin considered the concepts and logic of aesthetic philosophy to be an obstacle to understanding the social knowledge embedded in mass cultural phenomena and the space-time of everyday life. Neither traditional art, whose ideal is the identity of nature and form, nor idealist philosophy, which defines reason as the identity of thought and being, can comprehend the social hieroglyph because nature has been transformed by capital, and the isolated interiority of the aesthetic subject has disappeared into the mass. Through Benjamin's concept of mimesis as "nonsensuous similarity," and Kracauer's concept of the social hieroglyph as an allegorical form, the *historical image* is defined as a figure capable of representing and comprehending those dimensions of social and aesthetic experience under capital to which philosophy and art are blind. These two thinkers particularly valued film and photography not only for preserving and communicating this historical knowledge in an "alienated" form but also for redeeming the utopian potential of mass culture as a form of nontotalizing knowledge.

Chapter 6 extends this line of thought in another direction by examining Gilles Deleuze's two-volume theory of film in the context of the philosophy of history, specifically that of Michel Foucault. In *Cinema 1: The Movement-Image* and *Cinema 2: The Time-Image,* Deleuze argues that a tectonic shift marks the history of audiovisual culture in the twentieth century. The displacement of the movement-image by the time-image involves a turn both in the order of signs, requiring two different semiotics, and in the image of thought that characterizes the philosophical orientation of the two regimes. Although Deleuze insists that his two books are not "histories," in this chapter I argue that the shift from the movement-image to time-image can also be understood as the displacement of a Hegelian philosophy of history-in-images with a Nietzschean conceptualization of history articulated through new audiovisual forms in cinema, television, and digital media, no less than in the philosophical influence of Nietzsche in the writings of Michel Foucault, Gilles Deleuze and Félix Guattari, and other French historians and cultural theorists. In French film since 1958, a new orientation of the visible with respect to the expressible — of image and sound as well as movement and time — also marks a new conceptual relation with questions of history, memory, and politics wherein the figural is considered again as both time-image and historical image.

In the era of the figural, thought relies no less poignantly on opening a space in language responsive to the figural transformations of the eye than on releasing figures in space as discourse or expression. However, the machinic processes of the figural are also organized by technologies of control: the dream of the individual's total control over information is simultaneously the potentiality for absolute surveillance and the reification of private experience. The task of chapter 7 is to inquire whether we have indeed entered a new historical era, fueled by the increasing predominance of digital technologies and computer-mediated communications, that Deleuze called "control societies." If so, this era will be defined by its own specific knowledge practices, strategies of power, and modes of subjection. I argue that three fundamental questions need be asked to understand digital culture critically. First, how is the nature of representation changing with respect to the digital creation, manipulation, and distribution of signs? Second, how is the form of the commodity changing along with its determinations of the space and time of the market and the nature and value of exchange? And finally, how is our experience of collectivity changing; or in Deleuze and Guattari's terminology, how are our "collective arrangements" in social time and space being restructured by the new communication architectures of digital culture? In exploring these questions, I also argue that we need a social theory that is as attentive to creative strategies of resistance as it is to mechanisms of power and social control. Thus a social theory of digital culture, as a new regime of the figural and a mutation of the audiovisual archive, should be able both to critique the models of social control and surveillance imposed by "cybernetic capitalism" and to evaluate the new modes of existence that appear as contemporary communications technologies reorganize and reconfigure the lived spatiality and temporality of everyday life. In these new modes of existence, we might locate new possibilities for living, both resistant to, and critical of, the forces of global capital.

ACKNOWLEDGMENTS

All thought, one should admit, is the result of fortuitous encounters. This morning my three-year-old daughter placed in my hands Jacqueline Duhême's lovely book *L'oiseau philosophie*, wherein we read together Deleuze's words: "When one works, it is in an absolute solitude. . . . Only, this solitude is densely populated. Not with dreams, fantasies, or projects, but rather with encounters" (28; my translation).

This book is the result of myriad chance encounters, without doubt too numerous to mention. Among the most important inspirations for this book, however, were conversations with Hal Foster with respect to the 1996 questionnaire on visual studies published in *October* 77. I first conceived the possibility of this book in preparing my own response, and I thank the editors of *October* for allowing me to include my contribution here as part of chapter 1.

Chapter 2 first appeared in *Camera Obscura* 24 (1991): 11–44, with Liz Lyon and Raymond Bellour as indispensable interlocutors. Janet Bergstrom, Sharon Willis, Janet Wolff, and Peter Wollen also provided timely and important criticisms. "The Figure and the Text" was originally published in *Diacritics* 15, no. 1 (spring 1985): 34–50, and my thanks go out to Kimball Lockhart for his encouragement and editorial skills, and Raymond Bellour for his commentary. "The Ends of the Aesthetic" is a revised and expanded version of "Impure Mimesis, or The Ends of the Aesthetic," originally published in *Deconstruction and the Spatial Arts: Art, Media, Architecture,* ed. Peter Brunette and David Wills (Cambridge: Cambridge University Press, 1993), 96–117. Peter and David have been constant and valued interlocutors over the years as I have explored the consequences of Derrida's thought with respect to my own evolving arguments. John Guillory, Michael

Ann Holly, Keith Moxey, and Janet Wolff also supplied helpful advice and critical commentary. "The Historical Image" first appeared as "*The Last Things before the Last*: Kracauer and History," *New German Critique* 41 (spring–summer 1987): 109–39. Dudley Andrew, Miriam Hansen, and Tom Levin all provided encouragement and friendly criticism in the preparation of this research. "A Genealogy of Time" is a revised and expanded version of "A Genealogy of Time: the Nietzschean Dimension of French Cinema, 1958–1998," originally published in *Premises: Invested Spaces in Visual Arts and Architecture from France, 1958–1998* (New York and Paris: Solomon R. Guggenheim Museum and Centre Georges Pompidou, 1998). Dudley Andrew, my coconspirator in this project, was an inescapable influence as always. The essay originated in conversation with András Bálint Kovács. I would also like to thank John Hanhardt, Alison Gingeras, Bernard Blistène, and Charles Stivale for their input and encouragement. "An Uncertain Utopia—Digital Culture" is a revised and expanded version of several lectures: "Audiovisual Culture and Interdisciplinary Knowledge," originally published in *New Literary History* 26 (1995): 111–21; "Von Neumann's Architecture, You're Living in It!" previously unpublished; "Cybernetic and Machinic Arrangements," also unpublished; and "An Uncertain Utopia," which appears in *[me'diən]: Vierzehn Vorträge zur Medienkultur,* ed. Claus Pias (Weimar: Verlag und Datenbank für Geisteswissenschaften, 1999). As this chapter evolved, I benefited from the support and critical input of a number of friends including Raymond Bellour, Ralph Cohen, Douglas Crimp, Kate Nesbitt, Richard Sennett, Jennifer Wicke, Grant Kester, Lorenz Engell, and Claus Pias. In all cases, permissions to reprint have been acquired where necessary from the original publishers, and I thank them for their indulgence.

The reproductions of René Magritte's *This Is Not a Pipe* and *Les deux mystères* are made by the kind permission of Charly Herscovici. Many thanks to Lauren Rabinovitz for advice on how to make my images look better, and to Matt Reynolds for production help.

Throughout the final preparation of this book, Tim Murray was an invaluable friend and reader. I am also grateful for the comments of an anonymous reader at Duke University Press and, of course, Duke's own "man in black," Ken Wissoker. And finally, *gros bisous* to Dominique Bluher and Sarah Rodowick for just putting up with me throughout.

1. PRESENTING THE FIGURAL

The Idea is not the element of knowledge but that of an infinite "learning,"
which is of a different nature to knowledge. —Gilles Deleuze, *Difference
and Repetition*

The Idea of the Figural What does it mean "to have an Idea"? An
Idea is not a thought one possesses, nor is it a representation to one's
self. It does not even occur at the site of representation itself. An all
too rare event, to have an Idea is to confront a problem or question
that, no matter how inchoate or intangible, seizes us in thought and
launches us, almost unpredictably, on a peculiarly philosophical ad-
venture: the creation of concepts. Sometimes the concept is entirely
new, an autopoiesis. And sometimes the concept is adopted, though
in passing from the care of one philosopher to another it may lose its
cherished and comfortable identity to set off on a series of mad adven-
tures like some Don Quixote who leaves us trailing, like poor Sancho
Panza, in its wake.

There was a point in time when I wanted to write a book about *the
figural*. In my mind the name of this concept is indelibly associated with
the work of Jean-François Lyotard, in particular his magisterial *Discours, figure* and the writings on art of the seventies and eighties that
followed. And if this book takes the form it does now, it is partly because I felt the urgency of an unpaid debt. Most of the essays in this
book were written under the influence of, or in confrontation with,
Lyotard's writings on art and aesthetics. In homage to Lyotard, I can
thus present a first definition of the figural as a force that erodes the
distinction between letter and line: "The letter is a closed, invariant
line; the line is the opening of the letter that is closed, perhaps, else-

where or on the other side. Open the letter and you have image, scene, magic. Enclose the image and you have emblem, symbol, and letter" (*Discours* 268).[1] But at a deeper level, Lyotard's figural is more than a chiasmus between text and figure—it is a force that transgresses the intervals that constitute discourse and the perspectives that frame and position the image. Moreover, for Lyotard, the figural is inseparable from an aesthetic where the most precious function of art is to create the last preserve of nonideological meaning. But more on this later. In a larger sense, the figural defines a semiotic regime where the ontological distinction between linguistic and plastic representations breaks down. This opposition, which has been the philosophical foundation of aesthetics since the eighteenth century, is explicitly challenged by the new electronic, televisual, and digital media. In this respect, the electronic media have inaugurated a new regime of signs and new ways of thinking, which is why philosophy runs "after" the new media.

I will consider more deeply what this "after" means as a temporal concept in my discussion of Lyotard's concept of postmodernism. And at the same time, we will find that the "new" media include some very old friends. For the moment, though, I want to emphasize that although the concept of the figural has manifold roots, my thinking here proceeds along two principal branches that never cease to articulate one onto the other. On one hand, the figural demands a genealogical critique of the aesthetic and other philosophical concepts that are implicitly deconstructed in the new media. But this detour through the history of philosophy also inspires a confrontation with contemporary theories of sign and discourse in relation to image or figure. In this manner, *Reading the Figural* presents a philosophical journey where I seek out allies both for deconstructing the opposition of word and image and for creating new concepts for comprehending the figural as a transformation of discourse by recent technologies of the visible. Lyotard is also an exemplary figure here in his keen awareness of how thinking the figural requires a transformation of philosophical style tantamount to a performance of force within writing itself. Indeed, among the more interesting dimensions of each of the writers encountered in this book are not only the concepts they construct but also their performance of the figural within the space of their own thought and writing.

So if I have adopted the figural in part from Lyotard, the problematic nature of the concept owes as much to my reading of Derrida, Kracauer, Benjamin, Foucault, and Deleuze. Making the figural circulate among these philosophers is not a process of building an ever more accurate picture of a concept. To retain its power as a problem, the figural must also claim the powers of virtuality, becoming a nonrepresentational image that morphs continually with respect to the problems posed in each chapter. This is an act of thinking wherein the figural constantly shifts identity in its contact with different philosophers and where the philosophical questions themselves change when recontextualized by the concept of the figural. One can no more say that the figural is interior to the philosophy of Lyotard and thus adopted from him, since the concept is just as likely to resituate Lyotard on another plane of immanence where his philosophy must be rethought or thought anew.

I began thinking seriously about Lyotard in the mid-eighties. But the Idea of the figural had seized me some years before, indeed long before I was able to give it a name. Although Lyotard for one would undoubtedly have disparaged this idea, I like to think of the figural as my "Music Television epiphany." What MTV signified for me was an implicit philosophical confrontation between the history of contemporary film theory as a semiological endeavor and the increasing appearance of digitally manipulated images on American television. Computer-generated and manipulated images are now commonplace, of course. But when these images began appearing in television advertising, music videos, and other venues, it was impossible not to be astonished by how fluidly text was spatialized, thus losing its uniform contours, fixed spacing, and linear sense, and how precisely space was "textualized"; that is, how the Euclidian solidity of the image was fragmented, rendered discontinuous, divisible, and liable to recombination in the most precise ways. Suddenly the image was becoming articulable, indeed discursive, like never before. I do not want to imply, however, that my argument is founded on a technological transformation of discourse. And if later I draw an association between the figural and the virtual, this has little to do with the already debased informatic currency of the term. No matter how "figural" they may be, the so-called new media still fall within a long and complex genealogy whose lines of descent include both the history of philosophy and the history of art. The figural is something both new yet very old. Lyotard himself readily admits that the figural has an autonomous existence with a long history. The history of art, or more deeply the history of representation, is full of "authorless" examples of figurative text and textualized figures. Simply recognizing their existence already pushes the limits of modern philosophy's distinction between the arts of succession and those of simultaneity, but it does little to deconstruct it. Nonetheless, in their own peculiar transformations of discourse, perhaps the new media help us challenge in new ways the ontological gesture that separates the arts of time from the arts of space. In so doing, the visible is no longer banished from the realm of discourse, which is reserved for linguistic sense as the site of rational communication, and the articulable, or *énonçable*, can regain its powers of plastic transformation.

Lyotard's Leap into the Void: The Aesthetic before the New Media   At the beginning of this project, I was drawn to Lyotard not only for what he called his "defense of the eye" but also in recognition of his courage for asking, at a time when the influence of structuralism was still strong, What is discourse? How this question is asked affects not only a semiology of the image (whose opacity is either reduced to the grid of signification or valued as that which exceeds it) but also the concept of signification itself. The figural challenges the self-identity of discourse "to dissolve the present prestige of the system and the grid [*clôture*] in which the men of language believe that have confined all meaning" (*Discours* 12). Especially in the first half of his book, Lyotard argues convincingly that the limit of the Saussurean project—from the structural anthropology of Claude Lévi-Strauss, to Roman Jakobson's linguistics, and even to the earlier works of Jacques Lacan—was the inability to comprehend the problem of meaning as other than linguistic. Although Lyotard addresses neither photography nor cinema here, by extension his challenge must also confront a semiology of the image. The genius of Christian Metz, for example, was to have demonstrated early on that there could not be a cinematic *langue* as witnessed in his successive attempts to measure the image against concepts of the signifier, sentence, *énoncé*, text, and finally enunciation.[2] But this was an attempt to revise Saussureanism, to enlarge its terrain so that the image could be ringed by signification. Despite the brilliance of his arguments concerning image and signification, Metz maintained a concept of discourse that could not break with its linguistic foundations. Alternatively, the thought that most captivated me in Lyotard and Foucault was how "discourse" was transformed by the figural and so became a new concept.

Despite wrestling with Lyotard's texts early on, Derrida's critique of logocentrism, and above all his critique of Saussure in *Of Grammatology*, marked my first conceptual liberation from the linguistic signifier. Of course, whereas the early Derrida accomplished much in liberating the signifier from its linguistic shackles, his model was still very much a literary one. And despite his profound and original redeployment of concepts of spacing, *écriture*, and text, I have never been wholly convinced that deconstruction steps beyond a horizon delimited by a restricted concept of text.

Lyotard's *Discours, figure* (1974) should be revisited as one of the fundamental texts of poststructuralism because like Derrida, he understood well that a philosophical critique of structuralism had to demolish the twin pillars of Saussure and Hegel, indeed that Hegel's dialectic and theory of the symbol were the hidden engines of a structuralist logic. And like Derrida, Lyotard returned to Freud to articulate a nondialectical logic of signification, though in a very different way than Lacan, whose intellectual debt to Aléxandre Kojève's Hegel is omnipresent in the *Écrits*.

Lyotard's intuition, whose enormous debt to Freud's theory of phantasy is acknowledged throughout *Discours, figure,* is that figure and discourse cannot be opposed. Unlike the history of the aesthetic, which has much at stake in distinguishing them as incommensurable ontological territories, in Lyotard's view, figure and discourse are divided not by a bar but rather by only the slightest of commas. Nonetheless this comma does separate art and "discourse" in a way that erodes signification through spatialization. To read or to hear is not the same as to see. Or rather, in passing from text to image, the status of the eye changes. "One does not read or hear a painting," according to Lyotard. "Seated at a table, one identifies or recognizes linguistic unities; standing in representation, one seeks out plastic and libidinal events" (*Discours* 10).

Spatialization, then, occurs in two dimensions that are themselves incommensurable: designation and desire. *Discours, figure* is in fact a book whose argument is marked by this broad division. The first half is devoted primarily to the problem of discourse and the relation between text and figure. Here the role of designation or reference is fundamental, since it riddles discourse with a spatialization that the linguistic system cannot master. Where designation is formal or formed space, in the second half of the book, desire arises as an in-formal space, the force of the figural. Beyond or beneath the uncontainable spatial force of designation will be the unrepresentable force of primal phantasy where the figural expresses the disarticulatory powers of the death drive.

Before walking down this path, however, the problem of designation must be deepened. One does not approach the figural by deconstructing discourse or passing beyond it. Rather, in a first movement, Lyotard finds that figure resides in discourse as the intractable opacity of the visible. This is a "spatial manifestation that linguistic space cannot incorporate without being shaken, an exteriority that it cannot interiorize as *signification*" (*Discours* 13). Every discourse is haunted by perspective in that in order to *mean,* it must *refer.* Lyotard calls this function indexicality, though the concept functions in a very different way from the semiotic of Charles Saunders Peirce. In designating an object that it wants to present to the interiority of thought, discourse opens a view, indicates a vis-à-vis, over there, that rattles the invariability of both linguistic system and diacritical space with plasticity and desire, an expansive horizon. Indexicality means that discourse is shot through with the visible: the énoncé must point beyond its borders to objects positioned in space with respect to it. It is plunged into a gestural space that surrounds it, and it is riddled from within by deictic holes whose function is to indicate positionality in space (here/there) and in time (now/then).

In Émile Benveniste's view, these *indicateurs,* or "shifters" in English, are tokens, empty placeholders of subjectivity and position. But the "here" of Lyotard is grounded in the body. It indicates a correlative function between body and space that is incommensurable with the experience of language but nonetheless draws on it to indicate spatial and temporal location. Deictic markers have a curious status, then, since signification is inseparable from designation as, in Hegel's *Phenomenology,* a negativity that "spaces" language. "With shifters," Lyotard argues, "language is pierced with holes where the gaze insinuates itself, the eye sees outside and anchors itself there, but this 'outside' is itself returned to the primary intimacy of the body, its space (and time)" (*Discours* 39). Lyotard calls this a "diadeictical" relation. This is a sort of dialectic, though it is not a discourse because reference belongs to showing, not signifying—it is insignifiable. An indexical relation of a special kind, this sensate activity is a *Dasein* rather than a *Sinn,* whose movement is closer to the Bergsonian movement-image of Deleuze than the abstract movement of the dialectic, since it relates to the scanning of the eye and the mobility of the body in space. Nonetheless this is a negativity of a special type, an opening in space between eye and object as a kind of moving frame that is formal or formalizing. Indexicality gives us a formed space.

For Hegel, of course, this is a problem that the dialectic and the theory of the symbol must master. The sensate "this" (*das sinnliche Diese*) that we aim for does not belong to language: it is inexpressible and therefore neither true nor rational.[3] Lyotard's originality is to show that if language is powerless with respect to showing, as Hegel argues, it is not because the showable is *opposed* to the expressible but rather because it is too close to it. Rather than being opposed, the one the negation of the other in dialectical conflict, the visible and the expressible are bound in a heautonomous relation: though distinct and incommensurable, they are intimately related.

Discourse, then, is haunted by space in particular ways. There are, of course, *figure-images* given to be seen as organizations of plastic space. But there is also, in the very heart of discourse, a *figure form*—a nonlinguistic space within language that makes it *expressible,* in short, poetic or aesthetic. Therefore signification and expression are two different dimensions of discourse distinguished by their different relations to figural space: "Discourse has this space along its edges, a space that gives it its object as image; it also has this space at its heart, which governs its form. But do not be mistaken: the 'interiority' of figural space to discourse is not dialectical" (*Discours* 52).

Suddenly discourse, which wants to say everything and to make everything sayable, finds itself torn from within by both an unconscious of language and an unconscious of visibility. Each is formed from an interval defining a sort of negativity, or rather a negative space. In language, this is difference expressed as opposition that is ultimately rendered as the system of signification; in seeing, the spatial act of reference may express or indicate, but it does not *mean*. Signification operates through invariant codes, a rule-governed system of intervals where the logic of communication operates in a transparent space of pure reciprocity between sender and receiver. Alternatively, for Lyotard, visuality invades discourse as "a distance to be crossed that indicates the location where what I say is placed as a horizon that opens ahead of words and pulls them to it, the negativity that is the foundation of our spatial existence, mobility constituting depth" (*Discours* 56). Here the asignifying mobility of visual space functions as a space of transgression, at least for the ratio defined by language. The differences of the linguistic system and the distances of deixis are two forms of negativity, one rigid and one mobile, which are not dialectical. They neither cancel each other out nor transcend each other. Instead, discourse is redefined, not as the hierarchy of one to the other, but as the heterogeneous space of their cohabitation.

What of the figural in relation to signification and designation? Signification, or the order of language, is marked by structural opposition. But designation is formed from a sight that spaces the subject with respect to sign and discourse according to its internal indications of subject, place, and time. One is marked logically by opposition and the other by negativity.[4] In this manner, Lyotard shifts importantly the philosophical definition of discourse by demonstrating the complex imbrication of designation and signification within its very form and structure. Discourse is crossed by, and crosses between, two spaces or dimensions—that of subject and system—that spatialize it and hold it open. The figural, however, is marked by difference in yet another sense. The logic of difference is "neither the smooth negation that holds separate the elements of a (linguistic) system, nor this deep denegation that opens the referential or representational field with respect to discourse" (*Discours* 137). The figural is the avatar of another order whose relation to space, no less than discourse, is vexed. The figural is unrepresentable, beneath or behind representation, because it operates in an other space "that does not give itself to be seen or thought; it is indicated in a lateral fashion, fugitive at the heart of discourse and perception, as that which troubles them. It is the proper space of desire, the stakes in the struggle that painters and poets have ceaselessly launched against the return of the Ego and the text" (135). The blinding energy of desire *flows,* rather than is articulated, and it is these decoded flows that make language expression or poetry and painting an art. To the extent that space or representation belongs to the figural, then, it is produced differently from signification and designation, "for *the spacing or separation is not that of two terms* placed on the same plane, inscribed on the same support, and in principle reversible given certain conditions, but rather, the 'relation' of two heterogeneous 'states' that are, however, juxtaposed in an irreversible anachrony" (137). This difference is not another form of the negative. In its relation to primal phantasy and unconscious desire, the figural is an agent for the positivity of desire that returns to unsettle the "No" of discourse and that of perception. Difference is reborn here as the form of repetition characteristic of the death drive that undermines any concept of structure with its uncanny force.

The scandal of the figure is that it is both inside and outside of discourse. Language is no longer a homogeneous space marked by linguistic unities. The eye is in the word because there is no articulation without the appeal to an outside constituted as a visibility where objects are designated in space, as well as a spatialization that resides at the heart of discourse as an unconscious force — desire. Lyotard understands force, unlike Foucault or Deleuze and Guattari, as Freudian rather than Nietzschean. Nonetheless in this respect Lyotard is a curious ally with *Anti-Oedipus.* To the extent that force is desire, it is not a structure but rather a form, though a highly mobile and unstable one; it does not signify, yet it has "sense." The unconscious is not structured like a language, nor is it even a structure:

> To make the unconscious a discourse is to omit the energetic [*énergétique*]. To do so is to remain complicit with a Western ratio that destroys art along with dreaming. One does not at all break with metaphysics by finding language everywhere; rather, one accomplishes/fulfills it along with the repression of sensation [*sensible*] and *jouissance.* The opposition is not between form and force, for here one confuses form and structure. Force is nothing other than the energy that folds or wrinkles the text and makes of it an aesthetic work, a difference, that is, a form. . . .

And what do you believe is discourse? Cold prose hardly exists save at the lowest levels of communication. Discourse is thick. It does not only signify, it expresses. And if it expresses, it is because movement resides within it as a force that overturns the table of significations with a seism that makes sense. . . . Discourse calls the eye; it is itself energetic. To trace the path of the eye in the field of language, this fixed movement, is to follow the hills and valleys of metaphor, which is the accomplishment of desire, and one will see how exteriority as force, formed space, can reside in interiority as closed signification. (*Discours* 14–15)

This is how Lyotard radically redefines what is called "discourse." Discourse encompasses expression and affect, as well as signification and rationality, because it is also subject to a libidinal economy: the calm surface of linguistic system is always being churned by the force of desire.

There is a risk of scolding Lyotard for invoking yet another hermeneutic model of linguistic surface and libidinal depth here. And indeed there is some lack of care in the philosophical language he chooses in the book's introductory section, which is so deeply influenced by a similar language in Freud. For this reason, it is all the more necessary to insist that for Lyotard, discourse and figure operate as two different and incommensurable dimensions that nonetheless never cease to communicate with each other even within the space of the eye. Every "discourse," whether linguistic or plastic, has both textual and figurative aspects that operate as two dimensions of meaning: signification and "sense." Fortunately the English word "sense" shares much with the French. Where meaning is reduced in signification to a grid of differences systematically articulated as binary pairs, sense opens meaning to both spatiality and affect: direction, sensation, intuition. What separates these two dimensions, yet always rearticulates them in ever-renewable combinations, is what Lyotard calls his *utopie Freudienne,* the disarticulatory force of the so-called death drive. What Lyotard calls "depth" (*profondeur*) is not a negativity that refutes the flatness of surface. It operates in another dimension, the laterality or scansion, pure difference, that disunites and recombines both discourse and figure as the force of desire. Among the conceptual avatars of *Discours, figure*—Cézanne and Mallarmé on the side of art, Freud and Frege on that of discourse—figural space is presented as that which radically "exceeds the power of a reflection that wants to signify it, to render it in language, not as an object but as a definition" (*Discours* 19). This is fair warning to all books of philosophy, for "sense is always presence as the absence of signification. . . . Here is the death drive, which is always scheming with Eros-Logos. Constructing sense is nothing other than deconstructing signification. There is no model for this evasive figuration" (19). Depth refers, then, not to a topology or hierarchy but to a force or energy that flows uninhibited through figure and discourse, de-forming the presence of the image in space no less than that of meaning in language. The figural is neither figure nor figurative. Depth means that figural space falls "beneath" perception as the phantasmatic matrix that "reconnects the visible neither to the I-You of language nor to the One of perception, but rather to the 'it' of desire. And not even to the immediate figure of desire, but rather to its operations" (23).

These operations of desire are Freud's *Traumarbeit,* or even more profoundly, those of primal phantasy. For Lyotard, the dream-work —whose figures include condensation, displacement, considerations of representability, and secondary revision—presents an exemplary (visible) space where figure and text are engaged in a mutually deconstructive activity of a seeing that undoes saying. Moreover, these figural procedures are nonlinguistic—each draws on a spatial dimension that is excluded from the linguistic system. If, as Freud wrote, the dream-work does not "think," this places it on the other side of articulated language. It neither calculates nor judges; it transforms or perhaps de-forms (Freud's term is *umformen*) rational sense in particular ways. Condensation liberates an energy that erodes the unities of signification, morphing discursive space by destabilizing the spacing between letters and disregarding invariant graphic traits. "Considerations of representability" (*Rücksicht auf Darstellbarkeit*) stage the mise-en-scène of dreaming through selecting and juxtaposing visual and linguistic material, but also, more importantly, by strategically replacing portions of text with figures. Condensation, as a compression and distortion of both word- and thing-presentations, works together here with displacement to (un)form a rebuslike space whose materials have been selected for their figural potential. Secondary elabora-

tion functions, finally, to provide a veneer of signification to this sur-
real worked matter, to suggest a solution to the rebus, which, it must
be said, is to anchor the dream in a linguistic sense. But this satisfac-
tion, which rests on judgment, is a lure. Having no pretensions to uni-
vocity, the figural can neither lie nor mislead. If the dream-work has
sense, it will be found not in the order of language and judgment but
in the mise-en-scène of a force of transgression. This is the power of
the figural.

But this same activity exhibits a yet more profound division between
language and desire. The plasticity of the dream-work is not a model
of visual semiosis: "The dream-work is not a language; it is the effect
on language of a force exerted by the figural (as image or form). This
force transgresses the law: it impedes hearing; it makes seen. Such is the
ambivalence of censorship. But this mixture is only the first edition. It
is found not only in the order of dreams, but also in that of 'primal'
phantasy itself: discourse and figure at the same time, the work lost in
a hallucinatory scenography, originary violence" (*Discours* 270).[5] The
figural, then, is not primarily a montage or chiasmus between the said
and the seen; it is force or unbound energy, not simply unseen (the letter missed, an image not visible) but radically unconscious. It is a third
dimension, neither sayable nor showable.

To recapitulate, then, the force of the figural organizes space in three
incommensurable dimensions. The order of discourse is breached from
within by two different, if heautonomous, negations (opposition, division) and two kinds of spacing: that of the linguistic system organized
by invariant patterned differences, and that of reference or designation, which holds in perspective the sign and the object to which it
refers. There is no univocal discourse, then, since saying and showing are inseparable, if incommensurable, acts. Text is always already
figured; no amount of linguistic abstraction can banish spacing from
it. Figure and text together are thus part of discourse as if different
ratios of line to letter. The figural, however, operates in another dimension, that of unconscious desire, and returns to discourse as an infernal
repetition, the force of transgression. The figural operates on an "other
scene," that of the unconscious and primal phantasy. "The space that
they inscribe or that they engender," writes Lyotard, "is therefore an
other space. Through its incessant mobility it differs from that of the

system; from that of reference it differs in that it takes words for things" (*Discours* 275).⁶

Figure and text organize, in Deleuze's useful distinction, a *collateral space*. This is the order of discourse, the spacing characteristic of enunciation. And if the eye and position of the observer are introduced, the enunciative act is caught up in another circuit of relations that Deleuze calls *correlative space*. But the figural is not present in either of these dimensions, nor can it be represented by discourse, for it is not space but desire or force. Nonspatial, it is therefore nonrepresentational. Yet it can be apprehended in that the force of transgression acts on space, expressing itself in disordered forms and hallucinatory images. It is through these acts of "un-forming" that the different dimensions of the figural can be defined as image, form, and matrix.

The *figure-image* belongs to the seen, whether an actual or hallucinated image: "It shows me the painting, the film, an object set at a distance, theme; it belongs to the order of the visible as a revealing trace" (*Discours* 271). Here the figural operates as transgression or deconstruction of the percept, unraveling the contours of the image. The *figure-form* is unseen yet belongs to the visible as the architecture that sets it in place. It is the regulating trace or gestalt of the image, the scenography of representation. This is a Euclidian space, or an Apollonian good form that the figural undermines as a Dionysian force or "energetics indifferent to the unity of the whole" (277).

Image and form could belong to the order of discourse, whether linguistic or plastic. They are intelligible and therefore spatial forms. The matrix, however, is neither form nor structure, neither discursive nor visible. "The *matrix-figure*," writes Lyotard, "is invisible in principle, subject to primal repression, immediately intermixed with discourse, primal phantasy. It is nonetheless a figure, not a structure, because it consists in a violation of discursive order from the outset, in a violence done to the transformations that this order authorizes. It cannot be intelligibly apprehended, for this very apprehension would make its immersion in the unconscious unintelligible" (*Discours* 271). By the same token, the matrix can function as neither origin nor *arché*. Perhaps one could say that it is *an-archic*. "Far from being an origin, the phantasmatic matrix attests, rather, to the contrary: that our origin is the absence of origin, and that everything that presents itself as the object of a primal discourse is a hallucinatory figure-image, located precisely in this initial nonplace" (271).

As force, the figural exhibits all the qualities that Freud associated with the unconscious: absence of negation or contradiction; extreme mobility of libidinal energy and intensity of cathexes; intemporality; and dominance of the pleasure principle.[7] Unlike the qualities of discursive space, negation is unknown to it. This means, first, that desire is assertive and positive; as decoded (in fact, *uncodable*) flow, it is uncompromised by negation. A second consequence is even more destabilizing for a structuralist reading of Freud: the unconscious is not structured like a language. The positivity of desire means that unconscious "judgments" have neither modality nor quality. And equally important, as agent of the primary processes, the figural ignores the fundamental constraints of discourse; indeed, it derails perception, motricity, and articulated language as forms of the secondary processes. It belongs to neither the order of language nor representation — it is unrepresentable. "What I want to show is this," writes Lyotard. "The matrix is not a language, not a linguistic structure [*une structure de langue*], not a tree of discourses. Of all the orders of figure, it is the most remote from communicability, the most withdrawn. It harbors the incommunicable" (*Discours* 327). The matrix engenders forms and images, and even verbalizations that want to speak of them, but it itself is neither figure nor figuration, nor is it a discourse. The figural runs counter to representation, whether plastic or linguistic. What these distinctions make clear is the radical positioning of the matrix, which belongs neither to plastic nor to textual space. Neither visible nor readable,

> it is difference itself, and as such does not suffer even the minimum of structural *opposition* [*mise en opposition*] required for spoken expression or the forming or imaging required for plastic expression. Discourse, image, and form are all equally missing from it, yet it resides in all three spaces. Anyone's works are only the offshoots of this matrix; we might perhaps catch a fleeting glimpse of it through their superimposition, in depth. But the confusion of spaces that predominates "originarily" is such that words are being treated as things and as forms, things as forms or words, forms as words or

things; deconstruction bears no longer only on the textual trace as in the figural image, or on the regulating trace as in the figural form, but on the scene where the matrix is held, which belongs at the same time to the space of the text, to that of the mise-en-scène, and to that of the stage: writing, geometry, representation — each one deconstructed through the inmixing of the two others. (*Discours* 278–79)

Primal phantasy, then, is other to the system of language as well as visuality. As Freud insists in *The Interpretation of Dreams,* the objects of our internal perceptions are *virtual.*[8] Verbalizations or word-presentations are unconstrained by the rules of syntax. For its part, the image is disordered by the reign of the pleasure principle. Phantasmatic images, or thing-presentations, are "perceptions" unanchored by recognizable objects present in the external world. Moreover, the self-identity of images is fractured and polysemic no less than verbalizations that are rendered polyvocal. "The images the matrix generates are both sharply defined and blurred at the same time. The effect is as if multiple scenes, having certain segments or areas, some plastic element only, in common, were superimposed on the same film, but at the right exposure" (*Discours* 327–28).[9] Every phantasmatic "representation" is a figure of paradoxical sense whose outlines are clear, yet subject to continual change, for even the most singular image superimposes multiple sites, whose origins are contradictory drives and part-objects, and multiple temporalities in the confluence of (achronological) memory traces. Figural "form" is without unity because primal phantasy is always marked by the simultaneous activity of multiple forms or images as well as affects. Nor can desire operate as a unifying force, since primal phantasy is always the "expression" of multiple drives.

The force of the figural, then, deconstructs not only discourse but also the figure as recognizable image or proper form. This force is difference itself: "Not just the trace, not just presence-absence, indifferently discourse or figure, but the primary process, the principle of disorder, the incitement to jouissance. Not some kind of interval separating two terms that belong to the same order, but an utter disruption of the equilibrium between order and disorder" (*Discours* 334–35). In other words, the figural ignores the rule of opposition to ally itself with the force of difference. This is the secret and power of its "virtuality." In transgressing the intervals that constitute discourse, and the distances that constitute representation, the space of the unconscious, like the phantasized libidinal body, is neither unified nor unifying. It contains multiple scenes on the same stage and gathers in the same image incompossible spaces and times. For Lyotard, the example of primal phantasy stages most deeply the powers of the figural with respect to "aesthetic" form. Not a proper form, certainly, but "a form in which desire remains engaged—*form in the grip of transgression*—but it is also, potentially at least, *the transgression of form*" (350).[10] This is the fate of representation or discourse under the sway of the death drive: "To take the drive for a binding force would be worse than to take the unconscious for a language and to make the id [Ça] talk. Because, after all, there is some liaison in the unconscious—a phantasmatic and formal liaison, Eros. But the unconscious is not what it is (i.e., unknowable), except in so far as the liaison separates, comes undone, and it is here that the death drive reveals itself. . . . Now we understand that the principle of figurality, which is also the principle of unbinding (the baffle), is the death drive: 'the absolute of antisynthesis': utopia" (354).[11]

As I have already argued in *The Difficulty of Difference,* it is the role of art to make this "Freudian utopia" present in our everyday lives as a heterocosmic force. Paul Klee called this a *Zwischenwelt,* or "between-world," where the transformative, or better, transgressive force of the figural can operate. Klee's concept implies that desire opens a transcendental dimension whose possibilities for change are revolutionary and that functions universally, even though it is the special domain of artists: "I often say that worlds are opened and open themselves unceasingly in us, worlds that themselves belong to nature, but which are not visible to everyone. . . . I call it the *between-world,* because I sense it present between the worlds that our senses can perceive externally, and because internally I can assimilate it well enough to be able to project it outside myself in symbolic form."[12] There is a special force of transformation in everyone, transgressing both good form and common sense, which does not belong to anyone, though the artist has the special role of making it present in, shall we say, the spatially perceptible world. Here the special province of art is not to communicate but to transmit the incommunicable. Or as Lyotard would later state, "to present the unpresentable." The between-world is fueled by the virtuality of unconscious perception as "the genesis of a creation *that has no model.* The problematic is neither to constitute an intelligible world nor to make it recognizable; it is that of a '*between-world,*' an other possible nature that prolongs creation, making visible what is not, without, however, falling prey to a subjective imagination" (*Discours* 224).

Art neither visualizes nor symbolizes the figural in the usual sense. Lyotard finds that unlike the cubists, Klee did not "write" with geometric volumes; rather, he was concerned with the deconstruction of representation and the invention of what I have called a "nonspatial perception," which is also a space of the virtual and the unforeseen, a pictorial polyphony that is the special province of the Zwischenwelt. Where the figural inhabits art, space does not present an image; it bears witness to or exhibits a *work:*

> Klee's "between-world" is not an imaginary world; it is the exhibited workshop of the primary process. One does not speak it or "see" it; rather, it works. There the line does not note the signifiers of a discourse or the contours of a silhouette. It is the trace of an energy that condenses, displaces, figures, and elaborates without regard for the recognizable. "The essential is to decide to what ends the activity of making visible [*das Sichtbarmachen*] is exercised. To fix in memory what has been seen, or rather to also make manifest what is not visible?" Here the invisible is not the reverse of the visible, its back. It is the unconscious inverted—plastic possibility. (*Discours* 238)[13]

Where Deleuze presents the figural as a metaphysics of time, an *entretemps,* as we shall see in chapter 6, for Lyotard it is a philosophy of desire. The force of virtuality is not that of time but that of the primary processes, the force of unconscious desire.

The Freudian utopia of the figural was to find other forms in Lyotard's subsequent work, but in every case, desire is figured as a primal disarticulatory force whose condition is unrepresentability. There is an important link here between Lyotard and Deleuze, not only in their unremitting hostility to Hegel and Hegelianism, explicit or implicit, but also in seeking alternatives to the reigning traditions of philosophies of representation. Concepts of Idea, image, and phantasm circulate in their philosophies, though in very different ways. And in every case these concepts derive from a nonpresent perception that operates through a discordance of the faculties—the apprehension of a dimension that is not spatial in the sense of extension and that relates to force as virtuality.[14]

A key difference between the two, however, is how these concepts turn to the question of art: for Lyotard, the figural is an *aesthetic* concept in a way that it is not for Deleuze. (Or perhaps Deleuze implicitly invokes the more ancient concept of *aisthesis,* the dimension of sensation rather than art.) Lyotard persistently characterizes the primary processes as an unconscious "space" that preserves an aesthetic dimension for the figural. Moreover, here the figural preserves for art its critical dimension. Under capitalism, the integrative function of art is to fix or order desire through communication or representation, to turn and exhaust it in practical activity. But the aesthetic force of the figural—which derives from the ineluctable and uncanny disordering repetition of the death drive—is immediately revolutionary. It belongs to an order of sense or existence that is neither that of linguistic communication, nor figurative representation, nor practical activity. A Zwischenwelt, it falls between the practical perceptual and communicative operations of the reality principle.

Lyotard both revised and complicated his more strident and militant positions on art of the 1970s.[15] Yet this does not free us from pursuing the liaison between desire and transgression in his concept of the figural, and from inquiring into the ways in which desire functions as a "transcendental" concept in the Kantian sense, above all with respect to the question of art and politics. To examine this question, we must turn to Lyotard's concepts of the postmodern and the sublime.

I have examined two perspectives on the figural in Lyotard's work. The first primarily defines a discursive space where text and figure, letter and line, are mutually imbricated as two kinds of negativity, and two kinds of spatialization, that will never form a synthetic or symbolic unity. In other words, discourse is incapable of transmitting a univocal sense. The second dimension is that of desire, the dream-work, and primal phantasy. Spatial though not visible, unbound by either linguistic or perspectival negation, this is a virtual dimension where perception is freed from reality testing, and where words and things transform one into the other with the fluidity of hallucinated objects. More radically, even the scenography and enunciative structure of this "space" is perturbed by the uncoded flows of desire, producing a superimposition of contradictory points of view, incommensurable narrative scenes, and achronological layers of memory. Two dimensions of space, then, but what of the problem of time or history? In anticipation of chapter 5 of this book, where I will take up the question of *historische Bilder,* "historical images," as defined by Walter Benjamin and Siegfried Kracauer, the figural now appears as a question of time in Lyotard's concept of postmodernism.

To turn to the question of postmodernism may seem paradoxical, since one consistent hallmark across its variegated definitions has been an evacuation of historical sense. For example, Fredric Jameson's concept of the postmodern is just in its effort to define the cultural logic of postindustrial capitalism, one of whose features is to accumulate all of history into a single synchronic present. In retrospect, however, perhaps the period was too quickly named. For there is now, no doubt, a nostalgia for those postmodern 1980s when the limited historical sense of postmodernism was supposed to have evacuated any sentiment for the past. So already, not so many years after, we are confronted equally with that fact that postmodernism has a history, and with the question: What comes after?

Hence the problem of defining postmodernism as a style of art or architecture, or as a way of organizing space or sensation. To Lyotard's credit, he considered postmodernism neither as a historical period nor really as a style of art. One can say, however, that it is a historical concept that shares, in fact, a logic common to all historische Bilder: it is untimely. A suspension in the line of time, the critical art that Lyotard values is the ever-recurring expression of a future anterior. This is why Lyotard asserts, paradoxically, that a work can become modern only if it is *first* postmodern. To become modern in the sense of actual or contemporary, it must anticipate a coming time not yet present: "A work can become modern only if it is first postmodern. Postmodernism thus understood is not modernism at its end but in its nascent state, and this state is constant."[16] Or as David Carroll explains, "one of the primary functions of art is to keep the knowledge we have of it from ever being actual—either a present knowledge or one anticipated in a future that will some day constitute the present" (*Paraesthetics* 156). To inquire into the temporality of the figural is to understand that it is an untimely historical image as well as an imperceptible spatial one.

To the three dimensions of Lyotard's figural—discourse, figure, and desire—we may now add a fourth, the sublime, where the "avant-garde task is to undo spiritual assumptions regarding time. The sense of the sublime is the name of this dismantling."[17] In invoking the category of the sublime, the unrepresentability of the figural morphs from a spatial nature to a temporal one. In this respect, the "postmodern sublime" is badly named, for the experience of the sublime does not evolve; it is only historical in a special sense. It could be said even that the sublime is always a combination of "modern" and "post": "modern" in the sense of continually emerging in a recurring present; "post" in its suspension of the present in the anticipation of a nondetermined future. The two terms are incommensurable. What comes after the modern can be known only when an Idea or concept is attached to a representation that can express it. But the sublime is what throws the link between concept and representation into disarray. This is why the sublime is "witness to indeterminacy": thought is always caught in a suspended judgment whose anchors in either an a priori history of representation or a *sensus communus* have become ungrounded. The sublime *is* postmodern in this temporal sense regardless of art historical period. The question for Lyotard is therefore: At what point did the artistic expression of the sublime become possible as experimentation? This is tantamount to asking as well: At what point did art renounce representation?

I do not want to recapitulate Lyotard's history of the sublime here. It is clearly and concisely covered in his own published work.[18] But let it be said that while the experience of the sublime is outside history, as it were, the history of philosophy is marked by the search for concepts adequate to it, no less than the history of art is marked by the search for forms to represent it. In Kant, for example, the sense of beauty concerns a free harmony between the faculties of imagination or representation and concepts or reason. And judgments concerning the beautiful result from a universal consensus whose basis is this freedom. But the key quality of the sublime is not freedom but indeterminacy. Confronted with an absolutely immense or powerful event or object in nature or in art, the subject suffers a painful tearing of the faculty of conceptualization from that of imagination. The sublime can only be considered without the aid of reason, since the imagination fails to provide representations adequate to these absolutes. This pain, however, is mixed with a pleasure that attests to the striving of the imagination to illuminate what cannot be illuminated. Similarly, the inadequacy of images attests to the immense power of ideas through their function as "negative signs." In Lyotard's argument, this negation returns to the sublime as a force of nonpresentation. This force is exemplified by Lyotard as an optical pleasure reduced to nothing that promotes an endless contemplation of infinity. In other words, the reduction of optical pleasure yields an inversely related intensification of mental experience.

This optical pleasure reduced to nothing is a key feature of Lyotard's postmodern aesthetics. But since we do not necessarily need art to experience the sublime, why is the question of art so important? Perhaps it has do to with the presence and ubiquity of "representations" reduced to practical communication in our information culture? And in this respect, Lyotard's account of how optical pleasure becomes dissociated from the concept of representation in the history of art must be reconsidered.

One function of the Enlightenment for Lyotard was to turn art from the glorification of a human or divine name representative of a cardinal value to the micrological investigation of art itself. The gradual turn to micrologics that renounce totalizing schemes is a key feature of postmodernity. Serving the taste of the aristocracy, whether secular or religious, and circumscribed by the limits imposed by the guilds and academies, the nature of aesthetics in the classical period was bound by questions of *téchnē,* whose measure was representation in both the political and figurative sense. By sustaining supposedly universal norms of the beautiful, art served an integrative function. Here culture is defined as "public access to historical-political identifying signs and to their collective interpretation" (Lyotard, "Presenting" 64). For Lyotard, Dénis Diderot remapped aesthetics by making téchnē the "little technique" in the service of artistic genius. When art becomes the expression of genius as "an involuntary receptacle of inspiration" (Lyotard, "Sublime" 39), téchnē is freed from the norms of a school or program no less than those of culture or politics. (Of course, as we shall see in chapter 4, genius comes to serve other ends of the aesthetic.)

This yields three consequences. First, the artwork is detached from its integrative function and liberated from a mimetic function. Freed from the demands of representing nature, art comes to occupy its own world, not unlike Klee's Zwischenwelt. In the Kantian analogy, genius no longer represents nature; it represents like nature, that is, in perfect freedom. Similarly, art is freed from the definition of beauty deriving from nature, thus giving "monstrosity and malformation" their rights. Second, and in like manner, the consensus of public judgment dissolves. As there are no longer rules for making art, so neither are there rules for the reception of art. The "people" wander freely and individually through the galleries and museums, "prey to unpredictable feelings of shock, admiration, contempt, or indifference" ("Sublime" 39).

As the beautiful is gradually supplanted by the sublime, the philosophy of art is concerned less with the creator, who is left to the solitude of genius, than with the spectator and the experience of artworks, and this leads to a third turning in the concept of the aesthetic. Aesthetics, as the domain of judgments concerning art, comes to replace poetics and rhetoric, which were didactic domains meant to instruct the artist. Both genius and judgment contributed to the early modern notion of the liberal subject as a free, self-actualizing, and self-possessed individual, but this is not Lyotard's gambit. Lyotard notes that when the idea of the Beautiful is constrained by the cultural norms of a school, program, or project, art is defined by a notion of progress that projects artistic thought and activity along a linear continuum: one feels satisfied with predicting what comes next as deriving from what comes before. Representation evolves teleologically toward its ideal of beautiful forms. But as a "negative value," the sublime disrupts teleology with indeterminacy. The historical continuum is suspended in hesitation and agitation between pleasure and pain, joy and anxiety, exaltation and depression. And these are all affects demonstrating that "the sublime is kindled by the threat that nothing further may happen" ("Sublime" 40). Here the art object no longer conforms to natural models; rather, it is a simulacrum that presents the unpresentable. Art no longer represents; the artist creates events that are suspensions in the line of time and causality where the spectator suffers an intensification of her or his conceptual or emotional capacity.

That the sublime is witness to indeterminacy means two things, both of which return us to the question of micrology. If the negative value of the sublime reduces optical pleasure to nothing, the act of painting itself becomes a micrological investigation. Micrology signifies a turn in what artistic activity means as formal experimentation. Under the ideal of the Beautiful, painting explores the forms of existence demonstrable according to the laws of geometric perspective and *construzione legittima,* and progress in painting means the perfection of those forms in representation. But the sublime liberates painting from representation by asking it to show what is not demonstrable:

> That which is not demonstrable is that which stems from Ideas and for which one cannot cite (represent) any example, case in point, or even symbol. The universe is not demonstrable; neither is humanity, the end of history, the moment, the species, the good, the just, etc.—or, according to Kant, absolutes in general—because to represent is to make relative, to place in context within conditions of representation. Therefore, one cannot represent the absolute, but one can demonstrate that the absolute exists—through "negative representation," which Kant called the "abstract." ("Presenting" 68)

In taking on this task, painting becomes a philosophical activity, and abstraction takes on a new sense in the history of art. When painting becomes "abstract," representation is martyred. It becomes indeterminate, as does judgment, which is no longer regulated by a consensus of taste. As Lyotard puts it, painting becomes avant-garde, and art loses its integratve function:

> Avant-garde painting eludes the esthetics of beauty in that it does not draw on a communal sense of shared pleasure. To the public taste its products seem "monstrous," "form-less," purely "negative" nonentities. (I am using terms by which Kant characterized those objects that give rise to a sense of the sublime.) When one represents the non-demonstrable, representation itself is martyred. Among other things, this means that neither painting nor the viewing public can draw on established symbols, figures, or plastic forms that would permit the sense or the understanding of there being, in these idea works, any question of the kind of reason and imagination that existed in Romano-Christian painting. ("Presenting" 67)

This philosophically abstract quality makes "idea-works" of painting, thus placing it in the avant-garde of philosophy no less than art.

The martyrdom of representation turns painting to the task of demonstrating the existence of the invisible in the visible. This could mean, as in the nonobjective art of Wassily Kandinsky, the (non)representation of spiritual absolutes. But Lyotard has a different task in mind. Taking his cue from Maurice Merleau-Ponty, Lyotard sees Cézanne, for example, as investigating the elementary sensations hidden in ordinary perception as a way of ridding vision of its perceptual and intellectual prejudices. These *petites sensations* "constitute the entire pictorial existence of an object—a fruit, a mountain, a face, or a flower—without consideration of history of 'subject,' of line, of space, even of light" ("Sublime" 41). These prejudices include, of course, all the norms or rules that established figurative space as a space of representation since the quattrocento. In questioning and eliminating them, modern art sets out on a micrological research that interrogates, one by one, the "components that one might have thought 'elementary' to or at the 'origin' of the art of painting. They have operated *ex minimus*" (41). In other words, for Lyotard, the problems raised by form in modern art are driven by an ontological question, "What is painting?" which can be answered only through the reduction and subsequent investigation of its elemental components.[19]

The philosophical reach of modern art does not end here. The ontological questing of modern art produces a curious tension in Lyotard's argument. Once art and aesthetics turn to the question of the sublime, and once art sets off on its micrological investigations, painting is regulated by a series of "irreversible deviations in the directional course of art" ("Sublime" 40). Here the evolution of modern art is marked by teleology no less than that of classic art, as painting performs a series of ontological reductions concerning perspective, surface, color, support, and even the space of exhibition. At the same time, this optical reduction systematically reduces space or even places the question of figurative or object-al space under erasure (as when the canvas is renounced for body and performance art or in the staging of "events" and "happenings"). And as space disappears or becomes formless, the question of time recurs. The historical teleology of optical reduction and its concomitant pleasures, as well as the ontological line of thought in painting, continually encounter here another time, an indeterminate or unmeasurable time, no matter how evanescent, that releases thought from form and space. Hence the importance of Barnet Newman's sublime for Lyotard when writing in 1949 that he was less concerned with constructions of space or image in painting than with "sensations of time" ("Sublime" 36). This sensation was that of an ephemeral present or Now invoked in the titles of paintings such as *Here I, II*, and *III, Not Over There, Here, Now I* and *II*, and *Be I* and *II*, as if invoking strange deictic markers in relation to his canvases. But for Lyotard, this place is unsustainable; no thought can occupy it: "Newman's *now* is a stranger to consciousness and cannot be composed in terms of it. Rather it is what dismantles consciousness, what dismisses consciousness; it is what consciousness cannot formulate, and even what consciousness forgets in order to compose itself" ("Sublime" 37).

Here painting's withdrawal from grand historical or metaphysical themes, and its investigation ex minimus of its elementary components, brings it close to Adorno's position that

> the thought that "accompanies metaphysics in its decline" can only proceed in terms of "micrologies." Micrology is not metaphysics in crumbs, just as Newman's painting is not Delecroix in scraps. Micrology registers the occurrence of thought as the unthought that remains to be thought in the decline of grand philosophical thought. The avant-gardist effort records the occurrence of a perceivable "now" as something unpresentable that remains to be presented in the decline of grand representational painting. Like micrology, the avant-garde does not worry about what happens to the "subject," but about *is it happening?*, a raw state. In this sense it belongs to the esthetic of the sublime. ("Sublime" 41)

The stakes of this avant-garde are high for Lyotard. In an era when the triumph of globalization seems almost complete, capitalism presents its own sublime regulated by the Idea of unlimited wealth and power, and of information reduced to the flows of capital whose prodigious scales and lightning movements escape imagination. There is another way to put this that Lyotard only partially sees. When signs become "information" in the form of instantaneous and global data flows, representation in the older sense is equally de-realized. Information becomes an abstract or a negative sign in that it no longer relies on either spatial extension (analogy) or existential and temporal anchoring (indexicality), and in this sense it has supplanted the sublime's powers of intensification. For all who would contest it, then, this form of "hypercapitalism" presents a crisis of temporality as "the disappearance of the temporal continuum through which the experience of generations used to be transmitted. The distribution of information is becoming the only criterion of social importance, yet, information is by definition a short-lived element. As soon as it is transmitted and shared it ceases to be information but has instead become an environmental given: 'all is said'—we supposedly 'know.' It has been fed into the memory machine. The duration of time it occupies is, so to speak, instantaneous" ("Sublime" 43).

Ironically, then, capital has placed itself in direct competition with art for all that used to be called aesthetic experience. For Lyotard, the avant-garde is always at risk through either rejection, repression, or co-optation, but its place now has never been more fragile. Not only does capitalism collude with the avant-garde and seduce the artist, but now that the Idea of capital identifies itself with the sublime, it wants to render the avant-garde in art unnecessary. In this respect, it leaves art open again to a mythic and representational symbolism that promotes false collectivities or violent nationalisms.[20] Alternatively, the fate of art under capitalism is to reduce the avant-garde to the concept of innovation where history advances along a temporal continuum defined by the succession of always new and different art products. But Lyotard's sublime appeals neither to the continuity of the subject, nor to the totalization of metaphysical thought, nor to a consensus of public taste. And in this respect, the continuity of capitalist innovation, and the sublime suspension as the event or *Ereignis* of contestatory art, must oppose each other as radically different conceptualizations of time. Capitalism defines value as innovation. "[To] innovate" means to behave as if any number of things could happen and it means taking action to make them happen. In affirming itself, will affirms its hegemony over time. It also conforms to the metaphysics of capital, which is a technology of time. Innovation "advances." The question mark or the *Is it happening?* arrests. Will is defeated by occurrence. The avant-garde task is to undo spiritual assumptions regarding time. The sense of the sublime is the name of its dismantling" ("Sublime" 43).

For Lyotard, what is at stake in associating the sublime and the contemporary avant-garde is an ontological definition of art as a negating presence that reaffirms the here and now as a noncontingent and indeterminate possibility within an increasingly controlled society. The avant-garde task of the sublime is to produce a suspension in the line of time, in temporal experience itself. This is no longer an act of judgment ("This is beautiful") but a suspension of judgment ("Is it happening?") that in overreaching representation might open an interval where thought eludes the totalizing forces of capital. Lyotard's skepticism concerning art institutions and art pedagogy, however, leads him to barricade the last possibility of critique within the art object itself. Both the undeniable appeal and the limits of Lyotard's hopes for the avant-garde are expressed in this idea of a temporal ontology of the aesthetic. Where Derrida defines the frame as a (spatial) logic of controlled indeterminacy adjudicating the borders of aesthetic judgment and ontology, Lyotard's notion of the sublime defines a temporal interval without the concomitant critique of ontology. Perhaps, riffing on Yves Klein, this could be called Lyotard's "leap into the void": an interval defined by that moment of suspension between the act of leaping, when one's feet leave solid surfaces, and the hard landing of present history. This is an act of faith to preserve an ethics of time.

In Deleuze the tides of time flow in another direction, and one finds in art as in philosophy not the becoming of Being but rather the being of Becoming. Both Deleuze and Lyotard view art as experimentation. But for Deleuze this sense of experimentation is explicitly Nietzschean and not at all phenomenological or psychoanalytic. Art, like philosophy, has the capacity to renew itself continually because of its (un)grounding in a metaphysics of time as the being of Becoming is continually reasserted through eternal recurrence, as I will discuss further in chapter 6.[21] Lyotard's position is more Heideggerian in that art itself must assert and preserve its own ontology as an integrable Being that stands outside of history. It is on this second basis that we should inquire what is at stake for Lyotard in the postmodern sublime.

Lyotard, it seems to me, never wanted to let go of an idea of art as a separate world or dimension, indeed a space or territory functioning as the last reserve of a nonideological Being. Because art is always to be in excess of either knowledge or philosophy, it tends to appear as a black ontology. Unnameable, it continually reasserts itself, nonetheless, as an integral Being. Here is the vexed problem of art and epistemology. One can retain an idea of art as a separate sphere of activity, as does Deleuze, and at the same time argue, as does even Lyotard, that knowledge has value in its "little" articulations, nonteleological and nontotalizable. The comparison between Deleuze and Lyotard is instructive, because for the former the relation between art and philosophy can be expressed more simply. Both create—the former sensations, the later concepts—and each can motivate the other to think and create, each in its relatively separate domain. In Lyotard, the sublime end of art—to present the unpresentable—is to presume a suspended time whose becoming continually reasserts the Being of Art, or rather its ontological foundation in the question "What is Art?"

"What is Art?" and "Is it happening?" thus come to define a tautology where the questions of ontology and time continually circle one another. Art founds itself in the self-asking of this existential question, even if, in the same gesture, it suspends judgment. But only judgment is suspended; ontology and value still persist. Only the avant-garde and experimental art, in Lyotard's view, are capable of asking and leaving open this question. We have not yet left behind the crisis of political modernism.

The same may be said of Lyotard's earlier position. Here the limits of a "utopia of desire," which mark Lyotard's concept of the Event no less than that of the figural, are also the limits of a psychoanalytic politics. What is the problem of making the primary processes a first principle or the unrepresentable site of difference itself? Because an unlocatable or always already decentered origin (what Lyotard calls the *an-arché*) is nonetheless an origin. Desire or the primary processes have a site, a territory, and a horizon: the subject as defined by psychoanalysis. Clearly psychoanalysis has made an enormous contribution to critical social theory. But it is bounded at its heart by an unbreachable conceptual limit. No doubt desire is cultural as much as individual. And one should even say that it is cultural before being individual. But it overflows the subject only to return to the subject. Desire functions in psychoanalysis as a *bounded* infinity, and like the sign for that concept [∞], it pulses in a closed double loop that encircles subject and Other in a tautological space. This is not a revision of arguments I proposed in *The Difficulty of Difference,* where a similar appreciation and critique of psychoanalysis is proposed. I continue to be inspired by Lyotard's account of how the death drive and primal phantasy disorder the self-identity of the subject, returning difference and multiplicity to it. But to the extent that the figural defines for Lyotard an ontological ground for art, the subject-object duality, and along with it the identity theory of knowledge, cannot be overcome. Just as the concept of identification in film theory limits the radicality of the psychoanalytic concept in binding desire to the forms of the text, thus forging a determinate unity that runs from object to subject, so we must ask if Lyotard's concept of the aesthetic does not serve a similar end.

In this respect, David Carroll has presented the best defense of Lyotard's version of art as experimentation as a nondeterminable and nonteleological orientation whose aim is to interrogate the foundations of art. Here the ends of the aesthetic point to a specifically philosophical questioning whose consequences are political: "Art is considered to be a 'genre' without a specific end, a genre whose end is always in question and *to be* determined, never already determined. For Lyotard, the political 'genre' is also of the same undetermined nature. This means that neither art nor politics is really a genre at all. Their boundaries can never be conclusively delineated or fixed, the categories used to distinguish them from other genres can never be totally appropriate" (Carroll, *Paraesthetics* 168). The domains of art and politics have foundations, but their ground is unstable. And to the extent that art is defined by the question, if ever renewable, "What is Art?" then perhaps we can say that Art becomes, rather, a fluid ontology. In both art and politics, "The sublime serves to push philosophy and politics into a reflexive, critical mode, to defer indefinitely the imposition of an end on the historical-political process. By emphasizing the gap between Idea and concept, the notion of the sublime in the historical-political highlights the tension between the desire to surpass 'what is presentable' for something beyond presentation, as well as the critical awareness that no concept of the social is adequate to the Idea of freedom and none, therefore, can be considered to embody it" (182–83). In

Carroll's view, the sublime is a "paraesthetic" that functions as a critical safeguard against theoretical dogmatism in both art and politics.

The Idea of the sublime, then, is meant to maintain a place for art in an era when aesthetic experience is replaced by information and technology. What does the figural express after the end(s) of the aesthetic and the integrative function of art? Hegel may have announced too early (or we may be recognizing too late) the end of Art and indeed may have understood why a certain concept of Art was ending. In my own polemics with respect to postmodernism (which bracket this book in "Reading the Figural" and "An Uncertain Utopia"), my argument is neither with artists nor with contemporary artistic practice, but with the persistence of aesthetic concepts such as ontology, judgment, and value in even postmodern critiques of art. In my view, one of the most persistent features of the aesthetic has been to define an inverse ratio between the ontological and the historical. There is no concept of the aesthetic that does not ground itself in an ontology that projects a form of time, or rather timelessness, where Art must shore up its being over the erosions of history. And as I argue in chapter 4 of this book, the more Art strives to take shelter from the economic within the ontological, the closer it is bound by relations of exchange. In the sublime, and in many respects the figural, Lyotard wants to preserve in Art the last stand of nonideological Being. This is why I believe that the Idea of the figural demands, on one hand, a genealogical critique of the aesthetic and, on the other, a testing of the limits of an ontological conception of Art or the artwork. This project becomes ever more urgent as art, no less than critical thought, searches for its place after the new media.

Paradoxes of the Visual, or Philosophy after the New Media   To understand the figural as a transformation in the order of discourse, why is it necessary to turn to the recent history of philosophy (Lyotard, Derrida, Deleuze, and Foucault)? Or from another perspective, why should we pass through the history of the aesthetic to comprehend the distinctiveness of our contemporary, digitally driven semiotic environment?

Writing in 1929, Sergei Eisenstein, the great Soviet filmmaker and film theorist, proposed the following objective for all future work in aesthetics: "The forward movement of our epoch in art must blow-up the Chinese Wall that stands between the primary antithesis of the 'language of logic' and the 'language of images.'"[22] Eisenstein, who insisted on the explicit continuity of his theoretical and artistic work, thus bemoaned the tendency of philosophy to exclude the image from the purview of rational communication, which is reserved for speech or writing.

The genesis of Eisenstein's complaint can be traced to shifts in aesthetic theory during the Enlightenment that challenged Horace's claim of *ut pictura poesis* by attempting to strictly define the boundaries between the verbal and visual arts.[23] The fundamental exposition of this idea is, of course, Gotthold Lessing's *Laocoön* (1766). But this insistence on the fundamental difference between the verbal and visual has even deeper roots in the Enlightenment critique of classical philosophies. Generally speaking, eighteenth-century philosophy became increasingly concerned with refining and restricting the forms and categories of rational thought that were closely identified with the province of discourse — that is, verbal language or writing — as the sole proprietor of meaning and communication. In the domain of aesthetics, which emerged parallel to Enlightenment rationalism, sticky problems were thus raised concerning the interpretation of the plastic arts. These problems tended to be resolved in two ways that persist today.[24] One direction insists that to the extent that an image has a meaning, it must be echoed in a linguistic description. In this view, meaning is only possible as defined, expressed, or communicated through linguistic properties. Alongside this view develops an equally strong tradition in Western aesthetics that *valorizes* the image, either in its irreducibility to a sense or as its transcendence of the univocal and prosaic qualities of linguistic expression. In either case, word and image are still strictly defined in opposition to each other. Here words preserve the possibility of a singular and unambiguous expression over and against the "nondiscursive" properties of the image, which supposedly fails or exceeds the linguistic criteria of rational communication.

Obviously the forms of representation and communication that pervade and dominate our culture have long ceased to observe, and in fact may never have observed, the exclusive boundaries between verbal and visual expression that we have inherited from the Enlightenment. Everywhere around us, form exceeds concept. "Image" and "word" no longer respect each other's borders but freely intermix and interpenetrate in diverse media including advertising, print journalism, television, film, and computer imaging. But there are deeper problems at stake. Both psychoanalysis and deconstruction have achieved much in disputing the linguistic signifier's claim to founding a site of rational communication and free reciprocity between speakers. Despite their clear differences, Derrida's grammatology and Foucault's archaeology both dislodged writing from discourse, cracking it from within to reveal a spacing whose opacity opens onto the field of the visible. The identification of writing with discourse has thus been overturned in significant ways. Indeed, showing that writing is haunted by a spacing that deforms its contours and spins its linearity onto serpentine paths is an important dimension of the figural.

By dethroning speech or writing as the measure of "rational" thought and self-identical meaning, the critique of logocentrism frees us conceptually to consider visuality as a "discursive" concept, but only if we have disarmed a binary logic that supports an ontology of the visible no less than that of "writing." Recent debates in both media studies and art history concerning the coherence of visual studies inspired me to rethink the problem of the figural as a persistent theme of my research and writing over the past decade. Visual Studies holds together as a discipline through a consensus based on recognizing commonalties among "visual" media—painting, sculpture, photography, cinema, video, and new media—and the critical theories that accompany them. But just as Lyotard asks us to reconsider the figural by questioning our commonsense notions of discourse, as I asked in a short essay published in *October,* what happens if our "commonsense" notion of *the visual* is relinquished? What if we no longer grant the concept of visuality internal coherence by submitting it to a philosophical and genealogical critique? A brief survey of these questions shows how the figural operates as a transversal concept in the history of aesthetics.

My essay in *October* was written in response to a series of four questions sent to a group of international scholars.[25] The basis of these questions was to ask whether visual studies existed as a discipline, and if so, what its place was in relation to a more traditional history of art. As I saw it, there were two distinct though interrelated opinions woven through the initial reactions to *October*'s questionnaire. On one hand, each response acknowledged the emergence of a new area of study—

visual studies—as a matter of fact. On the other, despite the variety of responses—positive, negative, and ambivalent—each assumed that this emergence required a critique of long-standing notions of disciplinarity in the arts and the history of art.

I hold this position as well. However, I was struck by the way in which the idea of the visual or visuality was taken for granted. Film is a hybrid art, and it is not at all certain that it should be defined solely as a visual medium. Moreover, the respondents' confidence that visual studies existed as a distinct area of study derived from no consensus concerning its methodologies, but rather from faith in the self-evidence of the visual as a "natural" concept. As will be evident from my interest in how the problem of "audiovisuality" is raised by Foucault and Deleuze, I find it more productive to consider visuality as a paradoxical concept. Rather than accepting the self-coherence of the visual, the very interest of the hybrid nature of film—as well as the electronic and digital arts—is how they raise questions and problems that cannot be accounted for by traditional aesthetic theory.

In this respect, the critique of disciplinarity implied in the emergence of visual studies, no matter how it is defined, is based on two related questions that can be quite productive in their circularity. These questions may be summarized as follows.

Are the old disciplines dissolving because of a failure to conceptualize new phenomena? Thus visual studies acknowledges the increasing "visuality" of contemporary culture, or the ever-augmented power and currency of the visual as driven by the appearance of so-called new media—the electronic and digital interactive arts.

Or is disciplinarity under suspicion because of an internal critical and philosophical pressure? Disciplines seek to create intellectual empires and maintain their borders by asserting the self-identity of objects —painting, literature, music, architecture, cinema—and the knowledges that adhere to them. Both Derrida and Foucault have powerful critiques of how foundationalism produces regimes of knowledge based on presumptions of self-identity and the internal coherence of objects, ideas, and disciplines. Are we reaching the point philosophically where the coherence of disciplines can no longer be confidently founded on the self-identity of objects? I will argue as well that the figural rests uneasily in aesthetic categories of self-identity. In this manner, it may inspire a critique of how disciplines seek self-authenticating and self-authorizing foundations in ontological definitions of the arts.

Derrida, among others, has shown that the self-identity of a concept can be asserted and maintained only through a logic of opposition and hierarchy. The presumed coherence of visuality is the product of a long philosophical tradition of dividing the discursive from the visual arts. In his *Laocoön,* Gotthold Lessing codified the conceptual distinction of the visual from the poetic or literary. The currency of this distinction, widely held since the eighteenth century, remains undiminished despite the force of various artistic and philosophical challenges. No aesthetic judgment was valid, he argued, without clearly drawing borders between the arts based on succession and those based on simultaneity. In other words, Lessing argued for a strict division of the temporal from the spatial arts. From this moment on, the philosophical definition of the aesthetic became a matter of differentiating media through criteria of self-identity and then ordering them in hierarchies of value. Through Kant, Hegel, and beyond, the most temporal and immaterial arts, such as lyric poetry, ranked highest, since they were presumed to be the most spiritual; that is, they corresponded most closely to the immateriality and temporality of thought. This is a logocentric bias, since the instantiation of poetry in print in no way devalued the equivalence of speech and thought. Nor did it demand that "text" be treated as a spatial or figurative phenomenon. Conversely, the more material and gravity-laden arts rank lower in this schema. Simultaneity as "spatial" expression implies that the thickness of matter—pigments, earth, stone, bodies—resists and slows both expression and thought. The idea of the aesthetic in eighteenth- and nineteenth-century philosophy thus presumed a distinction between perception and thought in relation to matter or substance. Thinking, or the "play of ideas" in Kant's account, slows and thickens if expressed by the hand and absorbed by the eye. Yet it soars weightlessly if released by breath to enter the ear. The idea of reference or designation also plays in two directions. The spatial or visual arts wrest perceptions from matter and, by the same token, tend to be valued (or devalued) for their resemblance to the physical objects or events that inspired them. The linguistic or temporal arts derive value from the abstraction and immateriality they share with the pure activity of spirit or thought.

Since at least the eighteenth century, then, the idea of the aesthetic has relied on an opposition between the linguistic and plastic arts. Visuality or the visual arts are defined here as a quickening of thought in matter, pleasurable if not ultimately desirable. This is what simultaneity means for Lessing and the philosophical tradition that follows him. A sign coheres spatially and thus becomes a "visual" sign only by virtue of the brute and intractable qualities of a matter from which sense must be wrested with as much force as craft. The visual artist labors, but the poet soars.

In this conceptual schema, visuality is ineluctably associated with both perception and matter. But following the Pythagorean dictum that "man" is the measure of all things, it also presumes the presence of the body as both a perceptual origin and a manual agency that exerts force or action on matter. This is a central feature of all phenomenological accounts, including Lyotard's. From the fifteenth century on, space and visuality are thought together in relation to the dimensions and capacities of the human body—measured by the action of the hand in relation to the eye and the movements of the body in perspective with space. This is a fundamental dimension of "humanism." In its lived dimensions and forms, space is defined as the transformation of material by the labor of the human hand. Nature must yield to art in a physical struggle with material that surrenders its form to the artist's imagination. Here culture is defined by the transformation of nature in the artist's material struggle with stone and pigment. Conceptually, at least, space no longer exists separate from this transformation that renders the visual arts as arts of gravure. Space is created by the hand as material inscription, a physical working of matter; it is experienced from the perspective of the body's dimensions and capacities for movement.

Among the "new" media, the emergence of cinema, now more than a hundred years old, unsettled this philosophical schema even if it did not successfully displace it. In the minds of most people, cinema remains a "visual" medium. And more often than not, cinema still defends its aesthetic value by aligning itself with the other visual arts and by asserting its self-identity as an image-making medium. Yet the great paradox of cinema, with respect to the conceptual categories of eighteenth- and nineteenth-century aesthetics, is that it is both a temporal and "immaterial" as well as spatial medium. The hybrid nature of cinematic expression—which combines moving photographic images, sounds, and music, as well as speech and writing—has inspired equally cinema's defenders and detractors. For cinema's defenders, especially in the teens and twenties, film represented a grand Hegelian synthesis—the apogee of the arts. Alternatively, from the most conservative point of view, cinema can never be an art precisely because it is a mongrel medium that will never rest comfortably within the philosophical history of the aesthetic.

The emergence and proliferation of digital media exacerbate these problems. Unlike analogical representations, which have as their basis a transformation of substance isomorphic with an originating image, virtual representations derive all their powers from their basis in numerical manipulation. Timothy Binckley greatly clarifies matters when he reminds us that numbers, and the kinds of symbolization they allow, are the first "virtual reality."[26] The analogical arts are fundamentally arts of intaglio, or worked matter. But the transformation of matter in the electronic and digital arts takes place on a different atomic register and in a different conceptual domain. Where analog media record traces of events, as Binckley puts its, digital media produce tokens of numbers: the constructive tools of Euclidian geometry are replaced by the computational tools of Cartesian geometry.

Undoubtedly, the criterion of substantiality is a key concept of the aesthetic. And on this basis, distinctions between the analog and digital arts can be clarified. Comparing computer-generated images (CGI) with film shows that photography's principal powers are those of analogy and indexicality. The photograph is a receptive substance literally etched or sculpted by light forming a mold of the object's reflected image. The image has both spatial and temporal powers that reinforce photography's designative function with an existential claim. As Roland Barthes explained, photography is an "emanation of the referent" whose *noeme* is *ça-a-été*: this thing was; it had a spatial existence that endured in time.[27] Even film's imaginary worlds, say, the moonscapes of *2001* (1968), are founded by these powers. CGI, alternatively, is wholly created from algorithmic functions. Analogy exists as a function of spatial recognition, of course, but it has loosed its anchors from both substance and indexicality. It is not simply that visuality has been given a new mobility where any pixel in the electronic image can be moved or its value changed at will. The digital arts further confound the concepts of the aesthetic, since they are without substance and therefore not easily identified as objects. No medium-specific ontology can fix them in place. For this reason, it is misleading to attribute a rise in the currency of the visual to the apparent power and pervasiveness of digital imaging in contemporary culture. This is not simply because digital expressions permit new hieroglyphic mixtures of image and word, figure and text, or new ways of converting space into time and vice versa. The digital arts render all expressions as identical, since they are all ultimately reducible to the same computational basis. The basis of all "representation" is virtuality: mathematic abstractions that render all signs as equivalent regardless of their output medium. Digital media are neither visual, textual, nor musical—they are pure simulation.

One problem raised through reading the figural is to reclaim those arts where the relation between discourse and figure no longer rests easily on a division of temporality from spatiality. The hybrid qualities of the cinematic, and now digital, arts make clear that the distinction between the visual and the verbal on this basis has always been a lure, ensuring the subordination of a materialist theory of art to an idealist and logocentric one. Without question, however, the apologists of information are promoting a new form of idealism that I will discuss further in the final chapter of this book. To conclude my arguments here, I want to raise anew the question of technology and perception with respect to the changing claims of visuality and the figural.

The place of technology in the history of aesthetic judgment has always been a curious one. With respect to photography or cinema, it is paradoxical that the same idealist position of aesthetic judgment would increasingly abhor the technological production and reproduction of images yet assume the transparency of technology to writing. In my view, from woodcut, to printing press, to lithography, to photography, to cinema, and even to the phonograph record, a genealogy is defined in the history of the analogical arts. All are arts of gravure, a sculpting of the image in a physical support, a history that includes of course sculpture, architecture, and fresco. There is a fault line in this history, however, in that cinema, phonography, and video are two-stage arts that require a technological interface to mediate perception such as film projector, turntable and amplification, or the television monitor.[28] The history of the interface is a history of technological arrangements where body and perception are included in a machinic phylum whose spatial and temporal qualities become increasingly complex.

Evidently, in the transition from the analog to the digital, visuality is transformed, indeed problematized, not only as expression but also in relation to perception, that is, how body and eye are positioned in space and time according to specific conceptual and technological arrangements. Here the history of the technological interface presents some curious consequences for the history of visuality. The emergence of this "second stage" marks a fundamental discontinuity or disruption in the relation between hand and eye, where the space of material inscription disappears or rather is displaced with paradoxical consequences for the history of the aesthetic. As the enjoyment of art requires technological mediations or interfaces of increasing mechanical and/or electronic complexity, the more the continuum of perception becomes disjunct in space and time. Originarily, problems of aesthetic judgment assumed the reciprocal presence of artwork and perceiver. But in the two-stage arts, the relation between presence and absence of subject and object in space and time is refashioned in new and disturbing ways. Information recorded on a phonograph record, filmstrip, or videotape is not directly apprehended by the ear and the eye. Rather, it must be translated by the apparatus appropriate to each and reconfigured to a human scale, a process that comes to include, with ever greater complexity, the human as part of the machinic phylum. The eye and ear are displaced. Here Benjamin's "decline of aura" indicates not only representations that circulate independently of an authorizing context or copies becoming indistinguishable from originals but also the withdrawal of perception from a haptic continuum marked by continuity in time and space. Telegraphy, telephony, and all forms of broadcasting both complicated and amplified these qualitative mutations in space and time.

This fault line extends, of course, to the digital arts, establishing a continuity that bridges a sometimes all too facile distinction between the analog and the digital. As representation becomes more and more technological, the more we are convinced, in Walter Benjamin's apt phrase, of the "equipment free aspect of reality" [*der apparatfreie As-*

pekt der Realität].[29] With this idea, Benjamin wanted to articulate a curious dialectic. Cinema not only produced mechanical images whose illusion was to appear to be free of technological artifice; it also inspired the utopian longing for a reality free of technological mediation.

The desires embodied in idealizations of virtual reality are something else, however. The blue gardenia of the digital era is no longer to regain a reality that has been absorbed by its reproduction but to displace reality with an immersive virtual sensorium that wants to float free of its enormous computational apparatus. Here the digital interface wants to disappear no less than the mechanical one, but this disappearance is more a marriage than a separation of body and machine. It is striking in this respect how most histories of the computer interface articulate a discourse of liberation whose measure is the gradual closing of distance between body and machine. From mainframe and time-sharing devices to the personal computer, this is a dream not simply of eliminating the barriers of interactivity in space and time but rather of being included completely as a function of the machinic phylum; or in John Walker's words, "to transport the user through the screen into the computer."[30] Either the machine wants to enter the body as a direct neurophysiological connection, or more radically, the mind wants to shed the body entirely in downloading itself to the machine. This is a rather different dialectic with an important caution for thinking the figural. Because of the ease with which they enable the discursive to become spatial and the visual to become discursive, perhaps the digital arts are the most "figural arts." But at the same time, they are the most radical instance yet of an old Cartesian dream: the best representations are the most immaterial ones because they seem to free the mind from the body and the world of substance.[31] Ironically, digital machines seem far from becoming transparent devices. The more one dreams of an immaterial world of pure simulation, the more the body finds itself encased in technological supplements whose complexity is no less great than their fragility. The pervasiveness of digital technology in everyday life, the intractability as well as availability of digital machines, encourages a presence and visibility of the interface that promotes a constant self-consciousness of their social functions and creative uses as well as the fragility of information. Perhaps the telephone was once just as physically intrusive a device before becoming a ubiquitous and transparent technology. For the moment, however, the computer in all its variegated forms remains stubbornly present in our lives as a social and cultural problem.

This genealogy of the interface also describes a complex passage back and forth between the technologies of the image and those of writing as inscriptions in space and transformations of time. In this respect, photography and cinema share more with the printed word than the novel does with the oral tale. In both cinema and the novel, the collective space of storytelling—which unifies narrator and listeners in a reciprocal space and time—is disjoined. The narrative is fixed in form and content, circulating independently—in both space and historical time—in the form of a commodity. (In this respect, the book itself functions as an interface and should be considered more a venerated ancestor than an outmoded competitor for our new media.) Consequently narrative meaning shifts continually depending on the cultural or historical contexts through which it is received. What separates these modern arts from the woodcut, of course, is the absence of the hand and the increasing mediation of machines of a special type: those that produce uniform copies through a reification of time as a linear and sequential space.

The same may be said for the uniformity of perception with respect to groups. Film and broadcasting bind given collectivities in different spatial and temporal "architectures" of perception: one is unified in the space and time of projection; the other atomizes space while it unifies in time. The networked arts and communication atomize the flow of information in both space and time (though real-time interactions are also possible). However, it is also a many-to-many rather than a one-to-many medium where individuals produce as much as receive messages, often in an interactive way. It has often been noted that networked communications come to resemble oral communities even when they are fragmented in a distributed space that allows reciprocal, though often asynchronous, interactivity. Nonetheless this apparently tribal space is strongly marked by a kind of digital schizophrenia, well described in both its positive and negative aspects by Sherry Turkle in *Life on the Screen.* Not only communication but also personhood is fragmented in a distributed space. The power of computer-mediated communication in all its forms is to enable a collective and interactive dialogue that is freed from the limitations of space. But these monadic entities are united in a technology that also separates them, and their division is just as attractive as their unity. This is a freedom gained through the felt absence of consequences, for reciprocity is defined only by the virtual presence of avatars who, for all their other qualities, register not only the withdrawal of persons in the distributed network but also the absence of accountability for one's words and acts.

I will return to, and complicate, these arguments in chapter 6. My point here, however, is neither to critique the automation or mechanization of the arts nor to demonize the technological interface in either analog or digital media. Rather, I want to point out how odd it is that the aesthetic should want to ground itself ontologically through distinguishing space and time as separate dimensions or territories. And by the same token, perhaps the universal claim of both aesthetic experience and judgment has blinded the history of philosophy to the complex transactions that are taking place in relation to power and subjectivation as our semiotic environment is being remodeled. If we are entering a "posthuman" era, both culturally and philosophically, what does this mean?

Lessing's idea, and the history of aesthetics in which his thought is embedded, shows clearly what humanism has meant for five hundred years—that "man" is the measure of all things. No matter if, from the perspective of a universal time, this moment would hardly register on nature's clock. Images, for example, are organized from the height and distance of the human eye to preserve an illusion of spatial depth. Scale is organized in relation to human size. Colors, sounds, and textures are produced according to the physiological limits of human perception. This has been the basis of the analogical arts, whether of hand or machine inscription, for millennia.

The criticism of art suffers from the same illusion of mastery that makes "man" the center of all things and the measure of all values. The humanist perspective neglects the question of power, that is, the forces and relations of power served by specific organizations of space and time. It assumes the priority of "man" as an agent in space. But the composition of space-times as architectures of power also has collective and social dimensions that order and discipline bodies, movements, and communication. The historical organization of perspective also has an architectural force. It restricts, aligns, and regulates the body's movements in space, aligning body and eye with a space of "correct" perceiving. It comprises a series of constraints on what a body can do independently of individual will or consciousness. Think of the difference in experience between interacting with Tiepolo's *Stations of the Cross* at the Church of San Polo in Venice (in the way both church and artist intended, which is on your knees!) and viewing his paintings at the Accademia. One is not more free than the other; both channel the movement of bodies and direct the flow of perception while embedding artworks in distinct forces and relations of power. Architecture itself tells us more about the potentiality of the body, the forces it affects and that affect it, than any other enterprise. It is the design of spaces to live and work in, to travel across, and to communicate through, in ways that limit certain movements and enable others, and, as such, is an exemplary expression of power. Foucault's definition of how power encounters the body makes the point succinctly: divide in space; order in time; compose in space-time. An "architectural" theory of power thus diagrams forms of collectivity—distinct in their spatial and temporal organization—and demonstrates how movements of bodies and flows of information are both enabled and constrained.

Now it is said that we have entered a posthuman era, as if our age was somehow less inclined to misrecognition and idealism, and more committed to truth, than the one before it. The humanist era is undoubtedly undergoing a transformation, but for none of the reasons usually asserted. The transition from analog to digital media extends a displacement in perspective, or better, positionality, where what might define a perception as human is being reconfigured in ways that are still unclear. The digital arts seem immaterial because the transformations taking place are apprehendable only from a "machinic" rather than a "human" perspective. Hence the need of technological interfaces of greater and greater complexity to augment human perception and motor control. But as I have already pointed out, this genealogy has a long history. Nevertheless video and the synthetic or digital image do seem to mark a break with the genealogy of gravure that unleashes new powers for the figural and, at the same time, problematizes previous concepts of perception and the body. How many filmmakers have lamented the disappearance of the tactile handling of the filmstrip, of the days of stretching out a strip of 35 mm film to the light, judging by eye the space and duration of the cut? What does a strip of video-tape reveal to the naked eye? And one cannot even touch encoded in-formation, a symbolic abstraction locked away in disk arrays. We are continually asked to believe that the transformation of our semiotic en-vironment by digital machines has produced a friction-free space that launches our thoughts and expressions at the speed of light. Freed of our slow and gravity-bound being, we communicate universally in a weightless atmosphere. But we are not freed from relations of power. Looking back from the perspective of 2000 (and how dated this obser-vation will seem ten years hence!), what has been most fascinating and terrifying about the short history of the World Wide Web as a popular medium is how rapidly and thoroughly it was commodified. Created like the Internet as an open environment based on the free exchange of information and the communication of ideas, the Web has also be-come a space of surveillance and social control. It is a new architecture of power that is reorganizing the space and time of everyday life on a global scale. But new potentials of power are also new opportunities for criticism and resistance, and thinking the figural means that "visu-ality" needs to be considered not only as a discursive phenomenon but also as a transformation of relations of power and knowledge as well as subjectivation. Reading the figural means rethinking the aesthetic as a question of power.

As a concept, visuality is a space inhabited by paradox, and the figu-ral is my name for this paradoxical quality. What interests me most about contemporary visual studies derives neither from the presumed distinctiveness of media nor from cultural ethnographies of spectators. Indeed, the constant challenge I want to raise to both visual and cul-tural studies has to do with a philosophical problem: the invention and critique of concepts raised implicitly in the historical emergence of new media. For me the new media inspire "visual studies" through an im-plicit philosophical confrontation. Cinema and the electronic arts are the products of concepts that cannot be recognized by the system of aesthetics, nor should they be; they are *ahead* of philosophy in this re-gard. This is not to say that the new digital media are somehow more "figural" than the old analog media as the accomplishment of some ideal teleology. Nonetheless their invention, cultural form, and patterns of distribution and use are based on a set of concepts that recast the genealogy of visuality and the aesthetic in new contexts. They problematize the philosophical history of visuality and the aesthetic in ways that are still unclear.

Visual Studies for me is based, therefore, on the recognition that the new media demand a deconstruction of the concepts of both visuality and discursivity as well as the philosophical traditions from which they derive. This position requires both a genealogical critique of the aesthetic and a positive investigation of the concepts invented or suggested by new media that I have loosely designated under the signs of "the figural" and "audiovisual culture." Our era is no longer one of images and signs. It is defined, rather, by simulacra in Deleuze's sense of the term: paradoxical series where concepts of model and copy, the Same and the One, the Identical and the Like, are no longer easily reconciled or reduced by principles of unity and the selfsame. Within this framework, we need to begin reading the figural.

2. READING THE FIGURAL

A day will come when, by means of similitude relayed indefinitely along the length of a series, the image itself, along with the name it bears, will lose its identity. Campbell, Campbell, Campbell, Campbell.—Michel Foucault, *This Is Not a Pipe*

From the inauguration of modern philosophy in the eighteenth century, seeing and saying, imaging and speaking, and pictures and propositions have been considered as fundamentally distinct and often resolutely opposed categories. This strategy is not innocent. Over the course of two centuries, philosophy has barricaded itself within a concept of *speech* as the site of discourse, communication, meaning, and rational thought. This epistemological problem was unthinkable without the corresponding birth of *aesthetics* as a separate domain within the province of professional philosophy. For speech to maintain its identity, and poetry its place as the highest art (as attested by philosophers from Hegel to Heidegger), meaning in the "plastic" arts—architecture, painting, sculpture, and subsequently photography, cinema, and video—had either to be understood as reducible to linguistic sense or valorized as exceeding "rational" thought.

What philosophical resources could accomplish the excavation and dismantling of this ontological distinction between "linguistic" and "plastic" representations that still reigns in aesthetic theory today? This problem is crucial for the study of contemporary mass culture and the newest forms of mass communication. Cinematic, televisual, and other electronic media have already rendered this distinction obsolete, creating new systems of spatialization and temporality—indeed, new forms of thought—that modern philosophy is ill equipped to describe or understand. New modalities of expression have been inaugurated by the accelerated development of electronic and digital image processing as well as the "broadcast" distribution, rather than the "physical" distribution, of commodities, along with the economic and legal apparatuses that support them.[1] How can critical thought engage these new modes of expression and comprehend the forms of reading they have generated? Long ago the end of ideology was announced. But the wolf has not gone from the door; he has appeared in the electronic window as a TV evangelist. Although ephemeral, his image floats on an unending temporal stream. The era of signs is rapidly fading. We have already entered the age of the figural.

Rehearsing the Figural Painting, photography, video, and cinema have long proved resistant to models of description and explanation derived from classical semiology.[2] The electronic and digital arts are rapidly engendering new strategies of creation and simulation, and of spatial and temporal ordering, that linguistic philosophies are ill equipped to understand. In the physics of language, semiology represents Newtonian mechanics, and we already inhabit an increasingly dynamic and nonlinear discursive universe. Conceptually, the sign describes a thing; it must be replaced by a "becoming." Provisionally, I recommend the *figural*.

What I call the figural is not synonymous with a figure or even the figurative. It is no more proper to the plastic than to the linguistic arts. It is not governed by the opposition of word to image; spatially and temporally, it is not bound to the logic of binary oppositions. Ever permutable — a fractured, fracturing, or fractal space, ruled by time and difference — it knows nothing of the concept of identity. The figural is not an aesthetic concept, nor does it recognize a distinction between the forms of "high" and "low" culture. It describes the logic of mass culture itself; or rather a culture of the mass.

I am standing on a well-worn spot in the floor of the Church of San Polo in Venice looking at one of Tintoretto's versions of *The Last Supper*. The organic relation of this painting to the architecture of the church and to an ideology of religious devotion — as well as the presence of a physical deictic marker insisting that one occupy this exact place at this precise distance to appreciate "correctly" Tintoretto's ac-

Church of San Polo, Venice. Photograph courtesy of author.

Plaza, Centre Georges Pompidou, Paris. Photograph courtesy of author.

complishment—is testimony to the Renaissance philosophy of the subject as unique, selfsame, centered, and placed in society.

Two weeks later, I am on the plaza at Beaubourg absorbed within the crowd circulating past a giant-screen TV exhibiting an R. J. Reynolds documentary "Art in the Factory." No one will miss the multiple ironies of this documentary, where cigarette manufacturers enlighten assembly line workers by decorating the factory walls with abstract expressionist art to which, invariably, their backs are turned. However, the space of reception organized around the screen is as significant as its form and content. Where the Tintoretto places me as a unique point in space and time, on the Beaubourg plaza, "I" am dispersed into the crowd as a flow of randomized movements ordered only by an architectural space designed to channel the drift of the mass. Walter Benjamin forgot to tell us that the museum was a space of distraction no less than the cinema theater. And here the subject resembles no longer the distracted worker on the assembly line but rather the product on the conveyor belt.

Now at home alone watching *Melrose Place,* I am no less a part of an atomized collective. Though separated in space, I nonetheless share a temporal continuum with millions of others. From a singular point, to a molecular mass, to an atomized collective: these are three different images of subjectivity, reproduced historically within the structure of representation itself, that trace a line from auratic to postauratic art, and finally to the figural. What Siegfried Kracauer called the mass ornament, the spatial image of collective life, is now governed by seriality in leisure no less than labor. Tintoretto's painting announced the appearance of the democratic actor; today, government through "public opinion," the quantification and sampling of an anonymous, serialized mass, is the order of the day.

The disappearance of the "subject" no less than that of the aesthetic divides the figural from the problem of "postmodernism." In art critical discourse, postmodernism is for the most part a regressive concept. It reproduces exactly the terms, concepts, and values of modernism in its definitions of the artwork, the artist, and artistic value. Postmodernism has served only to reinvigorate the self-identity of the artwork by bolstering it in the commodity form characteristic of the current stage of capitalism.[3] Today artworks and aesthetic experience barely escape the form of pure exchange value, a fact well known by Sotheby's, the Saatchis, and multinational corporations. Contrariwise, the figural is a *historical* concept, not an aesthetic or stylistic one. The figural has nothing to do with the identification, criticism, or evaluation of artworks; it is entirely banal, prosaic, and quotidian. It dismisses the self-identity of the aesthetic, for it belongs to an era where "art" no longer exists save as a marketing strategy. Like the zombies in George

Romero's films, the form of self-consciousness in postmodern art is, paradoxically, not to know (or perhaps not to accept) that it is happily dead. And in this manner, it feeds voraciously, endlessly, and parasitically on the relics of the past. (For a savvy few, this is a source of darkly ironic humor, and sometimes even poignant political commentary.) Thus the figural will not be derived from an experience of art or by reflection on the forms of self-identity of the artwork. It represents a fundamental transformation of categories of expression and reading in the current era. Wherever analog information is replaced by the digital, the copy is disordered by simulation, and wherever physical distribution is replaced by electronic storage, retrieval, and retransmission, there one will find the figural.

Thus the figural is less a "thing" than a concept, designed to help characterize the social physiognomics of postindustrial capitalism and the information society. It characterizes the forms of spatiotemporal organization that are increasingly transforming urban space, audiovisual media, telecommunications, leisure; in fact, all the activities of everyday life. If the distinctiveness of our epoch is defined by transformations in economic practice, the structure and activities of the State, and the terms and conditions of philosophical knowledge, the figural is meant to describe a distinct mutation in the character of contemporary forms of representation, information, and communication. In short, the figural cannot adequately be described by the logic of identity characteristic of most extant aesthetic theories and philosophies of the sign and of language. To comprehend the figural, it is necessary to transform completely how the term "discourse" is understood by tracing out what Modern philosophy has systematically excluded or exiled: incommensurable spaces, nonlinear dynamics, temporal complexity and heterogeneity, logic unruled by the principle of noncontradiction.[4]

Foucault through Deleuze, or The Diagrammatics of Power You are still undoubtedly longing for a concrete example of figural expression. When I first composed this essay in 1987, I wrote that if we were a bit further along in the technological and economic transformations now taking place, you would be reading this essay not on the printed page but on the scanned space of a computer with a broadband network connection. My example might be to cite on your screen—with full color, sound, and movement—a series of MTV logos. The spatial and temporal heterogeneity of these images, their dialectical mixture of different forms and materials of representation, their procedures for dividing, mapping, and controlling movement are all of the greatest interest. Moreover, you should be able to exert those same controls over citation of the samples. With the appearance of HTML authoring, the World Wide Web, and QuickTime applications, this is all now possible. But this utopia is disingenuous, primarily because the marketing of existing technologies does not allow the consumer this amount of interactivity and control over time and movement, and network access and available bandwith are still limited. But if this technological utopia were possible, to restrict its use to the analysis of aesthetic form, governed by a philosophical tradition of aesthetics as establishing evaluative hierarchies through the strict differentiation of media and genres, is safe harbor from a much more disturbing event that has placed the Enlightenment conception of the subject at risk.

Since 1987 we have witnessed in developed countries the rapid proliferation of computer-controlled image and text processing and hypermedia, along with their forms of digital publication and distribution. What is beginning to change radically here is the philosophical basis for understanding the activities of "discourse" as well as reading. The analytic tradition in philosophy and linguistics has accustomed us to treating discourse has isolatable, formal unities: signs, words, statements, and syllogisms. The idea of the subject—as what stands outside these forms as the activity of mastery, understanding, and the ability to produce replete descriptions—is bolstered by the same criteria. Perhaps the most succinct and powerful effect of the figural is that it has abolished the criteria of unity and identity that are the product of Enlightenment philosophy. Transformations in communication, the media, and the management of multinational economies evidence that the figural era is already well ensconced, and for quite some time. Wealth belongs not to individuals but to corporations. The goals of advertising have ceased to be rhetorical—television does not market products for publics; it sells publics to advertisers. One thing has not changed. Communication still refers to the creation, distribution, and management of information and ideas. But the idea of communication as a linear channel between two points—the linking of addresser and addressee through a reciprocally comprehensible message—has ceased to be valid. "Discourse" is no longer linear and reversible; it is becoming increasingly entropic and dispersed; in the language of computer networking, it is "distributed" communication. Similarly, distinctions between subject and object are no longer clear-cut. This is understood well by those who finance, govern, market, and manage. The philosopher, whose function should be to develop concepts and tools for critical understanding, is panting to catch up.

More important than the analysis of forms is the creation of concepts that enable critical reading. Describing the shape of the figural in space and time is less crucial than understanding the logic that produces it. Siegfried Kracauer wrote that spatial images are the dreams of society. The task of post-Enlightenment philosophy is to discover whether the figural is producing an image of utopia or of nightmare. If I can read the figural through music videos, the architectural space of Beaubourg, or the serialized structure of telecommunications, then it serves its philosophical and critical function as what Gilles Deleuze calls a *diagram* of power.

Deleuze's conceptualization of a "diagrammatics of power" is described in his short book on Foucault. Deleuze's provocative reading demonstrates that more than any contemporary philosophical thinker, Foucault has transformed what is called "discourse."

There are three fundamental issues at stake in Deleuze's *Foucault*. The first simply states: Read Foucault again. For example, in chapter 1, "A New Archivist," Deleuze suggests that those who still consider the archaeological critique as "discourse analysis," in the sense given these words by Anglo-American linguistics, should read anew "Definir l'énoncé" in *L'archéologie du savoir*. Here the dissociation of verbal and visual signs, so characteristic of linguistic philosophies, is profoundly disturbed. In the English translation of *Foucault,* the choice has been made to continue to translate *énoncé* as "statement." But I shall insist that Foucault has irrevocably transformed this "discursive unit" to the point where it is no longer reducible to linguistic or "written" signs.[5]

Second, Deleuze argues that Foucault is not a philosopher of language in the restricted sense of the word. Rather, he is a philosopher of space, or rather spatialization, in the most complex and difficult way. (In contrast, Deleuze is a philosopher of time, which is why it is so interesting to read the one reading the other, as I will discuss in chapter 6.) Only by reading Foucault again can we understand how various concepts of space, spacing, or spatialization inform the questions Foucault has raised, or even how he attempted to think through these concepts in ways that cut across distinctions between verbal and visual signs, saying and seeing, propositions and pictures. For Deleuze, the archaeological "structure" of discourse, and the space of reading it inhabits, resides between the *visible* and the *énonçable.* The difficulty of these concepts lies in understanding that they are not historically given "forms." Rather, they define spaces of becoming or probabilities of emergence that are intimately linked to historically given forms of discourse and the power-knowledge relations they organize.

Finally, Deleuze insists that Foucault's work is not a philosophy of the subject in the usual sense. It is perhaps the most radical refutation of the concepts on which the Enlightenment version of the subject is built. This does not mean that philosophy should now reject the category of the subject; rather, the subject can no longer be described as identical to itself or as bounded by any interiorized space. It is defined only by the multiple and often contradictory places of possible discursive activity and actions on the body. For Deleuze, Foucault develops a supple mechanism for mapping the possible discursive and nondiscursive sites where the subject may emerge to be recognized or excluded. In works such as *Discipline and Punish* and *The Birth of the Clinic,* what is described are mutations or transformations in the architectonics of power. For these reasons, Deleuze characterizes the historical image of these transformations as a *diagrammatics.*

The most succinct way of defining the diagram is to call it a map of power — diagrammatics is the cartography of strategies of power. As such, the diagram produces a historical image of how strategies of power seek to replicate themselves in forms of surveillance, documentation, and expression on one hand, and in the spatial organization of collective life on the other. In *Discipline and Punish,* the "quartering" or subdividing of the plague town is one diagram; the Panopticon as the ideal of a disciplinary society is another. The diagram is an "exposition" of the relations between forces that constitute power and condition knowledge. It also renders as an intelligible image the fractured space where the visible and the expressible coexist as unsettled strata. Deleuze calls this space "the audiovisual archive." The visible and the expressible thus define two distinct regimes that are irreducible to each other. Each has its own rhythms, forms, and history. However, whereas Deleuze understands these two strata to be incommensurable, they nonetheless organize a complex *chasse-croise* that regulates what is made visible by processes or technologies of observation, and eloquent by procedures of expression.

Deleuze's description of regimes of visibility as organized by machines (*processus machiniques*) or technologies is interesting. What is rendered visible and thus knowable in an epoch derives from a historical *dispositif* in every sense of the word: architectural (the Panopticon as a disciplinary plan); technological in the sense of a strategic arrangement of practices or techniques; but also philosophical or conceptual. In French, the primary definition of a dispositif is a statement of summary or concluding judgment. The visible is therefore intimately linked to the expressible in that it enables énoncés that in turn "underwrite" conditions of visibility. (Visibility is not strictly equivalent to sight; rather, it refers to what can be rendered as intelligible and therefore knowable in a society.) A simple example is the circular relation between the strategic forms of observation and documentation in the operations of the clinic or the prison. But Deleuze's portrayal of Foucault's stratification of historical space is considerably more complex. Deleuze describes these strata by adapting Hjelmslev's distinction between planes of content and expression, each of which has a characteristic form and substance. Take as an example the Panopticon as a diagram of disciplinary power. Its plane of expression, which is discursive and conditions the types of énoncés that are possible, defines a specific form (eighteenth-century penal law) organizing a given substance (concepts of delinquency). Its plane of content, which is institutional, has its specific forms (the prison, school, or hospital built on the panoptic principle), whose spatial organization of power also regulates a given substance (the concrete possibilities of subjectivity within these institutions). If expression is linked to enunciative "procedures," this refers equally to the historically given forms of legal and juridical argumentation, architectural planning of panoptic structures, and regulations governing arrest, arraignment, and incarceration. The machines or technologies of the visible refer to actual institutional structures that impose conduct on bodies by organizing them in space and time.

Taking literally the metaphor of archaeological investigation, Deleuze defines these strata as the bedrock of historical thought: "Strata are historical formations, positivities or empiricities. As 'sedimentary beds' they are made from things and words, from seeing and speaking, from bands of visibility and fields of readability, from contents and expressions" (*Foucault* 47). On one hand, each historical formation comprises accumulated "deposits" of énoncés; on the other, every historical formation also comprises specific variations and combinations between technologies of seeing and procedures of expression. The specificity of formations derives from how the visible and the expressible produce and stratify énoncés. Thus these ensembles of the visible and the expressible do not derive from ideas, concepts, "mentalities," or subjects; they define their potential spaces of emergence.

What is ultimately at stake is how the possibilities of knowledge are defined in relation to power in given historical epochs. These strata, or more precisely their particular combination and distribution of the visible and expressible, constitute the positive forms of knowledge as historical a prioris. There are only "practices" of knowledge and strategies of power.[6]

Reading the Figural   The question of reading begins with how the space of discursive formations is segmented to maximize the legibility of its sedimentations of the visible and the expressible. Deleuze distinguishes three fundamental ways of sectioning archaeological space to examine relations within and across its corpus of énoncés: the correlative, the complementary, and the collateral. Each of these different sections organizes the activity of reading in different ways, depending on their particular stratification of the visible with respect to the expressible.

Correlative space defines the terms associating what can be said with what can be seen or observed. In *The Birth of the Clinic* this is the relation between "verbalization" and "spatialization," or how the legibility of objects, concepts, and subjects emerges in the organization of énoncés and vice versa. Foucault writes that the objective of *Birth of the Clinic* as an archaeology of the gaze (*le regard*) is to examine "the silent configuration in which language finds support: the relation of situation and attitude to what is speaking and what is spoken about" (xi). Therefore the "spectacular" organization of the clinic—how it establishes modalities of observation and derives knowledge from the disposition of bodies—is decisively linked to the problem of "language." The clinical gaze, for example, dematerializes language. It has the paradoxical ability to "hear a language" as soon as it "perceives a spectacle," but this language only resides in a natural syntax of things. This is a pure empiricism where the eye extracts the meaning of things seemingly without the mediation of signs. Diseases have their own alphabets, grammars, and syntactic organizations to which the eye alone is sensitive and in this manner "verbalized." However, Foucault measures the historical transformation of the clinical gaze into a "glance" as a division of the verbal from the space of observation. The body achieves new gravity and thickness. It is no longer a legible surface or pictured space traversed by a totalizing look. Rather, it becomes an object, an impenetrable surface guarding hidden but meaningful depths. Divided from language, the gaze is silenced, becoming "the non-verbal order of *contact*" (*Clinic* 122). It now requires instruments to translate the invisible interior of the body into a recognizable sense, not only the stethoscope and other technologies of auscultation, but also a system of signs that can document, classify, and otherwise map this hidden interior onto a legible space. If the gaze is ordered by empiricism, the glance is organized by a medical hermeneutic.

Complementary space designates the relation between the discursive and the nondiscursive as the institutional basis of power. Complementary spaces are diagrammatic in that a precise spatial logic orders the effects of power. In this manner, Foucault describes the Panopticon as "the diagram of a mechanism of power reduced to its ideal form; its functioning, abstracted from any obstacle, resistance or friction, must be represented as a pure architectural and optical system: it is in fact a figure of political technology that may and must be detached from any specific use" (*Discipline* 205). Deleuze insists on the spatial organization of this model. The abstract formula regulating panoptic power is not precisely "to see without being seen." The Panopticon only secondarily catches bodies in relations of force by deriving and delimiting their conditions of visibility. As an automated architecture of power for regulating collectivities, its primary function is to impose a given conduct on a given human multiplicity. One only requires that this multiplicity be reduced, caught up in a restricted space, and that the imposition of a conduct be accomplished through a redivision of space, ordering time in a serial fashion, and composing an architectonics of space-time. Therefore complementary relations exercise power through three fundamental operations: divide in space, order in time, compose space-time.

If the Panopticon is a factory of power, the plague town is a bureaucracy of power. In this it exemplifies the interaction of correlative and complementary relations. For example, in *Discipline and Punish*, the diagram of the urban grid derives from the seventeenth-century response to the spread of plague by rationally sequestering, subdividing, and mapping urban space to contain and control disease. The grid organizes a ceaseless process of observation and surveillance that is linked to equally relentless procedures of recording and documentation. "This enclosed, segmented space," writes Foucault, "observed at every point, in which the individuals are inserted in a fixed place, in which the slightest movements are supervised, in which all events are recorded, in which an uninterrupted work of writing links the centre and periphery, in which power is exercised without division, according to a continuous hierarchical figure, in which each individual is constantly located, examined and distributed among the living beings, the sick and the dead—all this constitutes a compact model of the disciplinary mechanism" (*Discipline* 197). This partitioning in space and time—a spatiotemporal architecture in the largest sense of the term—is a spatial image of power, or rather the strategic arrangement of elements through which power is exercised.

Collateral relations define the grouping of énoncés themselves—how they emerge, organize, and distribute themselves as historical formations of discourse. In choosing this term, Deleuze stresses that Foucault's definition does not derive the énoncé from speech alone; instead, it traverses the incommensurable spaces of the visible and the expressible. By tracing out the énoncé's strategic coordinations of the visible and the expressible, transformations of what is called "discourse" in different epochs, and how the organization of discourse is informed historically by the qualities of knowledge and power, can be more precisely understood.

What is immediately important for my argument is to follow Foucault in asking: if the énoncé is the fundamental "unit" of archaeological investigation, is it then defined by some principle of unity, especially one derived either from linguistics or from the study of language? In other words, is Foucault's notion of the énoncé fundamentally equivalent to the structure of propositions, speech acts, or sentences? Unquestionably, Foucault is testing his relation to structuralism, semiology, and analytic philosophy, and some of the most interesting pages of *The Archaeology of Knowledge* are dedicated to this problem.[7] For Foucault, the énoncé is irreducible to the structure of propositions whose value derives from being embedded in a hierarchical relation with axioms of a higher level within a closed and unitary system. The unity of propositions requires either the exacting logical structure of the syllogism or, paradoxically, the formal unity of aesthetic work. Indeed, the same proposition—for example, the famous "The cat is on the mat"—can serve radically different functions depending on the enunciative modality in which it is produced. Its appearance in a book by Dr. Seuss, rather than as a philosophical argument, will imply very different values, although each may be characterized by an exacting rhetorical or poetic system. More important, what is at stake is not the observation that the meaning of a phrase changes in different contexts but that the enunciative value of the phrase cannot be considered as identical to itself; it derives only from its position within a precisely ordered set of logical relations that are fundamentally historical.

Nor can the énoncé be reduced to the structure of performatives. This is a more interesting case because the presumed identity of the speech act is based on the exact correlation of a statement and an action: I promise, decree, agree. Foucault unbinds the supposed unity between events and words that must obtain in the formulation of performatives by demonstrating that the act itself does not remain the same throughout the series of statements: "Certain speech acts can be regarded as complete in their particular unity only if several statements have been made, each in its proper place. These acts are not constituted therefore by the series or sum of these statements, by their necessary juxtaposition; they cannot be regarded as being present whole and entire in the least of them, and as renewing themselves with each one. So one cannot establish a bi-univocal relation between the group of statements and that of speech acts either" (*Archaeology* 83–84).

If the énoncé cannot be reduced by the criteria of unity proper to propositional logic, aesthetic unity, or discourse analysis, neither will it be constrained by the criteria of grammar and the structure of natural languages; in short, énoncés are not identical to sentences. Foucault's comments in *The Archaeology of Knowledge,* though brief, are provocative. Genealogical trees, algorithms, balance sheets, graphs, and distribution clouds all "possess a highly rigorous grammaticality (since they are made up of symbols whose meaning is determined by rules of usage, and whose succession is governed by laws of construction)" (82). Yet none of these is equivalent to criteria defining units of natural language. "Any sentences that may accompany them," Foucault argues, "are merely interpretation or commentary; they are in no way an equivalent: this is proved by the fact that, in a great many cases, only an infinite number of sentences could equal all the elements that are explicitly formulated in this sort of statement. It would not appear to be possible, therefore, to define a statement by the grammatical characteristics of the sentence" (82).

This contrast of "natural" language with mathematical and statistical symbols is less provocative than Foucault's examination of the status of painting with respect to the énoncé. Here the relation between the visible and the expressible is most complex and its implications most far-reaching. It heralds, in fact, the first philosophical steps toward apprehending the figural.

In *The Archaeology of Knowledge,* painting receives some brief but interesting paragraphs. To examine the relation between painting and "discursive practice," Foucault argues, does not mean to transpose the silence of visual expression into commentary on the latent discourse of the painter as the "murmur" of his or her intentions. Rather, archaeological analysis pries loose the limits of practical knowledge that find expression equally in aesthetic practice and in the theories and institutional foundations of that practice:

> It would not set out to show that a painting is a certain way of "meaning" or "saying" that is peculiar in that it dispenses with

words. It would try to show that . . . painting is itself a discursive practice that embodies techniques and effects. In this sense, the painting is not a pure vision that must then be transcribed in the materiality of space; nor is it a naked gesture whose silent and eternally empty meanings must be freed from subsequent interpretations. It is shot through — independently of scientific knowledge [*connaissance*] and philosophical themes — with the positivity of a knowledge [*savoir*]. (*Archaeology* 194, translation modified)

The question here is how the problem of historical knowledge is embodied in the énoncé. The independence of painting from philosophical "themes" does not absolve the visual arts from the expression of "thought." On one hand, the problem of art cannot be understood as an autonomous realm separate from either discourse or knowledge-power relations; on the other, philosophy's claims for a monopoly on concepts, as embodied in linguistic propositions, are being subtly but unquestionably eroded.

This idea is more directly and provocatively expressed in the relation between resemblance and affirmation rehearsed in *This Is Not a Pipe*. This small book evidences Foucault's fascination with how the paintings of Paul Klee, Vassily Kandinsky, and René Magritte interrogate philosophy's exclusion of painting from the field of "enunciation." In so doing, they transform the identity of the énoncé itself.

In an account whose brevity belies its historical breadth, Foucault argues that two principles, resemblance and affirmation, governed Western painting from the fifteenth to the twentieth centuries. What he does not examine is the philosophical tradition that regulates the ordering of "aesthetic" signs according to these principles. Indeed, Foucault's description of the relation between affirmation and resemblance is more a product of the eighteenth century. Emerging with the birth of aesthetics as a philosophical domain in the work of Alexander Baumgarten and Georg Friedrich Meier, finding its most direct historical expression in Lessing's *Laocoön* and its development as part of a philosophical system in Kant, these two principles demand a separation between plastic representation, which organizes resemblance, and linguistic reference, which excludes it. "Visibilities" are organized by their capacity to resemble, and speech functions to bridge difference.

("On fait voir par la ressemblance, on parle à travers la différence" [*Pipe* 39].) Henceforth, Foucault argues, the universe of signs is divided into two systems that may neither merge nor intersect, and whose relation, though unstable, requires the subordination of one to the other. Kant's third Critique is not far away with its defense of the linguistic arts as the highest, and indeed the most mimetic, because they resemble the least. "What is essential," writes Foucault, "is that verbal signs and visual representations are never given at once. An order always hierarchizes them, running from the figure to discourse or from discourse to figure" (32–33).

Notice the simple but striking division that Foucault is on the verge of overturning. In the era of aesthetic philosophy that he is criticizing, expression is reserved for linguistic activity, which organizes "signs" and therefore meaning across difference; the field of the visible is that of the *representamen* as imitation or the silent repetition of things. Although resolutely divided, in Foucault's reading, these two orders nonetheless remain coupled in a powerful way: "Let a figure resemble an object (or some other figure), and that alone is enough for there to slip into the pure play of painting a statement [énoncé]—obvious, banal, repeated a thousand times yet almost always silent. (It is like an infinite murmur—haunting, enclosing the silence of figures, investing it, mastering it, extricating the silence from itself, and finally reversing it within the domain of things that can be named.) 'What you see is *that*'" (*Pipe* 34). Lacking eloquence, figures risk dissolving back into the world of things, from which they have barely separated themselves in the act of representation. To be meaningful, the visceral silence of thing-representations must be encircled and mastered by (linguistic) statements. Where the image resembles, the word refers and in so doing divides and differentiates. It is essentially a nominalist era.

Here Foucault recognizes in Magritte a fellow (maverick) philosopher, but not in the same way that Lyotard desires to have philosophers and painters keep company. Magritte recognized and articulated, before Foucault, the rule of these two principles in the history of signs and began to displace and reconceptualize them. In this respect, Magritte's painting becomes for Foucault "an art more committed than any other to the careful and cruel separation of graphic and plastic elements. If they happen to be superimposed within the painting like a legend and its image, it is on condition that the statement contest the obvious identity of the figure, and the name we are prepared to give it" (*Pipe* 35). But there is more at stake than the assertion that in Magritte's paintings the figure finally contests its affirmative bond with the text. Foucault's conception of what is called "discourse" floats throughout his work in the 1960s, as does the status of the énoncé, and this very indecisiveness is interesting. At times Foucault seems to accept at face value that the énoncé comprises a series of linguistic signs. However, in the short essays on Magritte and Klee, the place of the énoncé begins to shift and tremble; it no longer rests easily on the foundations of speech.

Foucault treats in detail two of Magritte's works: *Ceci n'est pas une pipe,* a drawing from 1926, and *Les deux mystères,* a painting from 1966. Foucault's arguments are neither commentaries nor interpretations. They present an extended reflection on how Magritte transforms the activity of reading in relation to figurative expression. In the era of resemblance and affirmation, the expressivity of the visible is absorbed by that of the linguistic. But if resemblance yields affirmation, if into the pure play of the figure there slips a "statement," then the énoncé is not identical to a proposition. Rather, it refers to a *collateral* space where resemblance and affirmation emerge from a specific division of the visible and the expressible in the Modern era. Representation-resemblance generates statements. Through reference and naming, signs stop the repetition of figures, linking words to things and thing-representations. In the theory of signs characteristic of the Modern era, the image of a pipe is read as "This is a pipe." And the space of the énoncé appears to be grounded in the following formulation:

      → "This is a pipe."

Magritte disturbs the collateral relation that divides figure and text into two separate streams, one characterized by simultaneity (repetition-resemblance), the other by succession (difference-affirmation). This does not simply mean that the text contradicts the figure or vice versa. Rather, it is a question of a chiasma between the two orders of signs that Foucault illustrates in the figure of the calligram. As a "sign," the calligram fascinates Foucault because it unsettles the linear flow of the sentence, shapes it into what it names, and thus submits affirmation to the law of resemblance. Conversely, it populates the

René Magritte. *Ceci n'est pas une pipe* (1926). © Charly Herscovici, Brussels, 2000.

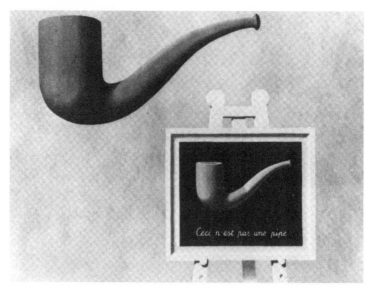

René Magritte. *Les deux mystères* (1966). © Charly Herscovici, Brussels, 2000.

FUMÉES

Eт tandis que la guerre
Ensanglante la terre
Je hausse les odeurs
Près des couleurs-saveurs

Et je fu
                m
                    e
                    du
                    ta
                    bac
                de NE
                Zo

Des fleurs à ras du sol regardent par bouffées
Les boucles des odeurs par tes mains décoiffées
Mais je connais aussi les grottes parfumées
Où gravite l'azur unique des fumées
Où plus doux que la nuit et plus pur que le jour
Tu t'étends comme un dieu fatigué par l'amour
Tu fascines les flammes
Elles rampent à tes pieds
Ces nonchalantes femmes
Tes feuilles de papier

"Fumées," by Guillaume Apollinaire.

figure with "discontinuous letters," teasing speech from the silence of graphic lines. In this manner, "the calligram aspires playfully to efface the oldest oppositions of our alphabetic civilization: to show and to name; to shape and to say; to reproduce and to articulate; to imitate and to signify; to look and to read" (*Pipe* 21).

But the aspiration of the calligram is unfulfilled; it does not challenge the ordering of signs that divides looking and reading into separate activities. The ordering of letters is too much confined by the shape of resemblance to be convincingly affirmative. The moment we read the deciphered sentence, the figure dissolves, and resemblance is shattered by naming. The calligram "never speaks and represents at the same moment. The very thing that is both seen and read is hushed in the vision, hidden in the reading" (*Pipe* 25). For Foucault, it is precisely Magritte's recognition of this unfulfilled subversiveness that is the secret of his painting. Recognizing that the power of the calligram is that it "can not yet say" and "no longer represent," Magritte reconfigures these two negations on the space of his drawing. Simultaneously, the collateral space of the énoncé is transformed.

Foucault calls Magritte's drawing an unraveled calligram (*un calligramme défait*). In *Ceci n'est pas une pipe* the calligrammatic text has been peeled from the support of the figure, restoring the two orders of signs to their "proper" spaces, but with a difference. The absence of letters in the figure and the negation asserted by the text disturbs the field of designation to which the calligram still belongs. "Magritte reopened the trap the calligram had sprung on the thing it described. But in the act the object itself escaped" (*Pipe* 28). Foucault characterizes the displacement from the Classical era to the Modern as the substitution of the age of meaning or signification for the age of representation. Just as earlier Velasquez's *Las Meninas* perfectly expressed the impending conclusion of the Classical era, the paintings of Magritte announce the end of Modernism as a philosophical epoch. Indeed, the apogee of Modern thought is no doubt ordinary language philosophy with its perfect faith in the collateral power of language—the ability of words to tie themselves convincingly to things, events, and actions. In Magritte's paintings, this faith collapses under its own weight like a dying star. Resemblance and affirmation are transformed as *similitude*.

The End of Modernism Saussure, one of the last great Modern thinkers, insisted that the relation between the signifier (sound-image) and the signified (concept) was arbitrary. Signification, the affirmation of meaning, occurs because words are divided from the things that they nonetheless name and master. In semiology, speech alone serves the collateral function of the énoncé. In the *Cours de linguistique générale,* for example, the importance of writing is belittled as being a "photograph" of speech.[8] Consigned to resemblance, it is a silent and graphic repetition of what is really meaningful. Resemblance only repeats once before affirmation appears to pin it like a dead butterfly on a collection table. Contrariwise, for Magritte it is the relation between "text" and "figure" that is arbitrary. With this discovery, the designative certainty of affirmation, in which "this" can always attach a name to a thing, dissolves, unleashing the power of repetition.

Similitude thus defines an order of signs where the function of designation has lost its centrality. Magritte's drawing is emblematic of a transformation in the collateral space of the énoncé, a shifting of its centers of gravity, where the visible is no longer excluded from the expressible. The two regimes are now linked by "a subtle and unstable dependency, at once insistent and unsure," where figure and text refer incessantly one to the other in embattled and contradictory ways (*Pipe* 26).

The Modern era believed in the equivalence of enunciation and affirmation. In the figural era, the link between reference and affirmation disappears, the visible and the expressible evince a greater codependence, and the self-identity of the énoncé—split along the fault line where figure and text displace each other—is no longer assured by a single affirmation. For example, in *Ceci n'est pas une pipe,* the designative function no longer stabilizes the relation between text and figure. "Between text and figure," Foucault writes, "we must admit a whole series of crisscrossings, or rather between one and the other attacks are launched and arrows fly against the enemy target, campaigns designed to undermine and destroy, wounds and blows from the lance, a battle . . . images falling into the midst of words, verbal flashes crisscrossing drawings . . . discourse cutting into the form of things" (quoted in *Foucault* 66). Within the frame of this simple drawing, figuration, affirmation, and designation no longer coincide, producing three contrary propositions in relation to a single énoncé. Moreover, the "propositions" themselves are neither wholly linguistic nor wholly figurative; they also derive complexly from this noncoincidence. In the first proposition, the drawing of the pipe serves the designative function ("this"), affirming that it is consubstantial neither with the series of phonetic sounds nor with the graphic traces represented by / "a pipe"/. The drawing, by referring to the text, affirms that it is ineluctably divided from it. The second proposition targets the sentence / "This is not a pipe"/. Here "this" refers to the demonstrative pronoun of the sentence, which is capable of referring only to that sentence, and is therefore neither equivalent to, nor substitutable for, the figure that floats above it. Finally, the third proposition designates

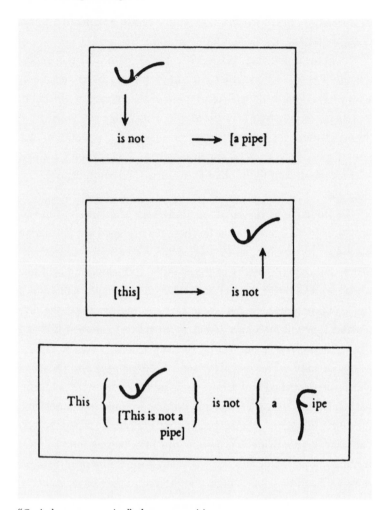

"Ceci n'est pas une pipe": three propositions.

the entire énoncé (ensemble of written text and figured pipe) as assert-ing that it can no longer be reconstituted as a calligrammatic merg-ing of word and image. The painting cannot be reduced to a unity. Split between figure and text, it keeps dividing, branching, and recon-stituting possibilities of meaning. In Foucault's reading of *Les deux mystères,* this process is even more explosive, producing seven contrary affirmations in the possible configurations and contestations that both group and divide figure and text. "Seven discourses in a single state-ment [énoncé]," writes Foucault. "More than enough to demolish the fortress where similitude was held prisoner to the assertion of resemblance" (*Pipe* 49).

The extent of the transformation of signs that has already occurred in the relation between the visible and the expressible is measured by this displacement of resemblance by similitude. According to Foucault, "Resemblance presupposes a primary reference that prescribes and classes" (*Pipe* 44). Resemblance belongs to the era of representation. It is governed by an originary authority, an authenticating model that orders and ranks all the copies that can be derived from it. Contrariwise, the similar is unleashed in a temporal continuum without origin or finality. Governed only by seriality, the similar multiplies vectors "that can be followed in one direction as easily as another, that obey no hierarchy, but propagate themselves from small differences among small differences. . . . Resemblance predicates itself upon a model it must return to and reveal; similitude circulates the simulacrum as an indefinite and reversible relation of the similar to the similar" (44). Lessing divided the linguistic from the plastic arts by opposing succession to simultaneity. Now the temporality of "discourse" has thoroughly permeated plastic space. The analog has been replaced by the digital.

Foucault's arguments concerning Magritte provide a foundation for understanding the nature of the énoncés that are forming the audiovisual archive of the figural era. But what mutations in the activity of reading are occurring, and what do they portend for the place and function of the subject?

By insisting on the incommensurability of the visible and the expressible, Deleuze characterizes the audiovisual archive as inherently disjunctive. Divided between processes identified with visibility and procedures identified with enunciation, these strata continually produce out of their very discontinuity the terms regulating possible knowledges. In *The Order of Things,* Foucault writes that "the relation of language to painting is an infinite relation. It is not that words are imperfect, or that, when confronted by the visible, they prove insuperably inadequate. Neither can be reduced to the other's terms: it is in vain that we say what we see; what we see never resides in what we say. And it is in vain that we attempt to show, by the use of images, metaphors or similes, what we are saying; the space where they achieve their splendour is not that deployed by our eyes but that defined by the sequential elements of syntax" (9). Different historical eras, and the different philosophies of language and representation belonging to them, may be defined by their particular negotiations of this division, which is one of the problems inspiring *The Order of Things*. But this disjuncture is important in and of itself. For Deleuze it is emblematic of the open-endedness and irreversibility of history as a space of becoming. This "movement" is coincident with neither a teleology nor an ideology of progress. Rather, it is a nonlinear dynamic—a potentiality without a predetermined outcome. The ratio between the visible and the expressible in a given epoch determines equally the essential rarity of énoncés as well as the potential creation of unforeseen concepts. The problem of the historical analysis of power as a diagrammatic, then, is largely a question of what forms of order, regulation, or control appear to manage this dynamic that produces equally the possibilities of liberation and domination.

In this respect, Deleuze asserts that there is no isomorphism, homology, or form common to seeing and saying or the visible and the expressible. At the same time, the figural era is best characterized by Foucault's formula describing the work of Raymond Roussel: " 'To speak and to show in a simultaneous motion . . . [a] prodigious . . . interweaving.' Speaking and seeing *at the same time*, although it is not the same thing, although we do not speak of what we see, or see that of which we speak. But the two comprise the stratum, and from one stratum to the next are transformed at the same time (although not according to the same rules)" (Deleuze, *Foucault* 67). The important thing is to describe how and where these transformations are taking place. If the function of designation is rapidly disappearing, this means that our culture is less one of the simulacrum than one where reading diagonally crosses the relation between word-representations and thing-representations. It is not a question of the primacy of print or visual media but a fundamentally new stratification of the audiovisual archive with implications for both expression and reading. The philosophical genealogy producing the Modern era divided the eye from the ear, such that the voice gradually insinuated itself into the place of thought. From the moment that written signs became the simple representation of phonetic sounds, and the voice became the emblem of thought present to itself, the eye began to inhabit a reduced space. The relation of reading to visibility took place as a peculiar displacement: the apprehension of the regular, linear continuum of print disappeared into the vanishing point of the flow of internal "speech." In contrast, the figural has exploded, fragmented, and accelerated regimes of visibility. This does not mean that the culture of the book will simply disappear, though its forms may change. But its dominance has been displaced, and along with it the nature of our forms of thought, which, as both Peirce and Vološinov have insisted, are inseparable from our collective experience of signs.

Foucault writes that similitude has the power to destroy identities. This is because the incommensurability of figure and text fractures the identity of the énoncé as well as the process of enunciation. Where designation no longer refers, the "common ground" between the signs of writing and the lines of image typical of the culture of the book are effaced. "On the page of an illustrated book, we seldom pay attention to the small space running above the words and below the drawings, forever serving them as a common frontier. It is there, on those few millimeters of white, the calm sand of the page, that are established all the relations of designation, nomination, description, classification" (*Pipe* 28). Now these borders are shifting and dissolving. In the era of electronic communication, the quotidian activity of the image that illustrates and the sentence that comments have been disrupted by similitude—an uncanny and paradoxical repetition propelled by the velocity at which the world of things recedes from the grasp of signs. Here is a formula for the chiasma of the figural: discourse that penetrates the form of things with its ambiguous power to negate and divide or differ; the independent weight of things congealing into signs that proliferate anonymously in the everyday life of individuals. No wonder that Foucault suggests Warhol as one of the first philosophers of the figural (Campbell, Campbell, Campbell . . .). Rather than closing in on itself, enunciation now obeys a centripetal force derived from the accelerated orbit of the expressible with respect to the increasing density of the visible. The velocity of regimes of visibility agitates énoncés like atoms in a particle accelerator. But what new "elements"—as concepts or possibilities of thought and imagination—will be created? What possibilities of liberation or alienation will they herald?

I will return to these questions in chapter 7. But to conclude here, two problems must be confronted concerning the appropriation of Deleuze and Foucault's writings for a theory of mass culture. The first concerns their positions on "art." For the most part, both draw their examples from the province of high modernism: Foucault writing on Magritte, Kandinsky, Klee, or Warhol; Deleuze on Syberberg, Duras, or the "figural" in paintings of Francis Bacon. These artists are assumed to belong to an aesthetic and philosophical avant-garde. To what extent can Foucault's and Deleuze's arguments be used to comprehend the more prosaic life of signs in contemporary Western culture? Second, I suggested earlier that it was possible to read a "mass image" defining the possibilities of collective life in the organization of architectural space, the distribution of televisual images, or other forms of social representation. The purpose of the diagram is to map the historical organization of power that reproduces itself in these phenomena, and in so doing to facilitate understanding of both the functioning of power and strategies of resistance. In the current era, if the identity of signs has been exploded by similitude, if meaning no longer derives from an authenticating model, and if the qualities of time render figure and text as equivalents rather than hierarchizing them, what mass image defines the physiognomy of the figural?

Foucault implies that similitude is a potentially transgressive category. But it is important to emphasize that this is not an argument for the critical capacity of "modernism" or the autonomous work of art. When the relation between resemblance and affirmation collapses, so too does the identity of a convincing plastic space. This does not mean, however, that painting or any other form of art disappears, or that art is obligated to refer only to itself. The extent to which "the image" insists on its self-identity—or to the extent that this relation is insisted on by arts institutions—is a measure of the degree to which the image has ceased to refer *to* things, by becoming *a* thing of a particular order. Nonobjective art? Such an idea is no longer possible.[9] What Clement Greenberg heralded as the utopian function of modernism only marked its progressive transformation into a commodity governed by exchange-value and the laws of capital. The quality of similitude has a utopian face, but it is also the figure of an increasing reification of signs.

Similarly, it must not be forgotten that the implication of film's, and now video's, "modernity" is a historical concept that does not necessarily incline these media to either an avant-garde or a nonideological aesthetic capacity. For example, the representation of continuous movement in both film and video is only ensured by a linear serialization of frames where the time and order of presentation are fixed, rendering perception as an activity rationalized according to the constraints of mechanical and electronic reproduction. Even on MTV, where varieties of fragmentation and discontinuous movement are the norm rather than the exception, the ineluctable temporal flow of the televisual continuum, measured and reproduced by the continuity of the sound track, ensures a centralized control that orders time and minimizes interactivity. The force of this acknowledgment cannot be ignored, especially when the ruptural capacity of figural discourse and other "hieroglyphic" forms is overemphasized by avatars of "postmodernism." No doubt, the circulation and dissemination of signs (above all through cinematic, televisual, and now digital media) has become the province of the figural. But the potentially disruptive force of the figural is constrained by at least three determinations. First would be the code of movement itself, with its overdetermined rationalization of perception and limitation of user interactivity. Second would be the reduction of the "hieroglyphic" image in the form of a commodity. For example, the accelerated "Eisensteinian" montage of the more spectacular credit card commercials is transformed by the ideology it delivers in thirty seconds: that in the current state of capitalism, one invests no longer in things but in the power of unlimited exchange. The explosion of signs is here the global circulation of international capital itself. Third would be the increasing serialization of the audience, that is, their constitution through the institutional forms of broadcasting as an increasingly atomized collective. In this respect, it is not surprising that Magritte's art has been so extensively plundered by advertising. But then, it is not really a question of theft. Both emerge from a discontinuous chain of events that mark the transition to the figural era.

The disappearance of designation is the most powerful consequence of the new digital technologies. But what forms of power, and what image of collective life, does this event augur for the figural era? The immense variety of expressive forms and capacities produced by digital technologies is derived from an elemental mathematic expression—the bit—and the technological expression of power in the figural era is the ability to manipulate totally the organization of quanta of information. Representation no longer exists in the sense of distinctive differences between media. Any sign can be stored digitally and reconstituted in another form; thus indexicality is no longer the measure of the "truth" of the image. The figural énoncé is virtual; it does not necessarily derive from any prior existence. Split from within by the noncoincidence of figuration, affirmation, and designation, signs proliferate in an endless temporal stream. The figural is the electronic and digital era par excellence.

The technologies of figural expression offer unprecedented control over the strategies of divide in space, order in time, and compose in space-time. This is a question not simply of what happens on the screen (cinematic, televisual, or computer) but of how these technologies serve to define, regulate, observe, and document human collectivities. The goals of interactive computing and communication that are in the vanguard of research on new electronic media, while genuinely utopian, must nonetheless be questioned, for the dream of the individual's absolute control over information is simultaneously the potentiality for absolute surveillance and the reification of private experience. The deciding factor involves political questions concerning the controls over centralization and access. Critical theory must therefore complement the aesthetic image of the figural with the "mass image" it portends. Without organized criticism and resistance, the liberating force of new information- and image-processing technologies will undoubtedly yield to the accelerating demands of a new capitalism, driven by a fantasy of infinite consumption and infinite access to the daily lives of individuals.

What is the "mass image" of the TV audience? The distribution cloud, rather than the geometric radii of the Panopticon, is perhaps the most characteristic mass image of the figural era. Dominated by statistical and demographic models, the television audience is no longer considered as a subject capable of expression; rather, it is a mass that is "randomly sampled." Broadcasters increasingly conceive of their audience as a virtual, mathematic space rather than a collectivity of individuals. In their currently developed forms, statistical and demographic research proliferate strategies that deprive the body politic of agency by converting it into a virtual — and therefore quantifiable, measurable, and "manipulable" — space; your "data image" matters and little else. Voting and public participation are less meaningful than an ephemeral "public opinion," whose absurdly small samples, margins of error, and control over what constitutes a "proper" question are a mockery of democratic ideals. Today a vote is a 900 number and costs you fifty cents. Credit cards accepted.

Here is another potential formula: randomized bodies, divided in space but unified in time. This serialization of the audience is analogous to the organization of televisual images as discrete and discontinuous spaces embedded in a temporal continuum. The Citicorp commercials of the late 1980s are exemplary, if unexceptional, in this respect. In these ads, spatial links are dissolved, regrouping images in distinct quanta. The fragmentation and diversity of these images are no less powerful than the temporality that binds them, representing the dream of a universally productive capital — in education, agriculture, and business — touching all peoples and dissolving all divisions of nation, race, gender, and class. Division or separation in space thus becomes unity or equivalency in time. The resulting utopia: capitalism with a human face, superimposed on the anonymous cipher of the Citicorp building. The labor performed there is no less powerful for its incorporeality: collecting information and organizing electronic financial transactions on a global scale. Temporality is the material and the continuum that is most fundamental for the exercise of power today. This is why corporations imagine bodies for themselves that are singular yet universal. By promoting an imaginary visibility in space, they belie their dreams of empire in time. Now that global financial markets are electronically linked, multinationals can boast along with the smallest convenience stores, "We never close." And their presence in the daily lives of individuals is just as ubiquitous. Multinational corporations seek an imaginary image of global unity across race, class, and gender difference. In their world, all beings are equal if they have access to electronic credit; only economic difference counts, and here the gap between the haves and the have-nots is ever widening. Here the traditional "subject of enunciation" has disappeared. Unleashed in a space of similitude, the singularity of the subject is displaced by repe-

"Citicorp, because Americans want to succeed, not just survive." Citicorp TV advertising campaign.

tition. An "individual" is appealed to less than a capacity to exercise electronic credit, a universal capacity for exchange in which the individual is him- or herself exchangeable for all others. The lesson here is that the potential for liberation or domination inaugurated by the figural will be decided by the following question: whether individuals are enabled to define, manipulate, and organize the temporal capacities inherent in the new technologies, or whether the new technologies will define, manipulate, and organize subjectivity by derealizing bodies and transforming categories of identity through the modalities enabled by digital information processing.

Between the visible and the expressible, no philosopher has been more attentive than Foucault to the chiasma where these activities ceaselessly haunt one another, always producing new forms of expression and reading. Foucault suggests that in the Classical era, designation and naming served as limits on this radically productive capacity. Designation permitted reading "to pass surreptitiously from the space where one speaks to the space where one looks; in other words, to fold one over the other as though they were equivalents. But if one wishes to keep the relation of language to vision open, if one wishes to treat their incompatibility as a starting point . . . instead of as an obstacle to be avoided, so as to stay as close as possible to both, then one must . . . preserve the infinity of the task" (*Order of Things* 9). Today the function of designation is being rapidly eroded by similitude, and thought relies no less poignantly on opening a space in language responsive to the figural transformations of the eye than on releasing figures in the space of expression. What it means to read—the attenuation of a gaze where language blossoms and disappears, dancing with a concept that inspires the visibility of a yet unnamed thing—is an activity undergoing constant historical mutation and renewal. This creative activity is as ceaseless as the attempts to control and delimit it. Therefore it is ever more crucial to define and encourage its utopian face.

When Walter Benjamin announced the era of mechanical reproduction more than sixty years ago, he knew that critical theory stood at a political crossroads. New technologies of the visible yield new procedures of expression, and along with them, new potentials for either reification or liberation. On the threshold of the figural era, we now face the same political choices.

3. THE FIGURE AND THE TEXT

The image is indeed located, with respect to the echo it might receive from language, halfway between the semi-transparency of written titles and dialogue and the more or less complete opacity of music and noise.—Raymond Bellour, "The Unattainable Text"

Film and the Scene of Writing *1971.* In "From Work to Text," Roland Barthes argues that an epistemological shift and a displacement of object have taken place in the field of literary theory. This shift of focus was in part the product of the seminars that inspired *S/Z,* Barthes's "writerly" deconstruction of Balzac's novella *Sarrasine.* In Barthes's criticism, the movement from work to Text in the field of literary understanding is understood as a transformation of the activity of *reading* through the critical deployment of seven figures: method, genre, signs, plurality, filiation (authorship), reading, and pleasure.

At the risk of an unjustifiable reduction, and noting that Barthes makes no direct reference to the undeniable influence of Jacques Derrida, this new object—the Text—may be characterized as that which opens the work on to the field of "writing."[1] For Barthes, the work is an empirical object, but the Text is a "methodological field" or a "process of demonstration." Therefore the movement from work to Text opens onto a reading whose purpose is to establish the intelligibility of the literary object through a process of transposition or rewriting. Whereas the work confines itself to the field of the sign, a logocentric space where reading is presupposed as an exchange of meaning or a reciprocal relation between author and consumer, the Barthesian Text is understood as an "irreducible plural" or an expansive "weave of signifiers," generated in the act of critical reading and recontextualization.

What is irreducible here is the potential relation between meaning and text, which is never one of pure identity. Rather than a consumption or exhaustion of the work, reading becomes instead an activity of free play, an infinite deferral of the signified. Again, Barthes's *S/Z* founds an exemplary practice in this respect. Rather than an interpretation or explication, what Barthes achieves is simultaneously a detailed picture of the processes and procedures of meaning subtending the "readerly" work and a complication of our notion of reading as a "writerly" activity. In fact, reading becomes a form of writing, the actualization of Text in new critical, theoretical, and social contexts.

1975. In "The Unattainable Text" (Le texte introuvable), Raymond Bellour begins by making direct reference to Barthes's essay: "That the film is a text, in the sense which Barthes uses the word, is obvious enough" (9).

"Obvious enough." That Bellour recognizes the full scope of his irony is by no means self-evident, and there will be further occasion here to question whether his idea of a film-text implies a relation to "writing" as Barthes defines it. There is little doubt, however, that Bellour is acknowledging the profound debt that film semiology owes to Barthes for its theories of the text and of reading. But of greater interest is Bellour's attentiveness to the paradoxical impasse with which film analysis confronts even the most radical literary theories. Here Bellour observes that textual analyses of literature such as *S/Z* benefit from the capacity to cite their object, the literary work. In other words, the passage from the readerly work to the writerly text in which the latter recasts the intelligibility of the former is facilitated because both work and text share the same matter of expression: they both occupy the field of writing. However, although this movement comprises a shift in the epistemology of writing, it ultimately questions neither the foundations of that epistemology nor the privilege that writing enjoys in the communication of knowledge.

So here is the paradox that Bellour cannot resolve, nor does he wish to resolve. On the one hand, the Barthesian notion of the text seems to be achieved literally by conventional processes of cinematic signification. (And here, perhaps, Bellour would emphasize along with Walter Benjamin the modernity of the cinema.) The cinematic text (since we agree over and against the prejudice of literary culture that it "has" one) is irreducibly plural. It resists characterization by the univocal sign because it conjoins five distinct matters of expression—phonetic sound, music, noise or sound effects, written inscriptions, photographic registration—and because its processes of signification, its textuality, are constituted irreversibly and ineluctably by movement of, within, and across images. Therefore it is by virtue of the qualities of plurality and movement, and a conjoining of spatiality and regulated temporality, that for Bellour the film is a *text,* but an intangible and uncitable one: "On the one hand, it spreads in space like a picture; on the other it plunges into time, like a story which its serialization into writing approximates more or less to the musical work. In this it is peculiarly unquotable, *since the written text cannot restore to it what only the projector can produce;* a movement, the illusion of which guarantees the reality" ("Unattainable" 25; italics mine). For Bellour, even though the film is the most "textual" of texts, it is *unattainable* (*introuvable*); its materiality cannot be grasped because it *resists writing.*

Because textual analysis in film as in literature takes the form of writing, Bellour considers the uncitability of the cinematic text to be a problem (though not an overwhelming or worrisome one) for two reasons. First, the Barthesian notion of the text is little more than a theoretical fiction or a methodological convenience that is valued for the readings it produces. And this is no less true for the methodology of textual analysis in film, as Christian Metz demonstrated so brilliantly in *Langage and Cinema.* Second, however, it often seems that the material intelligibility of the cinematic signifier is overwhelmed by the illusion of presence presented by the moving photographic image. Therefore, just as Barthes recasts the intelligibility of the readerly work (with its pretense to realism and presence) within the writerly text, so too does Bellour argue that knowledge of cinematic signification may only be achieved by breaking its fascination, stopping its movement, decomposing and transposing it into the alien modality of writing, even if one regrets losing what is most specific to it.[2]

There is much here that I agree with regarding the theory and practice of the textual analysis of film. But one cannot help noticing the symptomatic logic that confronts and defines the *problem* of the film-text in that textual analysis conceives the movement from image to script as the passage from illusion to knowledge. Bellour in fact recognizes this logic in Barthes ("That is why Barthes so strongly mistrusts everything that escapes the written" ["Unattainable" 20]) but ultimately does not avoid it. Are we then to assume that the image presents no knowledge, that it is wholly imaginary, with nothing of the symbolic residing within it; indeed, that it confounds intelligibility by escaping writing?[3]

Here even poststructuralist theory finds itself restating unconsciously an epistemological privilege that prioritizes writing in relation to figural discourses such as painting, photography, and cinema. Bellour, in fact, in casting about for what is specific to the cinematic text in relation to what it shares with literary, theatrical, musical, or pictorial arts, consistently refers to writing as the measure of citationality and therefore knowledge or rationality. To overturn this philosophical prejudice, it is necessary first to understand that "writing" has itself suffered a reduction in opposition to the image, moving or not, and that this reduction is in fact achieved by the logocentric tradition that still occupies and overwhelms the possibility of a semiotics of figural discourse. In contemporary film theory, this prejudice derives from the persistent biases of Saussurean linguistics, which measure the study of cinematic signification against the model of speech, a stable and repeatable code, and the univocal sign with all that follows — presence, identity, and the transcendental subject. One thinks here of the early essays of Christian Metz, for example, and the inevitable quandary of how to constitute a semiology of the cinema when that which seemed most fundamental to it constantly elided the forms (e.g., double articulation) by which language was constituted as an object of linguistic science. In this respect, one can only look askance at the renaissance enjoyed by the concept of enunciation and other speech-act models of cinematic signification in the 1980s, especially in European film studies.

But what if we were to attempt to overturn this prioritization, or at least to complicate it, opening up the problematic it presupposes? What if we were to assume that the figural and plastic arts, rather than standing outside of writing, were indeed themselves "written," that is, staged on the "scene of writing," as Derrida has considered it?[4] First, as I have already pointed out, the symptomatic place that writing now occupies in film theory as a kind of epistemological limit would have to be overturned. Second, it would be necessary to interrogate how the problematic of "writing" might encounter and redefine, indeed, might be redefined by, the potential intelligibility of figural discourses, including that of the cinema.

In sum, what would it mean for film semiology to recast textual analysis as a problem of filmic "writing"? Or to interrogate the continued presence of Saussurean concepts in film theory and to open up that field to a grammatological reflection? Two possible avenues have already been inaugurated in this respect, one by Thierry Kuntzel under the name of *figuration* and the relation of cinematic signification to the dream-work, the other being Marie-Claire Ropars's investigations into the possibility of a cinematic writing (cinécriture).

"With dreams displaced into a forest of script"   In "The Film-Work," a textual analysis of Fritz Lang's *M* (1931), Thierry Kuntzel takes up the movement from work to text in a manner that owes much to Barthes and Bellour while extending their ideas in a new direction. According to Kuntzel, the task of textual analysis is to demonstrate that the fiction film produces an ideological reading forged ultimately by its technological conditions of presentation. Here the task of a textual reading is impeded by the "code of movement" through which the film constitutes itself as spectacle: propelled by a linear movement whose speed and order of presentation cannot be altered (the speed of a sound film is mechanically regulated at twenty-four frames per second), film narrative imposes a controlled reading even at the level of its technological possibility. Recalling for the moment Barthes's comments in *S/Z* on the irreversibility of the proairetic and hermeneutic codes, film may now be understood to legislate the ideological constraints of the classic realist text to an even greater degree than that of the "readerly" novel itself. An analytical description that breaks the restricted spatial and temporal sequencing of film narrative therefore requires a specific kind of intervention in film's mode of presentation: "slowing or stopping its movement (continuity) to gauge the immobility (discontinuity) which sustains it, isolating visual or aural motifs, confronting and comparing them by means of reverse motion. This situation is to hear-view the film the way no cinemagoer can, and *to rewrite the spectacle in the form of a text* to scrape away layers of referential opacity masking the work of signification" (Kuntzel, "Film-Work" 41–42; italics mine). If one is to understand the condition of the film's textuality, the film must be broken down and reconstituted. In both of Kuntzel's film-work essays, this process of fragmentation and reordering, which owes so much to *S/Z*, is aimed at producing an account of film's figural activity: a particular weaving of visual and aural motifs that, like Freud's notion of the dream-work, is unavailable to conscious consideration save in the form of secondary revision.

For Kuntzel, textual analysis is therefore a specific activity of decipherment and transcoding in which the object of analysis is transposed from a "readerly" to a "writerly" modality. In this respect, Kuntzel offers two possible solutions to the paradox of *le texte introuvable,* both of which might be considered under the rubric of "filmic writing." On the one hand, the process of signification that structures the film-text must be understood as that which is repressed or denied by its readerly modality. Making explicit reference to Derrida's "Freud and the Scene of Writing," Kuntzel suggests that the resemblance of film's textuality to the dream-work implies a primordial writing or architext "beneath" its spectacular presentation. In Freud's terms, this figural writing is a "*Bilderschrift:* not an inscribed image but a figurative script, an image inviting not a simple, conscious, present perception of the thing itself—assuming it exists—but a reading" (Kuntzel, "Film-Work" 61; cited from Derrida, "Freud" 218). On the other hand, this "writing" implies an epistemological problem wherein both the rendering of the cinematic text and its reading must be reconsidered. The film must be represented differently. The intelligibility of its textual functioning is only possible at the price of transformation: the unraveling of the narrative's weave of images, sounds, and graphic traces, and the transposition of the film into "written text" through the activity of critical deconstruction that, paradoxically, restores the intelligibility of text by immobilizing the film.

Dream-work, figuration, Bilderschrift. Kuntzel's recourse to these terms is necessitated by the peculiar semiotic character of cinematographic forms. Although often considered as a predominantly visual representational system, film shares nothing of the immobility of conventional pictorial arts—the time of film's perception and meaning is fundamentally different from photography or the other plastic arts.

Film deploys itself in space and time like speech or writing, yet neither of these materials of expression can fully account for film's semiotic heterogeneity, which freely traverses the "proper" spaces of representation. Thus considered, any rigorous account of cinematic signification must critique the Saussurean concept of the sign with its account of a self-identical meaning produced by the union of (phonic) signifier and signified (mental concept). The problem of describing the film-text therefore poses acute problems for a semiology of speech.

> How to take hold of a textual "block" in which sound and visual motifs are articulated without recourse to a model which accounts for "semiotic practices other than those of verbal languages" (Kristeva, *Semeiotikē* 92). Freud elaborated such a model in *The Interpretation of Dreams* with his notion of "dream-work," the translation of a latent text into a manifest text. . . . This operation—this production —is subject to a requirement, the *consideration of representability* ("*égard aux moyens de la mise-en-scène*" in Jacques Lacan's formulation [511]): "Of the various connections attached to the essential dream thoughts, those will be preferred which admit of visual representation" (Freud 344). The manifest text is not to be read as a "drawing" [*dessin*]—or the film as spectacle—but as a network of signifiers, of terms which *figure* an absent term, a chain of signifiers, a signified in flight. . . .
>
> The figuration shapes the whole of the text's global structure: it translates into the dream's specific matter the logical relations, such as " 'if,' 'because,' 'just as,' 'although,' 'either or,' and all other conjunctions without which we cannot understand sentences or speeches" (Freud 312). (Kuntzel, "Film-Work" 55)

Because of this activity of figuration, of all the arts, film is closest both to reproducing the logic of the dream-work and to tacitly problematizing the modeling of all semiotic phenomena according to the structure of speech. Here, then, is a second justification for breaking down the phenomenal reading-time of film with its strictly regulated logic of succession and contiguity. It is only through this transformation that textual analysis can produce an account of the largely unconscious processes that determine the time of reading and the logic subtending all intelligible signs. For Kuntzel, film's replication of the discursive logic of the dream — which is closest to articulating the logic of unconscious thought with its mechanisms of condensation, displacement, and considerations of representability — comes to describe a generative system staging all semiotic phenomena. In "The Film-Work, 2," Kuntzel reformulates this argument in terms of Kristeva's differentiation between the *phenotext,* the phenomenological form of a signifying system, and the *genotext* that both subtends and exceeds it as those primary processes that traverse the so-called rational space of predicative syntax and stable or singular meanings. Following Derrida's essay on Freud, Kuntzel subsequently refers to this transversal space, which both "falls below" and "exceeds" speech and speech-oriented models of signification, as the "other scene"; in fact, the scene of "writing."

Kuntzel's position might be understood better by exploring another equally potent analogy. Characterized by an ineluctable forward movement, the reading that film presupposes underscores what both Roman Jakobson and Roland Barthes have characterized as the profoundly metonymic character of narrative. There is an implicit prioritization here, strongly characteristic of structuralism, in the degree to which narratological studies have dominated the semiotics of aesthetic communication. In privileging metonymy over metaphor, displacement over condensation, and narration over figuration, this prioritization is grounded on the one hand in a metaphysics of speech, put forward in the notion that only linguistics can found a scientific semiology, and on the other by a largely unconscious bias in favor of the oral tradition in narrative study. (Witness in this respect the profound influence of Claude Lévi-Strauss's mythological perspective as regards the former and the influence of Vladimir Propp with respect to the latter. And in the early essays represented by *Film Language,* Metz may be understood to repeat this bias to the extent that he could understand the inauguration of a film semiology only as a narrative semiology.)

Kuntzel, however, wishes to overturn this system of priorities. His textual analyses of both *M* and, in "The Film-Work, 2," *The Most Dangerous Game* (1932) can therefore be understood as revealing the force of metaphor in the figural activity of film, or the structuring of displacement by condensation. In this manner, a reading attentive to what Barthes terms the *plural* of the text is produced. For Kuntzel, the forward movement of the narrative-representational film is not exhausted by metonymy alone. Rather, it is better characterized as a *relay* of semic clusters or *constellations*. In "The Film-Work, 2," the idea of the constellation describes a complex figure that, replacing the concept of the sign, accounts for both the semiotic heterogeneity of the film-text and its particular dissemination of semes. This figure may be threaded with multiple matters of expression; specific and nonspecific codes alike, graphic, iconographic, and aural traces all participate in its structuring. Moreover, in the movement from one "constellation" to the next, the thread of various themes or motifs is freely mobile within the conjoined matters of expression, binding together and unraveling, giving complex space to the fiction in a plural weave of signifiers. Rather than a fixed and conventional signification, there is now movement and spacing within the text. The constellation is therefore an unstable, composite "sign" or a "floating figure, in its meaning, which the filmic discourse is going to insert into different signifying chains" ("Film-Work, 2" 13). In the earlier essay, Kuntzel characterized this composite figure as a "structure of superimposition of signifiers," which is precisely Lacan's definition of *Verdichtung* in "The Agency of the Letter in the Unconscious." The work of condensation is thus charged with particular force in any poststructural theory of cinematic signification: "To speak of the work of condensation within the textual system is to abandon the analysis of film-as-structure in order to follow a *process:* structuring. The film is not made up of segments of identical value, interacting (as in Saussure's definition of value) to produce filmic signification; the film is not spread out flat; it is only apparently successive. It has its own forces of generation, compression and relaxation" (Kuntzel, "Film-Work, 2" 20).

In "The Film-Work, 2," Kuntzel examines the force of condensation in the figure of the door knocker that opens *The Most Dangerous Game.* This uncanny object — carved in the form of a centaur who, pierced by an arrow, is ravishing a maiden — is understood to serve a dual function in the narrative. First it literally gives entrance to the fiction on the part of the spectator. Beneath the opening credits, a hand reaches into the frame and strikes the knocker three sets of three times. Disembodied, belonging as yet to no one and thus to everyone, this action epitomizes the staging of the spectacle by the camera so as to summon forth the spectator as the absent subject of the narration. Later, this

Semic constellations in *The Most Dangerous Game.*

DOORKNOCKER

CENTAUR   VIRGIN   ARROW

scene is repeated with a difference. It is now identified as the hand and view of Rainsford, the hero of the narrative, who has entered the film as the spectator's agent, relaying his or her look through the double staging of camera and diegesis. (A question, then, as Kuntzel points out, of a *double* identification that presupposes, in even the most classical fictions, a fragmented, dispersed, mobile subject.) Second, the door knocker condenses within a singular figure the paradigmatic axis of the film as it comes undone and is rethreaded in the form of the "constellations" of the centaur, the arrow, and the virgin. Each of these constellations accounts for a particular binding of semes in differing semiotic materials. The image of the centaur, for example, is refigured in the tapestry that adorns Count Zaroff's castle, as well as in the physiognomies of the insane Zaroff and his servant, Ivan. But more important, the dehiscence of this figure serves to distribute the principal themes of the narrative: the unstable transaction between bestiality and humanity, savagery and civilization, hunter and hunted. The figuration of the arrow also opens a particular signifying trajectory: it is Zaroff's favorite weapon for hunting the most dangerous game; it is the sign of his prowess; the first test to which Rainsford is put; and lastly the weapon by which Zaroff is defeated. The constellation of the virgin, however, differentiates itself in the following manner. Whereas the other two figures establish paradigms characterized by instability, iterability, and the reversibility of terms, the figuration of woman, played out in the character of Eve, is constant. The one paradigm that remains incontrovertible is that which governs sexual difference. The reversibility of the paradigm hunter/hunted that carries the plot forward as the conflict between men is foreclosed from the woman because she is the ultimate prey, the stake of both plot and fiction, desire and signification.

The idea of the "relay" is equally important for understanding how Kuntzel's emphasis on the figural force of condensation complicates the activity of reading. On one hand, the concept of relay accounts for the generation of text as the threading and linking of semic clusters through a process of repetition and displacement; on the other, it stages the possibility for understanding a reading-time that is asynchronous and nonidentical with the presentation-time of the film. Instead of a relation of succession and contiguity, " 'Relay' should be taken, beyond its accepted meaning in cybernetics, in the sense of a gap left in a tapestry at the moment of changing to a different color (a discontinuity of the text) which is filled at a later moment [*après-coup*] (a rhetorical pseudo-continuity)" ("Film-Work" 46). What the film-work presents is no longer a sequence of signs—a reading that is linear, progressive, additive—but a complex figural activity, a cipherment presupposing interpretation and a reading marked by temporal stratification and discontinuity. This would no longer be a reading "performed" by the thetic subject—the subject of linear time, predicative syntax, and progressive sense making—but of the fragmented subject, nonidentical to itself, revealed by psychoanalytic theory. It is, in Derrida's gloss, the subject of "writing": "The subject of writing is a *system* of relations between strata: . . . the psyche, society, the world. Within that scene, on that stage, the punctual simplicity of the classical subject is not to be found. In order to describe the structure it is not enough to recall that one always writes for someone; and the oppositions sender/receiver, code/message, etc., remain extremely course instruments" (Derrida, "Freud" 227).

To describe this complex space-time of reading, Kuntzel adopts the concept of *après-coup,* or deferred action, developed by Freud in his analysis of the Wolf Man. Here Freud demonstrated the structuring of the phantasmatic text as the continued deferral of the sense of an event, too traumatic or too pregnant with desire, until such a time as memory could present a context in which the event could be figured. Deferred meaning thus implies a particular structure of repetition where displacement serves the needs of censorship, and where condensation, with its flexibility of signifying materials, serves the figurability of desire. Thus the space and time of reading are understood as an activity of repetition and rememoration; or in another Freudian maxim favored by Kuntzel, it is a process of "remembering, repeating, and working-through." This notion of differed meaning is close to Derrida's description of semiosis as *différance.* Progress toward meaning is doomed to foreclosure and therefore repetition, causing the signifier to scatter and disperse while giving the text both momentum and volume. Drawing on concepts from Jean-François Lyotard's *Discours, figure,* Kuntzel explicitly compares this process to that of the enunciation of phantasy as described in Freud's essay "A Child Is Being Beaten." In Freud's analysis, this simple utterance is shown to be the originary matrix of a sadomasochistic phantasy, a "primal scene" that governs and perpetuates all subsequent stagings of that enunciation. Similarly, the opening moves of the narrative film—the figuration of the door knocker in *The Most Dangerous Game,* the circulation of the letter *M* that presages the terror of the child murderer in that film—are analyzed by Kuntzel as formulating a kind of architext or primary script that generates a "secondarily elaborated narrative" and governs its subsequent repetitions and figurations. It is here that Kuntzel's use of the dream-work as a homology for filmic textuality specifically engages the drama of psychoanalysis, inscribing within the figural discourse of the film the structure of phantasy life to which it gives enunciation. The "relay" that stages the discursive order of the film as the forward movement of the phenotext also responds to a logic that is other, "outside" the text, engaging the spectator in the *regressive* movement of dreams, desire, and phantasy life. In this manner, figuration stages the pleasure of the film-text as the mise-en-scène of desire.[5]

So the figure of the door knocker may be read as establishing a third vector in the first images of *The Most Dangerous Game,* as it generates a phantasmic matrix that gives form and movement to the relations of desire played out in the fiction. What is most suggestive here is that the self-identity of the text—the integrity of its body—must be placed in question. The work of condensation established by the figurability of the door knocker might then be understood as forging a correspondence between three discursive registers—that of narrativity, of figural representation, and of the enunciation of phantasy—whose boundaries are mobile, permutable, and by no means distinct.

Bilderschrift, Verdichtung, après-coup: by this series of terms Kuntzel describes the figural activity of film as that which corresponds most closely to the primordial "writing" that is the agency of the letter in the unconscious; or that which gives meaning only in the form of parapraxes and other gaps in language or by repetition in the form of a hallucinated object. The process of figuration that propels the text by continually reworking its semes, binding and dispersing them in a polyphonic system, also conducts the spectator through two coterminous spaces, that of the manifest and latent, phenotext and genotext, conscious and unconscious logic: "The sex and violence (the sexual violence) repressed by censorship, thus regain their dramatic force in this repetition which—in *displaced* fashion—masks and reveals them. The *reduplication* inscribes its *pathos* in the form of an 'echo' inside the image itself" ("Film-Work" 60).

This is the specific interest of Kuntzel's work for textual semiotics. What is at stake is not a language of film but a "writing" in images. And the logical relations (conscious and/or unconscious) that bind images into a discourse are intelligible only in the degree to which the presence of the visual field is broken and the text of the film is understood as figural script. To do so is to better understand the forms of reading presupposed by figural discourse as well as to produce reading differently. To do otherwise is to respect the image in the form of the real and of the self-identical sign that disguises the force of the uncanny residing within it as the staging of desire.

Hieroglyphics, Montage, Enunciation Unlike that of Kuntzel, the work of Marie-Claire Ropars-Wuilleumier in textual analysis has explicitly examined the question "filmic writing" [cinécriture] with reference to Derrida's philosophy. For Ropars, to introduce the problem of "writing" in film theory is to advance the critique of linguistically or phonetically based models of signification because cinematographic signification, like the "writing" of dreams, "exceeds phonetic writing and puts speech back in its place" (Derrida, "Freud" 218).

Like Kuntzel, Ropars presents filmic writing as replacing the cinematic sign with more complex concepts. Here she is inspired by the common interest of Freud, Derrida, and Sergei Eisenstein in pictographic scripts (the rebus, the hieroglyph, the Japanese ideogram) as the model for a figural activity that confounds the phonocentric model of signification. According to Ropars, Derrida, "through reference to hieroglyphics, in which no sign has unique value, . . . puts forward the hypothesis that writing develops a multidimensional form of signification, whose function is to shatter the unity and self-sufficiency of the sign, thus of meaning" ("Overall Perspectives" 1). As a model for cinematographic signification, the hieroglyph is of interest because of its mixing of phonic, graphic, and figural matters of expression, as well as its fundamental polyvalency. In the hieroglyph, a phonetic element can symbolize an object, transcribe an element combinable with other phonemes, or, through the juxtaposition of connected figures, formulate an entirely new concept: "Each sign can be covered in many directions, and bears the trace or the call of divergent associations, which break up its unity: for writing understood in this way, figurative even in the alphabet, fullness of meaning is shaken by the reference to the hiero-glyph, whereas the illusion of language, with enunciated or transcribed speech, develops it" ("Graphic" 147).

For Ropars, to the extent that hieroglyphic scripts seem to overturn the Western prejudice for the rationality of words as opposed to the image, their lesson is equally clear to Freud, Derrida, and Eisenstein: that of a "writing" that is not derived from speech. Moreover, Ropars argues that a theorization of cinematographic script in this man-ner contains a critique of logocentrism more radical than Derrida's. Through the intrinsic opposition of a theory of "writing" (écriture) to that of speech (*parole*), deconstructive philosophy leaves the radi-cal heterogeneity of scriptural form unaddressed. By focusing its cri-tique on the prioritization of speech over writing, the deconstructive project leaves unexamined the equally radical lesson of the hieroglyph, which reveals the prioritization of word over image. The cinema pro-vides a particularly fertile ground for examining this issue, since its semiotic potentiality relies on the mobilization of diverse materials of expression. And as I have pointed out in my discussion of Kuntzel, the stakes of this problem are higher for film semiotics. The historical development of cinema as a signifying practice has been dominated by an ideology of mimesis that, by determining the organization of images according to a schema of spatial continuity, linear exposition, and temporal irreversibility, has privileged film's realist vocation: the direct adequation of images to things. By posing visual representation as that which provides direct access to the real by short-circuiting sym-bolic expression or the mediation of "writing," the exploitation of film's mimetic faculty tends to sublimate signification in favor of iconic pres-ence. Similarly, the desire to marginalize film and film theory within the province of "popular culture" might then be understood as an effort to exorcise figural discourse, since by circumventing writing, it eludes and confounds the existing canons of philosophical knowing. As I have argued, this problem is at the root of the difficulties that film has posed for both linguistics and literary semiotics, and the efforts of Barthes, Metz, and Bellour are not exempt in this respect. That Der-

rida has not followed through this line of questioning in no way undermines the radicalness of deconstruction; it extends it into a new province. If the critique of logocentrism is based on the demonstration of
a scission internal to the sign and of the reversibility of the terms it
opposes — speech/writing, *phonè/graphè*, signifier/signified — then this
critique applies no less forcefully to the opposition of graphic and figural script or, in Freud's terms, a preference for "word-presentation"
as opposed to "thing-presentation." Because the cinema relies so profoundly on the mobilization and containment of difference through a
multiplicity of codes and materials of expression, the study of cinematographic signification can make a definite contribution to the field
of grammatology.

Thus Ropars's interest in hieroglyphic scripts resembles Kuntzel's
interest in the dream-work in that both provide a model of cinematographic signification based on a mixed and permutable "sign." Ropars
would like to enlarge the accepted notions of montage in this respect, since the cinema offers the possibility of disassociating image
and sound, fracturing one with the other; or further, combining and
recombining the figuration of things with that of letters in its representations. However, Ropars notes that the conventional narrative-
representational film too often modulates these possibilities of rup-
ture by aligning image and sound in an analogical representation of
their diegetic referent. It is the intention of her textual criticism, then,
to focus attention on those films in which one can detect "privileged
fracture zones" or where one can "define the remarkable relationships
seen forming between the activity of writing, conceived in the hieroglyphic form of editing, and written representation, understood as
mere graphic figuration" ("Graphic" 147). Of paramount importance
to Ropars in this respect are the films and theories of Sergei Eisenstein,
as well as other modernist filmmakers such as Marguerite Duras, Alain
Resnais, and Jean-Luc Godard. (I will leave unquestioned, for the moment, Ropars's implicit privileging of the "epistemology" of modernism through its association with writing.)

It should come as no surprise, then, that in a reading of Derrida's
"Freud and the Scene of Writing" in *Le texte divisé*, Ropars is struck
by his translation of *Zusammensetzungen* as "montage." By this term
Freud attempts to describe the syntactical force of connective relations

in the dream-work. In particular, Freud suggests that the juxtaposition of two images within the space of the dream, or the combination of two elements within a figure of condensation, presupposes a relation of intelligibility if not a logical relation per se. This caution is put forward only because the "rationality" of the dream, unlike that of speech, radically excludes the criterion of noncontradiction. The copresence of a concept and its antithesis is the foundation of its sense, not its dismantling. If Derrida finds in the dream the primordial work of the trace, it is precisely because dream logic is founded on the fracturing of the self-identical sign.

Because the film-work, like the dream-work, permits and even requires an interchangeability where words are sometimes figured as things and things are rendered with the syntactical legibility of words, Ropars argues that some of the most cherished notions of film semiology must now be overturned. She therefore proposes that the study of filmic writing should displace the problematic of the sign with that of the *text*. Following Barthes, Ropars opposes the text to the "work," which, founded on a speech-oriented communications model, renders as exchangeable the expressivity of the author and the comprehension of the reader through the agency of a common code. Similarly, Ropars argues in *Le texte divisé* that textual analysis should displace the study of film language, or the isolation of particular cinematic codes, as the object of film semiotics: "Textual analysis will consider a particular, already realized object — a film or group of films which appear as structured by the mobilization and weaving of codes — whereas semiological studies define language on its own terms by constructing its possible codes, which is to say the different systems of intelligibility authorized by its forms and materials" (14; this and subsequent translations are mine). By undermining the predominance of the study of codes in film semiology, textual analysis becomes the agency that, "by considering the route of signification as a process irreducible to the logic of the sign, permits the reinscription of film analysis, indeed the analysis of the cinema, within the general problematic of *writing*" (17).

In *Le texte divisé,* Ropars draws on Emile Benveniste's theories of enunciation and aesthetic communication for the dynamic model of the text she requires.[6] According to her reading, Benveniste attempts, on the one hand, to define the specificity of the system of language (langue) with respect to the diversity of its uses and, on the other, to understand the process of uttering (*énonciation*) with respect to the diversity of possible utterances (énoncés). To this end, Benveniste distinguishes between the operations of the *sign* and that of *discourse.* The function of the sign is identification, and its proper sphere of action is that of naming; discourse is concerned with the production of messages, and its sphere of action is that of enunciation. Moreover, the *process* of enunciation is understood both to constitute and to efface the effective boundaries between sign and discourse: the intelligibility of signs relies on their semantic modalization by discourse; the self-identity of discourse is dissolved by its division into signs.

What interests Ropars ultimately is how this distinction might describe the relation between the hieroglyph (like Kuntzel's condensation, a singular and permutable figure) and system (global actualization of "signs") in the generation of text, which is itself a singular discursive instance. This relation between a system and its singular moments seems to have much in common with the distinction between langue and parole, a cherished notion of Saussurean linguistics and a stumbling block for early film semiology, but Ropars argues against this interpretation. The relation between sign and discourse is not one of dialectical reciprocity but one of irreducible difference, a disjunction of language with respect to itself. The hierarchization of meaning, defined by linguistics as the problem of double articulation, can no longer be resolved by assuming the assimilation of parts to a whole. The two registers of signification are both irreducible to and inseparable from each other, and their coexistence introduces a fundamental heterogeneity into the functioning of language. There is no sign that is not always already a text, since its intelligibility relies on the system established by discourse; yet discourse cannot constitute itself except through the mobilization of signs. The production of sense relies on the differential movement between the two, and no identifiable transition can be discerned that definitely divides sign from text: "A hiatus separates them, putting into crisis any eventuality of hierarchical integration and therefore any unitary model of signification" (*Le texte divisé* 26). In sum, for Ropars, meaning is an effect of the *textual system,* and it is irreducible to any punctual source, be it author or reader. It has no decidable origins or stable codes from which it can be derived.

The textual enunciation therefore guarantees the possibility of meaning only as a process that relies equally on the temporality of the system as well as that of its constitutive moments. And it is here that we rejoin the paradox of *le texte introuvable,* for to interrupt the time of the system, to arrest the textual movement, is to recognize the sign while paralyzing the grounds of its intelligibility; to regain the momentum of the text is to dissolve the sign in the play of movement.

Ropars argues that in the history of film theory, the most exemplary examination of this problem is found in Eisenstein's writings of 1929 and after, where a theory of montage is built on the model of Japanese writing, poetry, and drama.[7] Eisenstein's thought on the relationship between the ideogram and cinematic signification, for example, has a special interest for Ropars's theory of filmic writing in two respects. First, in Ropars's reading, Eisenstein is said to argue that montage functions as much *within* as between shots. Therefore, as a principle of cinematographic organization, montage is transversal: it crosses the space of the shot through the multiple codes it brings into play in the construction of cinematic meaning. Furthermore, Ropars is fascinated by Eisenstein's comparison of the structure of montage to that of the ideogram, since both combine constitutive elements or "signs" based on a factor of resemblance to achieve a purely abstract concept. According to Ropars, Eisenstein was searching for an "abstraction of the sign, not in the representation vehiculated by its materials, but *in the negation of its representational dimension; a negation which may only be realized by a montage of a certain type*—conflictual not additional" (*Le texte divisé* 38; italics mine). The organization of a textual system according to the principle of montage is therefore opposed to the relation of succession and contiguity on which conventional denotation relies. Instead, it maximizes relations of conflict and discontinuity both within and between shots so as to figure a nonreferential space of signification. The process described by Eisenstein supposed that montage emphasizes the discontinuities that separate shots such that they can no longer be considered as extracted from the world, but rather as *frames* formally constituted by the camera: "From shot to shot conflict must be developed at all levels (lines, colors, lighting, volumes . . .). . . . Montage is first of all a fracturing of the order of the signifying process" (*Le texte divisé* 42). The possibility of a filmic writing is thus inhibited by the force of resemblance that attends photographic reproduction. What the ideogram represents in this respect is the possibility of a figural writing achieved through the combination of discrete entities with an iconic value into a signifying system whose value is purely symbolic (Eisenstein would say "intellectual"). Intellection is thus supposed to proceed through the apprehension of differences. A textual system constituted by montage, or what Ropars calls "hieroglyphic editing," would therefore have an epistemological status different from that of narrative-representational film. In addition, Ropars submits that Eisenstein's ideas were more radical in practice than in theory. For example, Eisenstein's theoretical definition of the montage cell as a minimal unit of signification (a cinematic sign, albeit a conflictual, unstable one) is exploded by its practical application. In its organization of a *text* through conflict at all levels of cinematic expression, montage tends to neutralize the self-identity of the shot, to fragment and open it out to signifying chains that are irreducible to any univocal sense. Quite similar, in fact, to Benveniste's comments on the irreducibility of sign to discourse and vice versa, the transversal activity of montage in the spatialization of cinematic text tends to resist or disallow its segmentation by the analyst. Ropars claims that this is indeed the experience of her analyses of *October* (1928), the work of montage accomplishes multiple chains of signification that are always combining and recombining into new configurations, new meanings that resist clear syntagmatic divisions.[8] In this respect, montage becomes the very "sign" of filmic writing. To the extent that montage finds its most radical actualization in the system of the cinematographic *text*, "it results in the production of signifying chains whose limits are undecidable and whose incessant work, both open and reversible, bars the production of any signified, which would be the freezing, closing, or fixation of this process" (*Le texte divisé* 49).

It is on this basis, however, that the theories of filmic writing presented by Kuntzel and Ropars part ways, for while the former deconstructs the epistemological privilege of writing with respect to figural discourse, the latter suggests that the deconstruction of the logocentric sign is accomplished de facto by a certain organization of filmic discourse. Moreover, whereas Kuntzel bases his theory of "writing" on a reconsideration of the *modes of interpretation and reading* that recast

À bout de souffle: Sequence 10

The paragrammatic formula: "Abdbs"

MALE VOICE-OVER:

Méfie-toi Jessica / Au biseau des baisers / Les ans passent trop vite / Évite évite évite / Les souvenirs brisés

FEMALE VOICE-OVER:

Vous faites erreur, Sherriff, / Notre histoire est noble et tragique / Comme le masque d'un tyran / Nul drame hasardeux ou magique / Aucun détail indifférent ne rend nôtre amour pathétique.

the social intelligibility of texts, Ropars builds a theory based on the "deconstruction" accomplished by cinematic *forms.* This difference in emphasis is exemplified in her analysis of Godard's *À bout de souffle* (1959).

Ropars's reading of *À bout de souffle* follows a double movement: the multiple play between two forms of writing—the "cinematic" and the "poetic"—that are continually interpenetrating and combining with each other. According to Ropars, "cinematic" writing circulates reflexively in the film in the form of graphic traces—movie posters, photos, cinema magazines—through which Michel, the Belmondo character, forges an imaginary identification, above all with the image of Bogart. The "poetic" surges textually in Ropars's most privileged "fracture zone," identified as sequence 10 in the film. This sequence develops within the space of a single shot. Having gone to the movies to see a Western, Belmondo and Seberg are shown face-to-face close-up, illuminated by the flickering light reflected from the screen. A male voice-off recites a text to which a female voice-off responds. This dialogue is scattered over two poems, one by Apollinaire, the other by Aragon, and is anchored diegetically neither to the characters, whose lips are otherwise occupied, nor by the sound-off of the supposed cinema projection.

Thus sound has become disconnected from image while poetic writing circulates in the form of disembodied voices. The cinematic sign is split by the disjunction of its two primary registers, and poetic writing occupies speech while running ahead of it in a network of assonance, homonymy, and homophony (*trop vite, évite, tragique, magique, pathétique*). In this brief moment, Ropars argues, the disassociation of image and sound made possible by montage has obscured the boundaries between figure and sign, speech and writing, and, in fact, the cinematic and the poetic, rendering them as open, multiple, and reversible. So two semiotic phenomena converge in this short passage: "*instability of the image,* both representation and support, film and screen, fiction and cinema; *disconnection of the voices,* parted from what it designates, torn apart by two equally impossible references. The divergence of the figurative and linguistic network stems from the relativity of their disjunction: a play of traces and cross-references, the text is directed at an image which comes undone under the pressure of another image itself reflected in the text; the editing circuit, having become reversible, sets up an open system of refusal between figure and sign" ("Graphic" 150; italics mine).

This short sequence might be inconsequential if it did not contain, in condensed form, what is for Ropars a *system* of the text of *À bout de souffle.* This system is organized by montage patterns, or "hieroglyphic editing," that tend to destabilize the registers of figural, scriptural, and vocal presentation. Each interpenetrates the space that is proper to the other, traversing both the mise-en-scène of the film and the fiction it stages. The circulation of "letters" forms a particularly dense network of association in Ropars's analysis of the film. For example, the line voiced from Aragon in sequence 10 ("Au biseau des baisers") is condensed into a paragrammatic formula (Abdbs) that, according to Ropars, circulates willfully in the film, inscribing itself at one point in a fragment of a movie poster ("Vivre dangeureusement, jusqu'au bout"), in the vocal alliteration of the Aragon poem ("souvenir brisés"), and in the title of a book enlarged on the screen (*Abracadabra*). It thus describes a circuit of traces that ultimately returns to the title of the film: *À bout de souffle.* In this manner, writing opens a privileged field that crosses freely between the *figural* (where writing is deployed in space, rooted in representation, or "immobilized," as Ropars says, like the photograph or graphic sign) and the *spoken,* which, far from referring back to speech as the origin and seat of meaning, implies instead the unleashing of a paragrammatic density in an explosion of phonetic traces. Therefore the activity of montage structures the enunciation of the text through a disjunction of cinematic signification with respect to itself. Here the hieroglyph is portrayed as a constant oscillation between figuration and scription—a form always divisible and combinable, and a signifying knot that directs meaning outward in ever more diverse yet related associational chains.

In Ropars's analysis, writing is associated not only with hieroglyphic script and free play but also, paradoxically, with a finality whose ultimate signified is death. Otherwise said, the written word circulates within a moribund economy. Through its references to the press, the novel, poetry, and finally the cinema, writing names a trajectory that seals identity. For Michel Poiccard, who is protected by the multiple guises that his closeness to the imaginary of cinema affords him, this means capture and extinction. The finality of the text, its narrative closure, is only ensured by naming Michel and thus "immobilizing" him. Moreover, in Ropars's reading, this economy is ultimately governed by sexual difference. It is here that the figuration of writing makes a startling reversal. In the fracture zone of sequence 10, writing not only becomes the "source" of speech but also is charged with warding off the graphic trace whose body seems both desired and prohibited, for the text of *À bout de souffle* renders this body as unequivocally feminine, sealing it in the figuration of Jean Seberg as Patricia. Entering the film with *New York Herald Tribune* doubly emblazoned on her body and in her voice, Patricia (who desires to be a journalist and a novelist) is immediately associated with "letters." In Ropars's reading, Patricia circulates in the film as the very embodiment of logocentrism: redundancy, repetition of the voice in writing; in short, "deadly monotony." Like Michel's former girlfriend who spells "pourquoi" in Lucky Strike boxes on her wall, Patricia demonstrates that the feminine body gives form to writing, stopping its circulation dead in its tracks.

The ambiguity of writing persists with the oralization triggered by Patricia. She can spread meaning as well as short-circuit it, and appears in turn as the body-turned-sign and the sign embodied, exerting a force of attraction mixed with repulsion: both letter and literature, writing and culture; an androgynous figure, who doubles

for Michel, in the double sense of the term: because she gives him
away (in French *doubler*) to the police, and because with his props
(hat, cigarette, dark glasses . . .) she takes on his role as protago-
nist . . . and his function as subject, master of vision and of the
viewer's interpellation. . . . The desire whose ambiguous object she
is thus seems inseparable from a dispossession of identity for the
one who desires her, M[ichel], sought in vain by a multitude of male
doubles, but who will stumble and die at the feet of a female double.
("Graphic" 155).

Narrative closure is thus guaranteed by the narcissistic doubling of the
female body whose sign—castration—brings finality, or the death of
the letter in the bridging of law and desire. In the final sequence of the
film, having informed on Michel, Patricia literally stands between him
and the law as the conduit bringing death.

Therefore writing occupies three intertextual spaces in Ropars's
analysis of *À bout de souffle*. First is the register of "letters" or literature, which comprises a complex network of citations from Aragon,
Apollinaire, and Maurice Sachs, as well as numerous other cultural discourses. Second is the register that is defined, through the agency of
hieroglyphic editing, by the reversibility of the "lettered voice" and
the "voiced letter," image and sound, figure and sign, that obliterates
the proper space of representation through a system of metonymy and
metaphor, displacement and condensation. Last but not least is the association of the feminine body (as visceral signifier of sexual difference)
with the written word, reducing the opposition of signs to a division
between the sexes. Here Ropars cautiously points out that the radical
potentiality of the first two registers is superintended by the last. By
formulating a paradigm (masculine/feminine) precise as it is powerful,
the textualization of the feminine body in *À bout de souffle* controls
the dissemination of letters in the film by restoring to it the status of
good fiction through the agency of a bad object. (In Kuntzel's analysis of *The Most Dangerous Game,* the paradigm of sexual difference, or
the constellation of the virgin, plays a similar role by stabilizing the reversibility of terms in the other paradigms.) Returning to sequence 10,
which poses Michel and Patricia face to face, Ropars notes that while
the doubling of images in the frame and of the voices on the sound-

track may present the sexes as equal, the division of texts does not: both poems are structured anagrammatically by the disposition of feminine subjects and names: " 'Jessica' added, or Patricia shortened in an 'amour *pathétique*' . . . which connects her to the anagram of Roma, the place of Michel's desire; Eve printed everywhere ('*Évite,* évite, évite' — why does M[ichel] only find the girls charming in Gen/*eva*?); 'dame' legible in 'drame hasardeux' . . . but how is it possible to read Adam or Abraham in it?; a multiform tree of Jesse" ("Graphic" 156).

The character of Patricia is thus deployed in Godard's film as "that dangerous supplement," a doubling of the letter in the voice and narcissistic double of masculine identity, bearing the sign of castration which either must be investigated and mastered or which masters and destroys.

> This intrusive outline, which underlines the success of writing, shows how dependent writing remains on a male subject whose doubled enunciation only borrows the woman's voice to seal the object of his desire in it. Let's not be deceived: the system of representation that associates the body with writing remains profoundly sexual; writing may be androgynous, but Patricia's androgyny is an attribute, even a defect, of the only female character, without weakening the male character's integrity, except through death. . . . In *À bout de souffle,* the doubling of sameness is resolutely projected onto . . . female images; in an imputation of feminine narcissism, it serves to divert the fascination exerted by the female body-text, displayed here as far [as] the poetic anagram. ("Graphic" 156)

Even while the feminine disturbs the linear progress of the text by displacing the proper space of cinematic signification in a hieroglyphic misalignment of image and sound, figure and sign, it nonetheless supports a contradiction where the stability of the fiction is restored by narrative and the "law" of sexual difference.

Despite a tendency to apply a sometimes idiosyncratic and recondite reading, the importance of Ropars's work in textual analysis resides in the following. Whereas most prior textual semiotics have concentrated on the mutual transformation of cinematic and narrative codes as a process in which the latter stabilize the former, Ropars's textual theory presents this transformation as a potentially destabilizing one that fragments narrative through the possibilities intrinsic to cinematic expression. However, in focusing attention on the *theory* that Ropars's textual criticism presupposes, one might inquire whether her notion of *text* falls short of that promised by hieroglyphic script and filmic writing. For example, there is little doubt that for Ropars this theory should be generated from a concrete critical relation with texts of a certain type—those whose systems of enunciation are governed by montage in its most dynamic sense. In *À bout de souffle,* this is demonstrated by "the film's paragrammatic density, the editing's ability to make the alphabet err into protean anagrams: when scriptural activity gets intense, we have seen the title and meaning come undone, and we have circulated fragments thus taken up from language along multiple channels—iconic or verbal, literal or vocal" ("Graphic" 158).

However, even if Ropars is led to underscore the explosive and centrifugal force of the hieroglyph, she cannot ignore its concomitant potential for textual stabilization. The potent difference that is understood to disfigure the integral body of the sign is also shown to be reduced by a given logic of sexual difference.

> The ambiguity of the scriptural text can be found in the female element which is supposed to embody it: there is a kind of ideological contamination here.... The fertility of the written word in the practice of filmic writing is equaled only [by] the suspicion it arouses when it is feminized in the fiction. In the same way as writing, the female figure appears as a force of disassociation; meaning she can just as well be a factor of separation, giving the sign back its evil integrity, as of disjunction, therefore of open dismembering and of spacing. ("Graphic" 158)

As Ropars points out more clearly in "Overall Perspectives," this association of the feminine body with writing reveals a profound duplicity in Godard's film, both fascination and suspicion of what Godard considers a "feminization of the medium." Writing circulates in *À bout de souffle* with a thanatopic urgency. The eruption of hieroglyphic editing in the film is thus understood as an exorcism of the danger of writing and of the difference that the feminine body presupposes. Writing appears in Godard's film then only "to be broken, erased, or transformed into a figure" (Ropars, "Overall Perspectives" 1). The epistemological urgency and the deconstruction that Godard directs at the cinematic sign is therefore guided by an economy of masochism on the part of the masculine subject. Here difference is deferred onto the fracture of the sign only to resolve itself in the death of the masculine heroes. (*Pierrot le fou* [1965] is an equally potent example in this respect.)

Thus part of the value of Ropars's work is the demonstration of a much broader phenomenon in cinematic signification: that of the reduction of the opposition of signs to the division of the sexes as a partial account of the rejection undergone by writing in the history of Western thought. However, my arguments here are directed not at the system of Godard's film but at the theory of the text presupposed by Ropars's reading. It is therefore necessary to unravel a paradox that should already be apparent. According to the management of sexual difference that superintends the system of hieroglyphic editing in Godard's films, *it is precisely the fracturing of the sign that guarantees the integrity of the enunciation and its coherence on the part of the masculine subject.* Since in several examples Ropars definitely associates a decentering of subjectivity with the deconstructive force of the hieroglyph, how are we to account for this aporia that both affirms and denies the integrity of the textual system and the subjective relations it "determines"? Does the question of "writing" in Ropars's theory interrogate the status of sign and text in film theory with the full force of deconstructive philosophy, or does writing refer to a more tangible entity, either that of graphic forms or that of "letters" in the sense of literary communication?

At the end of her essay on *À bout de souffle,* Ropars argues that "Godard's film asserts itself as writing inasmuch as it practices dismantling writing while drawing its resources from it" (159). It *is* a question, then, of "two writings." On the one hand, Ropars states that filmic writing in Godard is closely tied to a cinematic reflexivity: in the case of Godard, "the development of cinescripture [cinécriture] . . . implies a direct consideration of written form" (158). In *À bout de souffle,* this reflexivity takes the form of citations of cinema writing in the literal sense: film posters, the image of Bogart, references to *Cahiers du cinéma,* and so on. Rather than the reflexivity of *Vent d'est* or *Tout va bien,* where there is a direct appeal to recognize the mediation of cinematic discourse, here it is a question of a "filmic reflection" or a "cultural representation of cinema" (158). Like the dedication of the film to the poverty row studio, Monogram, this strategic reflexivity is one of citing or giving form to a popular discourse or popular writing of and on cinema.

But we already know that for Ropars this level of citation is in some degree parasitic. Its importance to the textual enunciation or its contribution to the film's "paragrammatic density" is formulated by the associational network that, condensed in sequence 10, distributes the textual system through a cabalistic process of fragmenting and recombining its proper name: *À bout de souffle*. And what is this sequence if not that moment where American popular narrative (the Western) meets French modernist letters (Aragon and Apollinaire)? The two dimensions of writing in the film, or the two networks of intertextual citation, are not equal. Ropars is quite clear in this respect: the former only "accompanies the fiction by reflecting it; the latter, which has to do with the semiotics of signification, causes the narrative to waver by temporarily breaking it off" ("Graphic" 158). The hieroglyphic dimension of Godard's text thus ensures, through the montage's eccentric spatial configurations, that modernist letters invade and disassemble popular fiction, molding that fiction in its image.

For Ropars, the text of Godard guarantees itself in writing, first through the presentation and thematization of graphic traces (the literal letter) and second with a direct invocation of modernist poetic letters. In the theory of the text that Ropars bases on the model of the hieroglyph, even if privilege is no longer granted to narrative, filmic writing is guaranteed nonetheless only by its conformity to a pre-given literary modality. In other words, film semiotics no longer discovers its founding moment in the narrative text, but rather in the poetic text. It is interesting to note in this respect that Ropars's description of the hieroglyphic dimension of the film-text conforms readily to Roman Jakobson's definition of poetic communication: "The poetic text projects the principle of equivalence from the axis of selection [the paradigmatic, metaphoric pole] to the axis of combination [the syntagmatic, metonymic pole]."[9] Therefore, in Ropars's theory, the ability of the film's paragrammatic dimension to disrupt the linear unfolding of narrative is managed not only by the paradigm of sexual difference; it is further controlled by a second paradigm, that which opposes poesis to mimesis. The epistemological standard of logocentrism, which reduces the intelligibility of figural discourse in the face of writing, is not fully "deconstructed" here; it has merely been displaced onto a generic division. Moreover, in Ropars's conclusion, this opposition resolves itself implicitly to a *stylistics* rather than a theory of signification or textuality. The "editing circuit" thus becomes the sphere of action of a pragmatics of the aesthetic text. Here montage is in danger of becoming the sign of "an artist creating his own semiotic" (Benveniste, cited in Ropars, *Le texte divisé* 5). Thus despite her attention to problems of Saussureanism in Benveniste, Ropars's own theory cannot decide whether the relationship between montage and enunciation is governed by the artistic development of a formal system or the pressure of a deconstructive reading. For Ropars, the value of the concept of enunciation is that it restores a sense of process and movement to the theory of the text by demonstrating the reversibility of sign and discourse, as well as all other hierarchically disposed elements of textual structure. By presupposing a disjunction of language with respect to itself, this concept opens a space in discourse for the subject to occupy. It is now necessary to ask whether this is a space where the subject stumbles and is lost, or is stood upright with the full force of an imaginary presence.

On this basis, we must finally decide whether the association of Benveniste with Freud and Derrida is in fact germane to Ropars's theory, or whether the theories supposed by enunciation, on the one hand, and écriture, on the other, might be incompatible. Here the complexity supposed by the concept of enunciation paradoxically restores to the text the self-identity of a system; it circumscribes the text, establishes its limits, and designates it as an object presupposing determinant formal and subjective relations. The writing that Ropars understands in the form of the hieroglyph and montage is ultimately reduced by this concept that ensures both the integrity of the textual body and the placement of a coherent (masculine) subject through the multiple inflections of the *voice:* that of *style* or literary voice, which defines the system of the text as an object of aesthetic communication and poetic language; that of the *author* (Godard), whose placement guarantees the status of cinema as writing, thereby inscribing it within the history of modernist letters; and finally that of mastery of the image or that fetishization of the letter where the coherence of the masculine subject is founded on the mastery of absence or the danger of loss that the feminine body is made to signify.

If Ropars initially rejects the Jakobsonian communications model of aesthetic signification, it is only to have it return in the form of the model of the poetic text that she implicitly adopts. And to the extent that the problem of meaning articulated therein is wholly assimilated to a problem of textual form on the one hand, and the reciprocity of addresser (author) and addressee (reader) on the other, Ropars's theory of the text seems to reproduce "the punctual simplicity of the classical subject." Here the theories of Kuntzel and Ropars must be opposed. For Ropars, the textual system is intrinsic: neither historical nor materialist, this conception designates the text as an empirical object whose form preordains certain types of reading by construing the relation between subject and text as one of identity. Kuntzel's theory, on the other hand, is extrinsic. It presupposes the fluidity of the semiotic process, and rather than predetermining the system of the text, it opens the text onto a discursive field where its potential meanings and subjective relations are capable of critical transformation as well as stabilization. Moreover, whereas Ropars's theory of reading emphasizes the determinations of textual form, Kuntzel restores the function of critical theory (which is both a political and ideological function) as establishing the terms through which textual meaning is formulated and disseminated in our culture.[10]

However, to the extent that she demonstrates a culturally determined relation between figure and sign, Ropars's analysis of sexual difference in filmic writing is invaluable. Bringing Derrida onto her own ground, Ropars has shown in film theory how writing has been associated with femininity in Western culture as that which disfigures the body of the logocentric sign, making it not one, not whole, not identical to itself. Here the threat of writing corresponds to that of sexual difference and more. Disassembling the integrity of the body in the voice, and of the sign in speech, Ropars's cinécriture participates in the deconstruction of distinctions of interiority and exteriority, presence and absence, and all subject/object distinctions. Yet in Ropars's theory of the text, the ghost of writing continually reinscribes the imaginary of the voice into the play of "writing." Understood as deconstructive readings, Ropars's textual analyses are forceful and superb. But as a theory of figuration and of the cinematic text, they are problematic in the degree to which they are overdetermined by models of literary speech and communication.[11]

In sum, to inaugurate a semiotic of figural discourse and hieroglyphic form, a full account of the contradictory place that writing now occupies in the field of film theory and textual analysis must be undertaken. It is part of the great value of the work of Kuntzel, Ropars, and others that they have demonstrated that the status of writing in film theory often presupposes an exorcism of the difference it signifies. The epistemological privilege granted writing in our culture is something more than the transcription of speech or the repository of memory. It is also that which constitutes itself by opposing the visual field, occupying it and reducing it. The intelligibility of figural discourse is thus constrained as that which either falls short of language or exceeds meaning, and whose significance must either be mastered by writing or built up into metaphysical fetishes such as "intuited" meaning or the sublime. In the postmodern era, the age of mass culture dominated by the social hieroglyph and what Baudrillard has characterized as the political economy of the sign, writing has been disfigured, cut loose in the visual field. Without a thorough critique, it now stands as a potential limit to cultural knowledge. This critique, moreover, must be carried through in the broader domain of the history of the aesthetic, as I will argue in the next chapter. But if film theory is to advance through deconstructive philosophy in its own province, which is that of the general intelligibility of cinematographic inscription, perhaps writing itself should now be placed under erasure, for what the textual analysis of film reveals in the examples of Kuntzel and Ropars is both the blessing and the curse of a "writing" held in place by logocentric thought. It is within the field of cinematographic signification — characterized by the heterogeneity of its matters of expression and the play of multiple signifying systems — that the potentiality of the hieroglyph as a mixed and permutable "sign" now occupies the field of its greatest reduction or liberation.

4. THE ENDS OF THE AESTHETIC

FOR CRAIG OWENS

Tout fleurira au bord d'une tombe désaffectée.—Jacques Derrida, *La verité en peinture*

With respect to the activity of aesthetic judgment, we are living in an age of reaction. Not only do the writings of the "cultural literacy" movement represent a reactionary politics, but their views also indicate a palpable withdrawal from history. Paradoxically, within their ranks, this phenomenon is cause for both celebration and mourning. In political economy, the end of History with capitalism triumphant has been proclaimed; at the same time, neoconservative educators agonize over the end of the aesthetic.

Exactly what has come to an end under the umbrella of the "aesthetic," however, is an open question. Take, for example, the debate initiated by Robert W. Pittman's 1990 editorial in the *New York Times,* "We're Talking the Wrong Language to 'TV Babies.'"[1] Pittman, "creator" of MTV and then a senior executive at Time-Warner, Inc., suggests that our cultural norms for processing information have decisively changed. Television represents a new "multidimensional" language, and its forms of reception have changed in kind: pre-TV adults process information in a linear and successive fashion appropriate to print culture; in contrast, the MTV generation is characterized by a heightened sensitivity to visualization and parallel processing—the ability to make sense simultaneously from competing information sources.

Pittman's rather McLuhanesque argument schematically represents two scandals from the point of view of the cultural literacy movement. First is the suggestion of the collapse of distinctive divisions—between aesthetic values (elite versus mass culture, for example) and aesthetic forms, especially the distinction between linguistic and plastic representation (the arts of time and the arts of space) — that have reigned unchallenged in philosophical thought for more than two hundred years. Second, and more obviously scandalous, is the suggestion that audiovisual media represent new forms of thought and new standards of literacy that render a previous culture obsolete. Here the anxiety is that the culture of *logos* is losing the high ground on a cultural battlefield where, in the information age, categories of thought are becoming increasingly nonlinear.

Pittman's sketchy arguments imply an end to categories that have traditionally defined the domain of the aesthetic and aesthetic judgment: the appeal to freedom, timeless and "universal" values, truth in representation defined by the identification of signs with nature, and the preservation of distinct divisions and hierarchies among representational forms. Yet he asks the "nonprofit sector and governmental organizations" to adapt to this sea change in the semiotic environment in order to communicate better with a youthful audience. The contradiction between the authority of Pittman's basic observation and the resistance on the part of the forces of cultural hegemony — represented not only by an influential community of intellectuals and educators but also by the NEH, NEA, the Department of Education, and other public and private organizations — is telling. As an executive of the largest entertainment and information combine in the world, Pittman represented the current historical stage in the development of capital celebrated by neoconservative economists and historians. As such he recognized clearly that the information economy is producing, and capitalizing on, new forms of signification and thought that outpace and bewilder the philosophers of reaction. The profound irony is that the cultural literacy movement continues to lobby hard for protectionism in the university because they cannot survive in a free marketplace of ideas. In like manner, they refuse to connect the imagined catastrophic end of the aesthetic to the ascension of capitalism they celebrate.

As challenges to NEA funding for "controversial artists" demonstrated, this debate is formulated as the question of what can be counted as "artistic" or "aesthetic" activity. The appeal to the universality of Western European values in this respect is curious, since the modern use of the term is a product of Enlightenment philosophy and less than two hundred years old. According to the *OED*, it had no widespread acceptance in English until the latter half of the nineteenth century. A history of the transformation of the Greek term *aisthesis*—referring generally to problems of sense perception and having its own complex history—into our modern sense of the term "aesthetic," as well as the range of meanings and activities it defines, would be of inestimable value but beyond the limits of my present argument. The keystone of this history, as Raymond Williams points out, would be to show how the aesthetic, "with its specialized references to *art,* to visual appearance, and to a category of what is 'fine' or 'beautiful,' is a key formation in a group of meanings which at once emphasized and isolated *subjective* sense-activity as the basis of art and beauty as distinct, for example, from *social* or *cultural* dimensions." [2] Our modern idea of the "aesthetic" has developed over time as a systematic retreat in philosophy from understanding the social and historical meaning of representational practices. Thus a critique of the "political economy" of art would have to confront two interrelated ideas: first, the autonomy of the aesthetic as an interiorized, subjective activity as opposed to social and collective ones; second, the value and self-identity of autonomous art as free of monetary value.[3] A deconstruction of the "aesthetic" might hasten the dissolution of this concept, already pushed to the extreme limits of its internal contradictions by the demands of contemporary capitalism, thus liberating new concepts for understanding transformations in the semiotic environment that are already taking place.

Jacques Derrida has introduced a number of questions that this genealogical critique should address in his reading—in "The Parergon" and "Economimesis"—of Kant's analytic of aesthetic judgment in the *Critique of Judgment.*[4] In these texts, Derrida demonstrates how Kant's conception of the ends and activities of art strategically obscure the inability of Enlightenment philosophy to bridge or to resolve distinctions between mind and nature, subject and object. From the eighteenth century onward, the problem of hierarchical distinctions among the arts is based on an interiorization of subjectivity that identifies "discourse" with speech and pure thought as distinguished from external perceptions derived from nature. This particular division of the verbal and the visual simultaneously elevates poetry as the highest art (because it is closest to speech and thus to thought) while identifying and ranking other artistic forms through an analogy with speech and linguistic meaning.

The question of aesthetic value is also paramount. Derrida investigates this question in neither historical nor materialist terms. At the same time, historical and materialist critics have failed to define important questions that are elaborated in Derrida's work on aesthetics. By rendering these questions explicit, and suggesting how they might be pursued, I want to establish some points of contact where an encounter between deconstruction and historical materialism may prove productive for cultural criticism. Thus Derrida's reading of Kant through the condensation "economimesis" elaborates the central issues that a genealogical critique of the idea of the aesthetic in Enlightenment thought must address. This is not simply a question of conjoining the "aesthetic" (mimesis as a process of imitation in relation to nature) and the "economic" and thereby demonstrating the allegiance of art to ideology as well as its reliance on capital. Derrida examines how the idealist elaboration of the aesthetic as an ontological question increasingly excludes consideration of the material and historical forces that are continually transforming representational practices and aesthetic experience. Idealist philosophy serves — through the elaboration of the aesthetic — to create an inverse ratio between the ontological and the historical. Derrida explores only one side of the question, namely, a critique of the ontotheological foundations of the "aesthetic." However, he does open the possibility of understanding how assertions of the autonomy and universality of the aesthetic become ever more strident as representational practices become increasingly dominated by patterns of consumption and exchange governed by the logic of commodities and the emergence of a mass public. In the current stage of development of capital, it is not that the aesthetic is now threatening to disappear, as the critics of reaction fear. Rather, it has never in fact existed, except as an ideology, in the terms elaborated since the eighteenth century in Western philosophy.

Derrida's reading of Kant is not about the interpretation of artworks, nor is he concerned with the goals and objectives of aesthetics.

Instead he performs a critical reading of how an idea of the aesthetic emerges in philosophy as one of its specific areas of inquiry. Kant is a predecessor as well as an adversary in this respect. To claim a specific territory for aesthetic judgments as essentially different from moral and scientific judgments, Kant critiques both Lord Shaftesbury and Francis Hutcheson, who equate moral and aesthetic judgments with matters of feeling, and Alexander Gottlieb Baumgarten's attempt to ground judgments of the beautiful in rational principles, thereby elevating aesthetics to the rank of a science. Thus Kant's third Critique is privileged for its exemplarity: its demonstration of how the conceptual identity of the artwork, and the organization of the domain of aesthetics, emerged in modern philosophy. By the same token, Derrida finds the problem of the example itself to be the most important and most fragile element of Kant's argument.

In *The Truth in Painting,* the chapter on the parergon in particular traces how the domain of aesthetic inquiry emerges in Kant's philosophy; that is, how the aesthetic attempts to define itself, to mark off its borders, and to give itself activities and ends distinct from other forms of philosophical work. In his opening paragraph, Derrida establishes a historical topography, beginning with the *Critique of Judgment,* which insists that the question of art be asked ontologically. As Derrida explains, this paradigm demands that "we must know of what we speak, what concerns the value of beauty *intrinsically* and what remains external to our immanent sense of it. This permanent demand—to distinguish between the internal or proper meaning and the circumstances of the object in question—organizes every philosophic discourse on art, the meaning of art and meaning itself, from Plato to Hegel, Husserl, and Heidegger. It presupposes a discourse on the limit between the inside and the outside of the art object, in this case a *discourse on the frame* ("Parergon" 12).[5]

Kant opens the terrain that modern aesthetic inquiry occupies. But the paradox of his analysis is that his solution to the specificity of aesthetic judgments *creates* the dilemma it was designed to resolve. The very insistence on enframing—defining on one hand the self-identity of art, and on the other the specificity of aesthetic judgments—is what in fact *produces* the divisions between object and subject, inside and outside, mind and nature, that the third Critique claims to transcend.

While enclosing and protecting an interior, the frame also produces an outside with which it must communicate. If the third Critique is to complete its teleological movement, this externality must also be enframed — a process creating a new outside, a new necessity for enframement, and so on ad infinitum. For Derrida, this is the *energeia* of parergonal logic.

For Kant, the principal goal and problem of the *Critique of Judgment* is to identify a bridge between his first two critiques, those of pure and practical reason. Citing Hegel's *Lectures on Aesthetics,* Derrida notes that the goal of the third Critique is "to identify in art (in general) one of the middle terms (*Mitten*) to resolve (*auflösen*) the 'opposition' between mind and nature, internal and external phenomena, the inside and the outside, etc. Still it suffered from a lacuna, a 'lack' (*Mangel*), it remained a theory of subjectivity and of judgment" ("Parergon" 3). Although Hegel reserves for himself the resolution of the subject/object dilemma, he credits Kant for having posed it astutely. Further on, Derrida cites Kant's own assessment of the problem: "Between the realm of the natural concept, as the sensible, and the realm of the concept of freedom, as the supersensible, there is a great gulf fixed, so that it is not possible to pass from the former to the latter (by means of the theoretical employment of reason), just as if they were so many separate worlds, the first of which is powerless to exercise influence on the second: still the latter is *meant* to influence the former. . . . There must, therefore, be a ground of the *unity*" (4).[6] Kant poses two separate, absolutely divided worlds across the following concepts: object/subject, nature/mind, external/internal, outside/inside, sensible/supersensible, natural concept or understanding/concept of freedom or reason.

In this respect, Kant's approach to aisthesis must be distinguished from that of Greek philosophy. Where classical thought elaborated a complex continuum between nature and mind, the material body and immaterial soul, aisthesis and noesis, Kant views them as divided worlds separated by an abyss. Yet some communication must exist between them. However, this abyss is not to be bridged by pure reason, that is, determinate concepts, since this would render aesthetic and scientific judgments as equivalent. A judgment of pure taste requires instead a logic of analogy, of telling examples, of symbols and figures; in other words, a discourse of and on the aesthetic that is governed ultimately by the logic of logocentrism. Here Derrida's reading of "economimesis" is paired with another special condensation: "examplorality." Through the rhetoric of "as if" introduced in Kant's third Critique by the discursive structure of the example, and a logic of semblance without identity originating in analogies referring to the model of speech, a bridge is extended between these discontinuous worlds. Although aesthetic judgment belongs to neither pure nor practical reason, Kant asserts nevertheless that it links them in a metaphysical system by demonstrating what is common to all three. This is a strange logic where difference and identity, the extrinsic and intrinsic, seem to cohabit peacefully.

In a work of pure philosophy, which should stand alone as a complete system of thought, "examples" define one instance of parerga. Indeed, Kant's first use of the term appears in the section "Elucidation by Examples" (§ 14) in "The Analytic of the Beautiful." Simply speaking, for Kant parerga include all things "attached" to the work of art yet not part of its intrinsic form or meaning: the frame of a painting, the colonnades of palaces, or drapery on statues. They are ornamental—an adjunct or supplement to the intrinsic beauty of the art work. Parerga border the work (as identity and activity) but are not part of it, they resemble the work without being identical to it, and they belong to the work while being subsidiary to it. As such, the question of the parergon initiates a series of divisions that define for Kant the proper object of the pure judgment of taste through a process of increasing interiorization.

On the part of the subject, aesthetic judgments, like theoretical judgments, may be empirical or pure. The former are material, sensate judgments concerning what is agreeable or disagreeable; they come to the subject from the outside by passing across the eye, the ear, or the tongue. Pure or formal judgments concern only the intrinsic beauty of the object; they are nonconceptual, a product of spirit produced by disinterested contemplation. The form of sense-objects is similarly divided between figure and play. Figure defines what is inseparable from the intrinsic architecture of the object—the design of the painting or the composition of music—and play is a secondary product of "charm," the agreeability of colors or the pleasantness of tones. But

according to Kant, though these secondary properties may not contribute to the proper pleasure of the artwork, like the frame of a painting they nonetheless have a specific, subsidiary function: "To say that
the purity alike of colours and of tones, of their variety and contrast
seem to contribute to beauty, is by no means to imply that, because
in themselves agreeable, they therefore yield an addition [*supplément*]
to the delight in the form [*Wohlgefallen an der Form*] and one on a
par with it. The real meaning rather is that they make this form more
clearly, definitely, and completely intuitable, and besides stimulate the
representation by their charm, as they excite and sustain the attention
directed to the object itself" (§ 14, "Parergon" 18). These distinctions
clarify how the parergon functions as a border. Without it there would
be no distinction between the self-identity of the aesthetic object—its
intrinsic form—and the extrinsic, aesthetic subjectivity that the artwork inspires as formal (immaterial) judgments of pure taste. As such
the parergon encloses the work, brackets it on four sides; yet it also
communicates with the outside, attracting or focusing the senses, so
that they may better intuit the work at hand.

The nature of this communication is significant. The object of Kant's
Critique is not art per se. Art or the making of art has no place in Kant's
philosophy. The philosopher has nothing to say, and should have nothing to say, to the painter or poet about the exercise of their art. The
role of the philosopher is to articulate, within her or his proper field,
the conceptual foundations that make artistic activity possible and permit it to be intuited and judged. This is a question of the analytic of
aesthetic judgment—the specificity of judgment rather than the specificity of art. Just as the analytic of the beautiful must enframe the work
of art, defining what is proper to it as an object of pure taste, what is
proper to the subject in this experience must be delimited exactly in
the conditions of aesthetic judgment.

Aesthetic judgment therefore requires a specific formalization of the
object-subject dilemma; it concerns the delimitation of the proper objects of pure taste and an analytic of the subjective feeling of pleasure
or displeasure arising in relation to them. Kant's meticulous delimitation of the conditions of object and subject in aesthetic judgment,
however, have not yet answered the fundamental question of the third
Critique: how does judgment define the base or foundation of philo-

sophical inquiry by constructing a bridge between pure and practical reason? Derrida notes that in Kant, "Understanding and reason are not two disjunct faculties; they are articulated in a specific task and a specific number of processes, precisely those which set articulation, that is, discourse, in motion. Between the two faculties, in effect, an articulate member, a third faculty comes into play. This intermediary, which Kant rightfully calls *Mittelglied,* middle articulation, is judgment (*Urteil*)" ("Parergon" 5). The modality of aesthetic judgments is similarly tied to the forms of speech. Derrida writes that "we are familiar with the example: I stand before a palace. Someone asks me whether I think it is beautiful, or rather whether I can say 'this is beautiful.' It is a question of judgment, of a judgment of universal validity, and everything must therefore be in the form of statements, questions, and answers. Even though the aesthetic affect is irreducible, judgment demands that I say 'this is beautiful' or 'this is not beautiful'" (11). Judgment formulates itself as statements, questions, and answers. It is a kind of dialogue, but of what sort? Across a series of divisions—between interlocutors engaged in "aesthetic" conversation, between the subject (spectator) and the object (palace), and within the philosophical subject internally divided in its faculties—a filigree of words is woven. Within the space of the statement, universal communication must occur freely between spatially detached and isolate parts.

Everything eventually returns to the power of logos to breathe life into judgment and harmonize the faculties. The key to understanding how aesthetic judgment illuminates the process of philosophical judgment, however, is expressed in the following question: how can aesthetic judgments appeal to a *universal* consensus and communicability when their origin is radically subjective, individual, and nonconceptual?

This appeal to universality informs Kant's famous emphasis on the disinterestedness of aesthetic judgments that is defined on the one hand by freedom and on the other by a noncognitive pleasure: the *Wohlgefallen* proper to the object of pure taste. Freedom, as the realm of the concept of the supersensible, is especially important in Kant's attempt to unify his philosophical system. This indicates, first of all, that aesthetic judgments are detached from all contingent demands or extrinsic motives, especially economic ones. There must be an absolute lack of interest in the object's existence; otherwise the critic cannot operate with perfect freedom. The spectator must have nothing at stake. If the critic invests in the object, as it were, his or her judgment cannot transcend its subjective origins and pretend to universal communicability.

The criterion of universality is also tied to the way Kant uses the idea of freedom to divide and differentiate the activities and ends of the work of art from those of nature, quotidian labor, and science. In this respect, it defines the aesthetic subjectivity of those who create as well as those who judge.

The division of art from nature is the greatest and most important territorial border in the third Critique. Doubtless, Kant preserves the classical distinction between *physis* and téchnē, where nature as mechanical necessity is opposed to art as the arena where human freedom is most clearly exercised. Ultimately, the Kantian definition of mimesis—which weaves a bold analogy between how God represents himself in nature, the artist in fine art, and the philosopher in judgment—attempts to bridge these oppositions by deriving its "rules" from nature, but only as a free production rather than mechanical repetition. Like every freedom protected by "laws," however, these rules restrict more than they allow. They instigate hierarchies of rank and privilege, empowerment and disenfranchisement, elevated and lowered beings. In this respect, freedom is first of all human freedom; the work of art is always the work of "Man" (*ein Werk der Menschen*). In Kant's example, the work of bees ("cells of wax regularly constructed"), despite their order and symmetry, cannot be considered works of art. This is the first move in a parergonal logic that divides humanity from animality— raising "man" and his productions above nature while not being strictly separate from it—in order to bring humanity in general by degrees closer to divinity.

However, in this hierarchy, mechanical repetition and ends-directed labor are not restricted to animals alone. Derrida points out that Kant's comments on the relation between nature, art, and imitation are placed between two remarks on "salary." The first, "On Art in General" (§ 43), divides liberal or free (*frei*) art from salaried or mercenary art (*Lohnkunst*). The second, "On the Division of the Fine Arts" (§ 51), declares that "in the Fine-Arts the mind must occupy itself, excite and satisfy itself without having any end in view and independently of any salary."

Art appears only in the absence of economy; its significance, value, and means of circulation may not be defined by money. "By right," Kant states, "we should not call anything art except a production through freedom, i.e., through a power of choices that bases its acts on reason" (§ 43). Thus the hierarchy that orders beings in nature according to the relation of humanity to animality replicates itself as a scale evaluating the activity and labor of individuals. In Derrida's reading of Kant:

> Art in general . . . cannot be reduced to craft [*Handwerk*]. The latter exchanges the value of its work against a salary; it is mercenary art [Lohnkunst]. Art, strictly speaking, is liberal or free [*freie*], its production must not enter into the economic circle of commerce, of offer and demand; it must not be exchanged. Liberal and mercenary art therefore do not form a couple of opposite terms. One is higher than the other, more "art" than the other; it has more value for not having any economic value. If art, in the literal sense, is "production of freedom," liberal art better conforms to its essence. ("Economimesis" 5)

Craft is based on a vulgar economy and quotidian use. For Kant, however, the artist is no common laborer, as Derrida summarizes in three points. First is Kant's suggestion that "free art is more human than remunerated work" ("Economimesis," 6). Just as the play of freedom in artistic activity elevates humanity above the instinctual activity of bees, the "liberal" artist is more fully human than the wage laborer. Second, Kant implies that just as man's elevation in nature empowers him to enlist the utility of animals toward his ends and "higher" labors, so too may the freer individual, the artist, enlist the mercenary work of the craftsperson, or use the vulgar tools of craft, without the value of art being implicated in an economy of usefulness and exchange. Oppositions deriving from nature/man and animal/human are thus reproduced as hierarchies defining the relative value of individuals and their labor, subordinating remunerated work and the lesser freedom of the craftsperson to the higher ends of the artist.

Similar criteria divide art from science and in turn reproduce hierarchical distinctions between mechanical and aesthetic art on one hand and in aesthetic art between agreeable and fine arts (*schöne Kunst*) on the other. For Kant, there is no law applicable to the imagination save what is derived from understanding. When the imagination proceeds only according to a determinate law, the forms produced are determined by concepts. This is the ideal of scientific knowledge where the imagination is subordinated to the elaboration of concepts of understanding. The Wohlgefallen appropriate to scientific statements, for example, only derives from a formal perfection in harmony with concepts; it is experienced as the "good" and has nothing to do with the beautiful as such, which, for Kant, is resolutely nonconceptual.

Unlike the scientist, the pure artist (Genius, in Kant's account) does not require reflexive conceptualization to accomplish exemplary works of fine art. By the same token, the lesser forms of art, and the pleasure defining them, are all characterized by their relative proximity to the conceptual. In Derrida's gloss, "An art that conforms to knowledge of a possible object, which executes the operations necessary to bring it into being, which knows in advance that it must produce and consequently does produce it, such a *mechanical art* neither seeks nor gives pleasure. One knows how to print a book, build a machine, one avails oneself of a model and a purpose. To mechanical art Kant opposes aesthetic art. The latter has its immediate end in pleasure" ("Economimesis" 8).

In a similar way, aesthetic art divides into two hierarchic species, for aesthetic art is not always fine or beautiful art. *Pure* taste has, in fact, a literal meaning for Kant. It elevates or lowers the aesthetic arts according to the criterion of whether their pleasures are empirical or spiritual. Within aesthetic art, the "agreeable arts" — for example, conversation, jest, the art of serving and managing dinner as well as an evening's entertainment, including music and party games — seek their ends in enjoyment (*Genuss*). The Wohlgefallen appropriate to fine art, however, involves pleasure without "enjoyment" — at least in the sense of an empirical, if incommunicable, sensation. Being purposive only for itself, it can have no finality in the sense of satisfying a physical appetite or filling an empirical lack, thus yielding Kant's basic definition: "Fine art . . . is a way of presenting [*Vorstellungsart*] that is purposive on its own and that furthers, even though without a purpose [*ohne Zweck*], the culture of our mental powers to [facilitate] social communication. The very concept of universal communicability carries with it [the requirement] that this pleasure must be a pleasure of reflection rather than one of enjoyment arising from mere sensation. Hence aesthetic art that is also fine art is one whose standard is the reflective power of judgment, rather than sensation proper" (§ 44, *Judgment* 173).

Pure pleasure and pure taste belong only to judgment and reflection; at the same time, judgment and reflection must be without concepts. Only on this basis do the criteria of freedom and noncognitive pleasure ensure the universality of aesthetic judgment as particularly human by subtracting out the creaturely distractions and temptations of worldly life. If fine art involves the "production of freedom," this is freedom from economic or political interest, and from the finality of scientific investigation or ends-directed labor, as well as a pleasure free of physical appetites.

If the experience of fine art is resolutely without *concepts,* then why should philosophy take an interest, if only the moral interest involving practical reason and concepts of freedom, in the beautiful? This is linked to a second question. Because the definition of judgments of pure taste seems to recede from both the social and the creaturely toward an interiorized, immaterial subjectivity, how does the experience of fine art advance the culture of mental powers with respect to social communication? In other words, how is the pleasure—without enjoyment or concept—of art returned to the space of philosophical communication in the predicate "This is beautiful"?

These questions are answered by considering the curious role of mimesis in the third Critique. The version of mimesis that Derrida reads in Kant is governed not by a logic of semblance or imitation but by a logic of analogy. For example, Kant defends philosophy's moral interest in the beautiful because despite its lack of conceptual grounding, the judgment of taste nonetheless *resembles* logical judgment because of its universality. Thus in aesthetic judgment the philosopher may

> talk about the beautiful as if [*als ob*] beauty were a characteristic of the object and the judgment were logical (namely a cognition of the object through concepts of it), even though in fact the judgment is only aesthetic and refers the object's presentation [*Vorstellung*] merely to the subject. He will talk in this way because the judgment does resemble [*Ähnlichkeit hat*] a logical judgment inasmuch as we may presuppose it to be valid for everyone. On the other hand, this

universality cannot arise from concepts. For from concepts there is no transition to the feeling of pleasure or displeasure (except in pure practical laws; but these carry an interest with them, while none is connected with pure judgments of taste). It follows that, since a judgment of taste involves the consciousness that all interest is kept out of it, it must also involve a claim to being valid for everyone, but without having a universality based on concepts. In other words, a judgment of taste must involve a claim to subjective universality. (§ 6, *Judgment* 54)

By similar criteria of "universality," and despite the abyss that essentially divides humanity from nature, Kant renders art and nature as equivalent, since they both share the lawfulness without a law, or purposiveness without purpose (*Zweckmässigkeit ohne Zweck*), that governs their beautiful forms. In both cases, logical relations of identity and nonidentity rest side by side like discordant notes that nevertheless ring with a strange harmony.

In this way, Kant's implicit theory of mimesis asserts the superiority of beauty in nature and derives the beautiful in art from its relation to nature. But that relation is defined not by a logic of the copy but by a rhetoric of production and reproduction. In finding common ground between art, nature, and genius, mimesis requires a logic of equivalent activities, not one of mirrors. This implies a third distinction that divides the artisan from the artist as the difference between a reproductive imagination and a productive imagination that is originary, spontaneous, and playful. In Derrida's view, the value of play in Kant defines a form of productivity that is purer, freer, and more human, as opposed to work that is ends directed, unpleasant, and exchanged against a salary.[7] Reproductive imagination is therefore a vulgar realism — reproduction in the form of likeness, or repetition as identity. In contrast, productive imagination — regardless of whether it applies to acts of creating or of judging aesthetic objects — is characterized by a paradoxical freedom that is the imagination's "free conformity to law."

The liberties implied here, as well as their limitations, are central to how Kant's notions of mimesis mediate difficulties of subject and object. On one hand, the free play of imagination is limited by the forms of the object intuited: "Although in apprehending a given object of sense the imagination is tied to a determinate form of this object and to that extent does not have free play (as it does [e.g.] in poetry), it is still conceivable that the object may offer it just the sort of form in the combination of its manifold as the imagination, if it were left to itself [and] free, would design in harmony with the *understanding's lawfulness* in general" (*Judgment* 91). A judgment of beauty becomes possible, then, when the harmony of form in the object is intuited as analogous to a harmony in the subject that the imagination would form with respect to the understanding if, paradoxically, the imagination were left in perfect freedom to conform itself to the lawfulness of understanding.

Resemblance, then, limits the freedom of the imagination, if for no other reason that it may function as an aim, purpose, or end. And the more semblance between sign and referent, the more extreme are these limitations. On the other hand, without an underlying "lawfulness" there would be no ground for uniting understanding, moral judgments, and judgments of taste, and no language with which to communicate them. By a process of analogy, this sense of lawfulness without a law and purposiveness without purpose, whose original territory is that of nature, informs and "naturalizes" every reference in the third Critique to representation, signification, or language.

In a similar way, nature limits what is most "wildly free" in the production of art through its (silent and nonconceptual) "dictation" of rules to Genius. "Genius," writes Kant, "is the talent (natural endowment) that gives the rule to art. Since talent is an innate productive ability of the artist and as such belongs itself to nature, we could also put it this way: *Genius* is the innate mental predisposition (*ingenium*) *through which* nature gives the rule to art" (§ 46, *Judgment* 174). In this manner, the forms of analogy derived from mimesis begin to efface all the oppositions — mind/nature, subject/object, supersensible/sensible — that divide Kant's philosophical system. As Derrida explains,

> All propositions of an anti-mimetic cast, all condemnations leveled against imitation are undermined at this point. One must not imitate nature; but nature, assigning its rules to genius, folds itself, returns to itself, reflects itself through art. This specular flexion provides both the principle of reflexive judgments — nature guaranteeing legality in a movement that proceeds from the particu-

lar — and the secret source of *mimesis* — understood not . . . as an imitation of nature by art, but as a flexion of *physis,* nature's relation to itself. There is no longer here any opposition between *physis* and *mimesis,* nor consequently between *physis* and *téchnē.* . . . ("Economimesis" 4)

This process of naturalization also effaces the role of economy in artistic production. If the pure pleasure of judgment and reflection is free of concepts, ends, and interests as well as empirical sensation, it is also free of exchange. The aesthetic implies an ideal freedom for humankind, by analogy like nature yet entirely separate from it, conceived as a "nonexchangeable productivity." "Nevertheless," writes Derrida, "this pure productivity of the inexchangeable liberates a sort of immaculate commerce. Being a reflective exchange, universal communicability between free subjects opens up space for the play of the Fine-Arts. There is in this a sort of pure economy in which the *oikos,* what belongs essentially to the definition [*le propre*] of man, is reflected in his pure freedom and his pure productivity" ("Economimesis" 9).

Through mimesis, then, art does not imitate nature in the sense of reproducing its visible signs. Art does not reproduce nature; it must *produce like* nature, that is, in perfect freedom. And paradoxically, for Kant the moment in which an artistic production is most fully human — in other words, most clearly and unnaturally fabricated by human hands — is the moment when it most clearly replicates the effects of the actions of nature. Thus Kant writes, "In [dealing with] a product of fine art, we must become conscious that it is art rather than nature, and yet the purposiveness in its form must seem [*scheinen*] as free from all constraint [*Zwang*] of chosen rules as if [*als ob*] it were a product of mere nature. It is this feeling of freedom in the play of our cognitive powers, a play that yet must also be purposive, which underlies that pleasure [*Lust*] which alone is universally communicable, although not based on concepts. Nature, we say, is beautiful [*schön*] if it also looks like art; and art can be called fine [*schön*] art only if we are conscious that it is art while yet it looks to us like nature" (§ 45, *Judgment* 173–74). In their most ontologically pure forms, artistic productions resemble nature most clearly when they have most clearly liberated themselves from natural laws. Art and nature are most analogous in the purity of their freedom from each other. This is Kant's most daring move in the teleological orientation of the third Critique, since it turns the chasm between mind and nature, subject and object, into the ground for their unity.

At this point Derrida reemphasizes how a divine teleology, in fact a process of ontotheological naturalization, underwrites the logic of economimesis, securing the identification of human action with divine action. This is already apparent in the hierarchies of value and identity established by the opposition of free and mercenary art. However, this identification does not necessarily subordinate humanity to a God in whose image it has been fashioned. Rather, like an identification with an other on the stage—or better yet, like a good method actor—the artist produces in his or her activity a divine subjectivity. In this way the logic of economimesis secures the figure of Genius as the exemplar of a divine agency in art where the artist creates—without concepts as a pure and free productivity of the imagination—in a fashion analogous to the way God produces his works in nature. In the third Critique, "Genius as an instance of the Fine-Arts . . . carries freedom of play to its highest point. It gives rules or at least examples but it has its own rules dictated to it by nature: so that the whole distinction between liberal and mercenary art, with the whole machinery of hierarchical subordination that it commands, reproduces nature in its production, breaks with *mimesis,* understood as imitation of what is, only to identify itself with the free unfolding-refolding of the *physis*" ("Economimesis" 6). For Kant, fine art is the art of genius, and genius is a gift of nature, an endowment of its productive freedom. And what nature gives to genius, genius gives to art in the form of "nonconceptual rules."[8] In so doing, genius "capitalizes freedom but in the same gesture naturalizes the whole of *economimesis*" (10).

The same divine teleology that ranks and orders artistic labor and subjectivity also organizes a hierarchy within the fine arts. If genius "capitalizes" freedom by submitting it to a circle of (immaculate) exchange, then some forms of artistic activity have greater value than others, and this value derives from how the exercise of freedom exemplifies the action of God in nature. According to the same logic wherein art and nature are most clearly alike when, in their beautiful forms, they are most different, Kant asserts that poetry is the highest form of expression as well as the most mimetic, because it most radically rejects imitation. Because the factor of resemblance in signs limits the freedom of the imagination, the imagination is most free and open to play in contemplation of linguistic signs because of their arbitrariness, their noncontingent relation to the natural world, and because the gift of language most clearly marks the abyss separating the human from the instinctual and creaturely. Because of their relation to language, among liberal artists, poets are the most free and, in conferring the freedom of the imagination to humanity, are most like God. This relation between God and genius defines the "immaculate commerce" informing Kant's theory of aesthetic communication, and Derrida recognizes the tautology:

> An infinite circle plays [with] itself and uses human play to reappropriate the gift for itself. The poet or genius receives from nature what he gives of course, but first he receives from nature (from God), besides the given, the giving, the power to produce and to give more than he promises to men. . . . *All that must pass through the voice.* . . .
>
> Being what he is, the poet gives more than he promises. More than anyone asks of him. And this more belongs to the understanding: it announces a game and it gives something conceptual. Doubtless it is a plus-law . . . [*un plus-de-loi*], but one produced by a faculty whose essential character is *spontaneity.* Giving more than he promises or than is asked of him, the genius poet is paid for this more by no one, at least within the political economy of man. But God supports him. He supports him with speech and in return for gratitude He furnishes him his capital, produces and reproduces his labor force, gives him surplus value and the means of giving surplus-value.
>
> This is a poetic commerce because God is a poet. There is a relation of hierarchical analogy between the poetic action of the speaking art, at the summit, and the action of God who dictates *Dichtung* to the poet. ("Economimesis" 11–12)

At the origin of all analogy, then, is the word of God; in the third Critique everything returns to logos as origin. For this reason, Derrida argues that the "origin of analogy, that from which analogy proceeds and towards which it returns, is the *logos,* reason and word, the source as mouth and as an outlet [*embouchure*]" ("Economimesis" 13). Kant's privileging of oral examples, the "exemplorality" of the *Critique of Judgment*, underwrites the crucial function of mimesis in Kant's attempt to resolve the dilemmas of subject and object formulated in his philosophical system.

I have already discussed how Kant's portrayal of "pure" judgments of taste relies on a rejection of empirical sensation and a withdrawal of the physical body. Curious, then, how the centrality of the mouth figures in the *Critique of Judgment*. Above all, in the section "On the Division of the Fine Arts," it organizes a hierarchy among the arts, and in the terms of aesthetic value (taste or disgust), by defining them with respect to the expressive organization of the human body. For Derrida, the figured circle of the mouth, and the circularity of immaculate commerce in spoken communication, organizes a parergonal logic of the subject in Kant. Just as the "frame" of painting had both to protect the intrinsic purity of art and to open up commerce with the outside, the mouth establishes a privileged border between the interiority of subject and an outside that must be represented and communicated to others, whose purest form of expression is speech. For Kant, individuals who lack any "*feeling* for beautiful nature" are those who "confine themselves to eating and drinking — to the mere enjoyments of sense," or who would prefer the trick of imitating a nightingale's song "by means of a tube or reed in [the] mouth" to the song of the poet celebrating nature in lyric. Therefore the purest judgment of taste, the truest art, and the purest Wohlgefallen pass through orality, but only in a nontactile, nonsensuous fashion. Singing and hearing thus represent "the unconsummated voice or ideal consumption, of a heightened or interiorized sensibility," as opposed to "a consuming orality which as such, has an interested taste or as actual taste, can have nothing to do with pure taste" ("Economimesis" 16).

The purest objects of taste, as well as the best judgments, pass in and out of the subject on the immateriality of breath, rather than through vulgar consumption or emesis.[9] Similarly, in Kant's *Anthropology*, hearing prevails over sight among the "objective" senses, that is, senses that give a mediate perception of the object. Unlike sight, hearing is not governed by the form of objects that may yield a determinate relation, a restriction of freedom in the play of ideas. Conversely both voice and hearing have a sympathetic relation to air, which passes outside of, and into, the subject as communicative vibrations. "It is precisely by this element," writes Kant in § 18 of his *Anthropology*,

> moved by the organ of voice, the mouth, that men, more easily and more completely, enter with others in a community of thought and sensations, especially if the sounds that each gives the other to hear are articulated and if, linked together by understanding according to laws, they constitute a language. The form of an object is not given by hearing, and linguistic sounds [*Sprachlaute*] do not immediately lead to the representation of the object, but by that very fact and because they signify nothing in themselves, at least no object, only, at most, interior feelings, they are the most appropriate means for characterizing concepts, and those who are born deaf, who consequently must also remain mute (without language) can never accede to anything more than an *analogon* of reason. (cited in "Economimesis" 19)

This identification of speech with reason and a pure interiority of thought ensures that a logocentric bias organizes the division and ranking of the fine arts in the *Critique of Judgment*. Kant bases his categorization of the fine arts—speech (*redende*), the visual or formative (*bildende*) arts, and the art of the play of sensations (*Spiel der Empfindungen*)—on an analogy with verbal communication whose fundaments include word, gesture, and tone. Where aesthetic value is concerned, the decisive criterion is a nonsensuous similarity where lyric, because of its relation of nonidentity with the signs of nature, is most like them because it allows the imagination to respond freely and without determination. Despite his potential iconoclasm in this respect, Kant ranks painting higher than music because of its ability to expand the mental powers that must unite in the activity of judgment. The problem here is the temporality of music, which, unlike painting, does not bring about a

> product that serves the concepts of the understanding as an enduring vehicle, a vehicle that commends itself to these very concepts. . . . The two kinds of art pursue quite different courses: music proceeds from sensations to indeterminate ideas; the visual arts from

determinate ideas to sensations. The latter [arts] produce a *lasting* impression, the former only a *transitory* one. The imagination can recall the lasting [impressions] and agreeably entertain itself with them; but the transitory ones either are extinguished entirely or, if the imagination involuntarily repeats them, they are more likely to be irksome to us than agreeable. (§ 53, *Judgment* 200)

Comparatively speaking, Kant disparages music not only because it is ephemeral but also because temporally and spatially it undermines the freedom and autonomy of subjective contemplation. Whereas the spectator can interrupt the temporality of painterly contemplation by averting his or her eyes, he or she cannot interrupt a musical performance, which often "extends its influence (on the neighborhood) farther than people wish, and so, as it were, imposes itself on others and hence impairs the freedom of those outside the musical party" (§ 53, *Judgment* 200).[10]

Returning to the *Anthropology,* Kant argues that sight is the most noble of the senses because it is the least tactile and least affected by the object; therefore one assumes that among the plastic arts, painting will benefit from this nobility. However, whereas sight may be the most noble sense, hearing for Kant is the least replaceable owing to the intimate relation between speech and concepts. Here again Kant refers, in a rather objectional way, to the situation of deaf-mutes who, through the absence of hearing, will never attain "true" speech and thus reason: "He will never attain real concepts [*wirklichen Begriffen*], since the signs necessary to him [gestures, for example] are not capable of universality.... Which deficiency [*Mangel*] or loss of sense is more serious, that of hearing or of sight? When it is inborn, deficiency of hearing is the least reparable [*ersetzlich*]" (cited in "Economimesis" 22).

For similar reasons, among the discursive arts, poetry (*Dichtkunst*) is superior to oratory (*Beredsamkeit*) because the latter, especially as a public art, potentially deceives and machinates, treating men "like machines" (§ 53, *Judgment* 99).[11] It is a mercenary art that promises more than it gives while expecting something in return from its audience, namely, the winning of people's minds. Therefore, in the third Critique, poetry is the highest art because "it is the art which imitates the least, and which therefore resembles most closely divine productivity. It produces more by liberating the imagination; it is more playful because the forms of external sensible nature no longer serve to limit it" ("Economimesis" 17). By the same token, poetic genius is the highest form of aesthetic subjectivity because in its analogous relation to the divine logos, it is the most free and confers the most liberty on the imagination of individuals: "It expands the mind: for it sets the imagination free and offers [*darbietet*] us, from among the unlimited variety of possible forms that harmonize with a given concept, though within that concept's limits, that form which links [*verknüpft*] the exhibition [*Darstellung*] of the concept with a wealth of thought [*Gedankenfülle*] to which no linguistic expression [*Sprachausdruck*] is completely adequate [*völlig adäquat*], and so poetry rises [*sich erhabt*] aesthetically to ideas" (§ 53, *Judgment* 196). In Kant's view, by freeing us from the limits of external, sensual nature, poetry binds linguistic presentation to the fullness of thought, rendering the presence of ideas to thought, in a way that no other art can. And even if, as a figured "aesthetic" language, it is inadequate to the absolute plenitude of the suprasensible, it is nonetheless closer to truth. Unlike rhetoric, which uses the figurative potential of language to deceive purposely and to limit freedom of the imagination, poetry fully discloses that it is mere play that can nonetheless be used to extend the power of understanding.

Derrida rightly insists that Kant derives a theory of value from the arbitrariness of the vocal signifier, that is, its difference with respect to external sensible nature. The difference, immateriality, and interiority of the vocal signifier align it with the realm of freedom:

> Communication here is closer to freedom and spontaneity. It is also more complete, since interiority expresses itself here directly. It is more universal for all these reasons. . . . And once sounds no longer have any relation of natural representation with external sensible things, they are more easily linked to the spontaneity of the understanding. Articulated, they furnish a language in agreement with its laws. Here indeed we have the arbitrary nature of the vocal signifier. It belongs to the element of freedom and can only have interior or ideal signifieds, that is, conceptual ones. Between the concept and the system of hearing-oneself-speak, between the intelligible and speech, the link is privileged. One must use the term

hearing-oneself-speak [*le s'entendre-parler*] because the structure is auto-affective; in it the mouth and the ear cannot be dissociated. ("Economimesis" 19)

The nature of this freedom is marked in every case by a profound interiorization, a retreat from the external signs of nature into a purely subjective autonomy whose measure is the autoaffective structure of logocentrism. Here we must try to bring together the analytic of judgments of pure taste and the analytic of the beautiful while rethinking the relation between subject and object as well as mind and nature, implied by Kant's theory of signification in the third Critique. In this manner, the circle of orality passes again through three otherwise autonomous realms: those of nature (God), art (poetry), and philosophy (judgment).

The self-identity of judgment as a mental power separate from cognition (understanding or pure reason) and desire (practical reason) derives only from the feelings of pleasure or displeasure that belong to it. Nevertheless Kant insists that the philosopher should take a moral interest in the beautiful in nature in spite of the nonconceptual and disinterested pleasure devolving from judgments of pure taste, for this Wohlgefallen would not be explicable if there were not a principle of harmony (*Übereinstimmung*) between what nature produces in its beautiful forms and our disinterested pleasure in them. Although the latter is detached from all determined ends or interests, there must be some means of demonstrating the analogous relation between the purposiveness of nature and our Wohlgefallen.

This demonstration cannot take place through pure concepts of understanding. However, for Kant this harmony is legible, or perhaps it would be better to say audible, in the impure mimesis, the relation of identity in nonidentity, that determines the autoaffective structure of logos as the origin of analogy in the third Critique. There must be "language" in nature, or at least the traces of a formalization organizing the apparent disorder of nature as legible signs. Otherwise the beautiful in nature could never be intuited. The experience of Wohlgefallen itself, which binds imagination and language in the predication "This is beautiful" is evidence enough for Kant that there is poetry in nature of which God is the author, even if a theological proof is ultimately insufficient for him. Through his insistence on an analogy between moral judgments and judgments of taste, Kant asserts in § 42 the superiority of natural beauty and attests to its aesthetic legibility in a judgment of pure taste, that is, our ability to "read the 'ciphered language' [*Chiffre-schift*] that nature 'speaks to us figurally [*figürlich*] through its beautiful forms,' its real signatures which makes us consider it, nature, as art production. Nature lets itself be admired as art, not by accident but according to well-ordered laws" ("Economimesis" 4). Later, Derrida summarizes this idea by stating that for Kant, "Beautiful forms, which signify nothing and have no determined purpose are therefore *also, and by that very fact,* encrypted signs, a figural writing set down in nature's production. The *without* of pure detachment is in truth a language that nature speaks to us. . . . Thus the in-significant non-language of forms which have no purpose or end and make no sense, this silence is a language between nature and man" (15).

This analogy between nature and art is parergonal, forging an identity between otherwise exclusive realms, those of humanity and nature: nature speaks but silently; it writes but figurally; it is endowed with interest that can only be taken in a disinterested way. With the controlled indeterminacy that marks every parergon, the realms of nature and humanity are given a common language yet denied the space of reciprocal communication; they must remain extrinsic to each other. But this does not mean that a dialogue will not take place. Finding the beautiful in nature and art, we may experience them both aesthetically. However, the extrinsic form of aesthetic objects, activities, and situations has less to do with the power of judging than with the peculiarities of an internal (silent) dialogue between imagination and the understanding that arises in the subject, but only on one necessary condition: that the purpose or ends of this experience remain indeterminate and inscrutable, and therefore without finality. While intractably dividing object and subject, the "disinterestedness" of the aesthetic nonetheless inspires communication by inscribing the circle of the mouth on the (philosophical) body of the subject. The purposelessness of both nature and art opens up a dialogue in the necessary interiority of aesthetic judgment. In Derrida's assessment of Kant, this "purposelessness [*le sans-fin*] . . . leads us back inside ourselves. Because the outside appears purposeless, we seek purpose within. There is something like a movement of interiorizing suppliance [*suppléance intériorisante*], a sort of slurping [*suçotement*] by which, cut off from what we seek outside . . . we seek and give within, in an autonomous fashion, not by licking our chops, or smacking our lips or whetting our palates, but rather . . . by giving ourselves orders, categorical imperatives, by chatting with ourselves through universal schemas once they no longer come from outside" ("Economimesis" 14).[12]

In this way, the nonconceptual pleasure inherent in judgments of pure taste is associated with the play of freedom as "a lawfulness without a law, and a subjective harmony of the imagination without an objective harmony" in a movement of idealizing interiorization (*Judgment* 92). Everything recedes — from the extrinsic, the empirical, and the corporeal — into the subjective, the internal, and the spiritual. This is why one must not consult the aesthetic object with cognition in mind. Rather, it is a subjective, interiorized investigation of the origin of a pleasure that is nonconceptual and thus nondiscursive.

This is the final ground for the essential disinterestedness of aesthetic judgments. To say that an object is beautiful, and to demonstrate that the philosopher has pure taste, everything returns to the meaning that the subject can give to the representation [*Darstellung*], excluding any factor that would make the subject dependent on the real existence of the object. For this reason, Derrida states that the Wohlgefallen, the pleasure proper to art in the Kantian sense, takes the form of an autoaffection, an interiorized and self-authenticating dialogue. In *Of Grammatology*, the logocentric circle of autoaffection is critiqued as a self-producing and self-authenticating movement that identifies reason and fullness of being with the temporality of speech. Thinking, at least the pure thought of philosophy, is represented as hearing-oneself-speak, a formula Derrida reprises in relation to Kant's *Critique of Judgment*. The comparative authenticity and veracity of poetic speech, its capacity for mimesis without semblance, the indissociable relation between the mouth and the ear, the irreplaceability of hearing, the association of speech with interiority, with concepts, and with internal sense — all these factors mark an insistence that the position of logos in Kant's system is not one analogy among others. The linguistic signifier is that "which regulates all analogy," writes Derrida, "and which itself is not analogical, since it forms the ground of analogy, the *logos* of analogy towards which everything flows back but which itself remains without system, outside of the system that it orients as its ends and its origin, its embouchure and its source" ("Economimesis" 19).

In Derrida's chapter on the parergon, this internal speech also represents a discursive invagination of the aesthetic. Something in the pure alterity of the beautiful initiates a silent, internal dialogue between the mental powers of imagination and understanding that in turn externalizes itself as speech, ensuring its communication in judgment. This is not a dialectic, at least in the Hegelian or Marxian sense, but rather a series of discrete exchanges rendered as equivalent because they share a common modality. In this manner, autoaffection, in the proper Wohlgefallen, becomes for Kant the possibility of mastering the opposition between mind and nature, the inside and the outside, and the subject's relation to the object. Similarly, although the Wohlgefallen that breathes life into aesthetic judgment is the property of the subject, it is itself not intrinsically "subjective":

> Since this affect of *enjoying something* remains thoroughly subjective, we may speak here of an autoaffection. The role of imagination and thus of time in the entire discourse confirms this. Nothing which exists, as such, nothing in time and in space can produce this affect which affects itself with itself. And nevertheless, *enjoying something,* the *something* of enjoyment also indicates that this autoaffection extends beyond itself: it is pure heteroaffection. The purely subjective affect is provoked by that which we call the beautiful, that which is said to be beautiful: *outside,* in the object and independent of its existence. From which, the indispensable, critical character of the recourse to judgment: the structure of autoaffection is such that it is affected by a pure objectivity about which we must say, "This *is* beautiful," and "This statement has universal validity." Otherwise there would be no problem, no discourse on art. *The wholly other affects me with pure pleasure while depriving me of both concept and enjoyment. . . .* Utterly irreducible heteroaffection inhabits—intrinsically—the hermetic autoaffection: this is the "*grosse Schwierigkeit*": it does not install itself in the comfortable arrangement of the overworked subject/object couple, within an arbitrarily determined space. . . .

And all the same time it is there, pleasure, something remains; *it is there, es gibt, ça donne,* pleasure is what is given; for no one, but it remains and it is the best, the purest. And it is this remainder that gives rise to speech, since it is discourse on the beautiful that is primarily under consideration once again, discursivity with the structure of the beautiful and not only a discourse arising out of the beautiful. ("Parergon" 13-14)

Just as there could not be beauty in nature if there were not, by analogy, a poetry of nature, a discourse could not emerge from the beautiful if the beautiful were not itself discursive. This is why the orality of poetry has the most pure affinity with that of aesthetic judgment: not only because they are the most purely internal and auto-affecting but because art and judgment share the same frame, that is, the circle of the mouth. Judgment must speak or state the beautiful, even if the beautiful eludes it conceptually, to supplement beauty's nonconceptual lack and return it to the space of philosophy. The auto-affective circle that produces the judgment of pure taste also informs how God figures his order in nature, how the gift of "natural" cre-ativity is transmitted to genius, how genius bestows the gift of form on poetic language, and in turn how a judgment of pure taste is engen-dered by contemplation of the beautiful forms of poetry or of nature. As parergons, there is an essential relation here between the frame and the signature, on one hand, and the circle of the mouth in relation to exemplorality, on the other. Just as the inscription of the signature ensures an external authorizing presence within the purportedly pure aesthetic interiority delimited by the frame, so the figure of the mouth, and the circularity between speech and hearing, ensures a passageway between mind and nature, the inside and the outside, subject and ob-ject, where heteroaffection and autoaffection fly into and out of each other, gliding on the wings of speech.

This peculiar oscillation in the analytic of pure taste replicates exactly that of the analytic of the beautiful, defining the status of both as parergons. The frame is supposed to decide what is intrinsic to the artwork, defining its ontological character as such. The frame is there to divide and exclude, separate the outside from the inside, and to con-trol any commerce between them. Yet it must also be a bridge, for the whole point of the third Critique is an extrinsic appeal—the relation between the spectator and the artwork and how that confrontation between two unique identities, between subject and object, produces a unity in the form of judgments of pure taste. The parergon is therefore a logic of "controlled indeterminacy" or of a ceaseless vibration between inside and outside, the intrinsic and extrinsic, subject and object, the reflective and the determinant, the singular and the universal, the conceptual and the nonconceptual, mind and nature. In short, the ontological question of "what is," which is meant to define the integral being of art and of aesthetic subjectivity, seems paradoxically to appeal to, and be infected with, the outside in the very asking of the question. The frame of Kant's analytic thus functions itself as a parergon. In Derrida's words, it is "summoned and assembled like a supplement because of the lack—a certain 'internal' indetermination—in the very thing it enframes" ("Parergon" 33). This indetermination is, in fact, the ontological uncertainty of the very idea of the aesthetic:

> The analytic *determines* the frame as *parergon,* that which simultaneously constitutes and destroys it, makes it hold (as in *hold together,* it constitutes, mounts, enshrines, sets, borders, assembles, protects —so many operations assembled by the *Einfassung*) and fall at the same time. A frame is in essence constructed and therefore fragile, this is the essence or truth of the frame. If such a thing exists. But this "truth" can no longer be a "truth," it defines neither the transcendent nor the contingent character of the frame, only its character as *parergon.*
>
> Philosophy wants to examine this "truth," but never succeeds. That which produces and manipulates the frame sets everything in motion to efface its effect, most often by naturalizing it to infinity, in God's keeping. ("Parergon" 33)

A parergon is only added to supplement a lack in the system it augments. No simple exteriority defines the space of parerga, for they also constitute an "internal structural link . . . inseparable from a lack within the *ergon.* And this lack makes for the very unity of the *ergon*" ("Parergon" 24). (Indeed, the *Critique of Judgment* is itself parergonal, which is why Derrida decides to read a work of philosophy as if it were a work of art. It is a detachable volume within Kant's system of philosophy while being at the same time functionally inseparable. The third Critique must bridge the gap opened between the first two and thus complete Kant's system of transcendental idealism, enframe it from inside, making the system visible in its entirety.) The frame is summoned to give an ontological presence and shape to a space that otherwise threatens to dissolve in aporia; the circle is there to give form to what is otherwise an absent center, and to provide a concept for an otherwise conceptless blank space. This is another way of saying that the aesthetic is an imaginary concept, but in the psychoanalytic rather than Kantian manner. Feeding a regressive fantasy of presence and autonomy, it detaches the work from the field of history by resolutely excluding any social meaning, including the economic and the political. Thus the frame functions as "the invisible limit of (between) the interiority of meaning (protected by the entire hermeneutic, semiotic, phenomenological, and formalist tradition) *and* (of) all the extrinsic empiricals which, blind and illiterate, dodge the question" (24).

In this respect, I would like to conclude with some brief remarks on the division between the verbal and visual in Kant, as well as Derrida's rather cryptic but frequent references to the work of mourning in the Kantian experience of pure taste and the Wohlgefallen appropriate to it.

As I argued earlier, the eighteenth century produced a hierarchical opposition between the verbal and the visual, linguistic and plastic representation, as ontological categories that can no longer be sustained, if indeed they ever could. Kant does not produce this hierarchy in as definite way as Lessing before him or Hegel and Heidegger after him. Kant's ideas concerning the division of the fine arts are not specifically iconoclastic, nor is he concerned, as Lessing is in *Laocoön*, with defining and preserving territorial borders among the arts, thereby reproducing the ontological drive of the aesthetic within a definition of the *differencia specifica* of various artistic media. There is one exception—poetry. Here an ontological imperative unites object and subject: the question of the aesthetic and that of judgment in the autoaffective identification of speech, reason, and freedom that defines the logocentrism of the third Critique. In Derrida's gloss, "Kant specifies that the only thing one ought to call 'art' is the production of freedom by means of freedom [*Hervorbringung durch Freiheit*]. Art properly speaking puts free will [*Wilkür*] to work and places reason at the root of its acts. There is therefore no art, in a strict sense, except that of a being who is free and *logon ekon* [has speech]" ("Economimesis" 5).

Although poetry is the highest art for Kant because imitating the least, it is most free, the principle of nonsensuous similarity is not the only criterion for ranking the arts. If so, music would have to be ranked higher than painting. But here the preference for private as opposed to public experience emerges at the same time that sight, while being the noblest sense, is subordinated to hearing as the least replaceable. Both the privilege of the poetic and the exemplorality of the third Critique point to what amounts to a transcendent principle, ranking the arts according to their ability to exhibit "aesthetic ideas." For Kant, *Spirit* (*Geist*) is the animating principle that defines the purposiveness of mental life. "By an aesthetic idea," writes Kant, "I mean a presentation of the imagination [*Vorstellung der Einbildungskraft*] which prompts much thought, but to which no determinate thought whatsoever, i.e., no [determinate] *concept*, can be adequate, so that no language [*Sprache*] can express it completely and allow us to grasp it" (*Judgment*, § 49, 182). Further on, Kant summarizes: "In a word, an aesthetic idea is a presentation of the imagination which is conjoined with a given concept and is connected, when we use imagination in its freedom, with such a multiplicity of partial presentations that no expression that stands for a determinate concept can be found for it. Hence it is a presentation that makes us add to a concept the thoughts of much that is ineffable, but the feeling of which quickens our cognitive powers and connects language, which would otherwise be mere letters, with spirit" (185). The intervening example entails Kant's reading of a poem by Frederick the Great, about which Derrida has much to say. I restrict myself to pointing out that the graphic presentation of speech in writing finally combines all the elements adhering to a judgment of pure taste. Lack of semblance produces a surfeit of freedom; the wider the abyss between an external representamen and its internal apprehension, the higher the pitch of mental powers whose agitation breeds concepts. Through the eye, the noblest and least tactile sense, comes the purest, most immaterial, and most interior hearing. All interest has finally withdrawn: the poet withdraws into writing, itself the best representation of speech, if only a supplementary one, because of its nonsensuous similarity. Yet only this pure, interior speech animates it as Geist, gives meaning and value to language that would otherwise be mere letters, just as, paradoxically, the King returns political economy to the third Critique through his patronage. In sum, lack of semblance, maximization of freedom and the subjective powers of desire, absolute interiorization: this is the formula that only poetry provides. And despite the implied preference for poetic writing and the silence of reading, only logos can return meaning to spirit as hearing-oneself-speak, and in the third Critique this is true for every art, spatial or temporal, plastic or linguistic.

Thus Kant participates importantly in forging the division between the verbal and the visual as it emerges in eighteenth-century thought. But the ontological surplus that adheres in the former is so powerful that Kant seems indifferent to the latter. The formal status of the plastic and musical arts is taken for granted. They can be dispensed with quickly to move on to more pressing business. However, this absence of reflection on the "lower" arts—despite the process of division and hierarchy that seems to demand it—nonetheless continues to function through a sort of repression. It returns in the third Critique through the supplementary logic of examples; for example, verbal images like that of judgment as a "bridge" linking the abyss separating understanding and reason, but more importantly in the square of the frame and the circle of the mouth. The square and the circle as figured spaces are crucial to Derrida's reading.[13] In the *Critique of Judgment,* the figural incessantly inhabits and haunts the logocentric space that attempts to exorcise it, and the more the space of logos attempts to purify itself in the language of philosophy, the more figural and analogical that language becomes. While representing the drive for enframing and enclosure that informs the ontological imperative of the aesthetic, the parergon simultaneously presents its empty center, in fact, the absence of a center as ontological lack. In this manner, Derrida's genealogical critique demonstrates the breadth and complexity of what must be deconstructed in the idea of the aesthetic. This does not mean restoring to philosophy the task of assessing the meaning and value of the visual arts, for this only overturns the hierarchy by restoring the ontology in another way; it does not deconstruct it. What is most important is understanding how philosophy has produced the problem of the self-definition of the arts, as well as the autonomy of fine art and of aesthetic meaning, as a response to the very indeterminacy or undecidability of all ontological questions.

The foregoing references to the revenants haunting the third Critique lead finally to Derrida's comparison of the Wohlgefallen of pure taste to the work of mourning. According to psychoanalytic theory, mourning is a process where the subject replaces mentally the loss of a loved object. The death of the object is what gives rise to mourning, which is why the idea of the aesthetic appears in an era marked by ever increasing reification, culminating in our own age. The work of mourning is also characterized by a process of interiorization, in fact, a process of incorporation that erects the lost object within the subject as an idealized image. The historical irony of the idea of the aesthetic derives from understanding that the rise and decline of an ideal of Art does not develop across a continuum; rather, they are two sides of the same process. Derrida is correct in reading in this irony the tautological orientation of transcendental idealism. It is not that Art dies and therefore must be mourned; this is the anxiety of the cultural literacy movement. Rather, it is the unconscious fear that Art may never have existed — and will never be able to exist in the economic age that desires it as a supplement to alienation and lack of freedom — that accounts for the ideologies subtending transcendental idealism.

But everything blossoms beside a deconsecrated tomb. I thus offer in conclusion the following funereal image. In a simply but elegantly appointed auditorium, two Old Masters in identical gold frames lean uncertainly against an off-white background. They are neither attached to the space nor hung from it, for their stay here will be a short one. Indeed, they may never be seen again, for although they are too big to fit in your wallet, they will store easily in a vault. They are in transit, and above them hangs a sign not unlike the ones found in railroad stations and airports the world over. It reads "Sotheby's Founded 1744" and records the value of these works, which shifts second by second, in dollars, pounds, francs, marks, lira, and yen. The caption to this image reads "Dede Brooks Makes Her Bid: Sotheby's president wants her auction house to be a stock exchange for art."[14]

This image presents the ultimate irony of the cultural literacy movement, as well as the affectations of taste and connoisseurship that have

Dede Brooks makes her bid: Sotheby's president wants her auction house to be a stock exchange for art.

so profoundly marked the institutional development of art history. We are in the last stage of the era of the aesthetic. The split in consciousness that attempts to repress the economic and the political in the aesthetic has never been so severe. Similarly, we now occupy an age when the economic has almost completely possessed what is called the aesthetic as well as the most advanced technologies of representation available to us. It is hard to comprehend how this dialectic can develop further, although there is no guarantee that it will not. Nonetheless it renders ironic in ever more powerful and visceral terms the hue and cry for the restoration of traditional concepts of "value" and hierarchies of evaluation, of the self-identity of the artist and of aesthetic work as free from value, and of the necessary relation between beauty and nature. Paradoxically, this work of mourning is possible only because the political and economic society that the neoconservatives most fervently pray for has reached an advanced stage of development. And if Art is finally and incontrovertibly being converted into capital, this is because the ideology of the aesthetic was itself seeded and nurtured by a capitalist political economy. This is the historical lesson that Derrida's philosophical deconstruction of the aesthetic enables us to examine and work through. The contradictory consciousness of the neoconservative movement derives from the refusal to understand that their ideology of the aesthetic, whose disappearance they fear, derives from the political economy they celebrate as globally triumphant. This has been true for nearly three hundred years. Thus the more they cheer on the triumph of capitalism, the deeper they dig their own cultural graves.

This conclusion should cheer those interested in a contestatory art, and a contestatory cultural criticism, to the extent that they themselves can work through, and indeed liberate themselves philosophically from, the idea of the aesthetic.

5. THE HISTORICAL IMAGE

I sometimes wonder whether advancing age does not increase our susceptibility to the speechless plea of the dead; the older one grows, the more he is bound to realize that his future is the future of the past—history.—Siegfried Kracauer, *History: The Last Things before the Last*

A Plea for the Dead Toward the end of *The Order of Things*, Michel Foucault offers the following reflection on the problem of historical knowing:

> All knowledge is rooted in a life, a society, and a language that have a history; and it is in that very history that knowledge finds the element enabling it to communicate with other forms of life, other types of society, other significations: that is why historicism always implies a certain philosophy, or at least a certain methodology, of living comprehension (in the element of the *Lebenswelt*), of inter-human communication (against a background of social structures), and of hermeneutics (as the re-apprehension through the manifest meaning of the discourse of another meaning at once secondary and primary, that is, more hidden but also more fundamental. (372–73)

To suggest a comparison between the work of Siegfried Kracauer and Michel Foucault may appear disingenuous. Kracauer himself would have warned against making too much of the exact contemporaneity of his last work, *History: The Last Things before the Last*, and Foucault's book for this would assume a necessary relation between two historical thinkers simply on the basis of their sharing a common time.[1] Obviously Kracauer and Foucault occupy different discursive contexts, and in fact, both are the product of different times. Yet there is a problematic that bridges this distance, one that operates obsessively as the "positive unconscious" of Foucault's book (appearing undisguised only in these last pages) while presenting itself as the manifest objective of Kracauer's: a redemption of the power and specificity of historical thought as a particular form of knowledge.

This unlikely and polemical juxtaposition might begin to account for the sense of the uncanny that strikes the "modern" reader who happens on Kracauer's book *History: The Last Things before the Last*. For example, without effacing the real differences between Kracauer's and Foucault's thought, one can nonetheless assert that both would insist that historical knowledge is possible only on the basis of an experience of finitude and the fundamental discontinuities of history, and both use the same term — "regularity" — to assert that the coherence of historical thought in no way implies the force of chronological, linear, or homogeneous temporal schemata. More important, both ultimately understand history as an intermediate yet privileged epistemological space that unceasingly erodes (without surpassing) philosophy's pretensions to universal understanding by demonstrating its temporal aspect and its failure to comprehend the minutiae of everyday life.

For the reader used to thinking of Kracauer as a "classical" theorist, other surprising affinities with "modern" thought abound. Kracauer's critique of Hegel, which is one of the most comprehensive motifs of the book, situates him within one of the key problematics of Frankfurt school writings on history. Yet the nature of that critique, with its insistence on the discontinuous and nonhomogeneous structure of historical space, most closely resembles Althusser's.[2] Nevertheless, to understand Kracauer's fundamental contribution to a philosophy of historical knowing, one must first attempt to situate his final book not only with respect to the full scope of his writings but more importantly with Kracauer's specific yet oblique relation to other Frankfurt school writings on the philosophy of history, crucially those of T. W. Adorno and Walter Benjamin. The work of Walter Benjamin is especially important, and it is strange in retrospect that it has taken so long for Anglophone readers to recognize the intellectual correspondences between these two thinkers. The neglect of Kracauer's book on history, and the general misunderstanding of his later work written and published in English, is scandalous but may be explained by a specific historical paradox. Kracauer was a thorough reader of Benjamin, and the earliest translation of Benjamin's writings, *Illuminations,* reached English readers only in 1969, the same year as Kracauer's book on history was published posthumously.[3] Moreover, although Benjamin's thoughts on history thoroughly permeate Kracauer's book, Benjamin's voice is still a distant one, echoing against the influence of Dilthey and Husserl. This voice is also distant because it is drained of its revolutionary power. Kracauer, though still a committed materialist, was, at the time, no Marxist, nor does his critique of historical knowing carry the force or political commitment of Benjamin's "Theses on the Philosophy of History," for example. However, it is precisely the context of Benjamin, I would argue, that is needed to understand Kracauer and, in certain respects, to read him against himself. In short, Kracauer seems to take for granted lessons from Benjamin of which his time and place were not yet aware.

Two essays by Benjamin in particular continually assert themselves in Kracauer's argument—the introduction to the *Trauerspiel* book and the "Theses on the Philosophy of History." Not coincidentally, these are Benjamin's last work and one of his earliest. More explicitly, Kracauer notes with surprise in his introduction that his apparently "new" interest in problems of historical knowing revealed a long, complex genealogy. This genealogy, which seems to originate first in a clarification and justification of his *Theory of Film,* subsequently reveals a lifelong project—"the rehabilitation of objectives and modes of being which still lack a name and hence are overlooked or misjudged" (*History* 4)—that includes his *Die Angestellten,* his novel, *Ginster,* his study of Offenbach, and most fundamentally his 1927 essay on photography. *History: The Last Things before the Last* comprises a curved universe in which the momentum of Kracauer's thought follows the arc of a long backward glance. The more he pushes forward, the closer he seems to his point of origin. And just as Benjamin was finally able to place the theological orientation of the *Trauerspiel* study side by side with a materialist perspective in the "Theses on the Philosophy of History," Kracauer's last work finds its most significant dialectical juxtaposition in a parallel between history and photography, originally explored in his 1927 essay "Die Photographie."[4] Photography and film have a privileged vocation for what Benjamin and Adorno call the capture and constuction of "historical images." For the attentive social reader, the historical image illuminates not only the play of forces wherein the commodity relations of capitalism permeate and reify the everyday experience of individuals and the forms of collective life available to them but also the play of resistance and the utopian desire for other modes of existence whose expression is otherwise occluded in the history of capitalist societies.

The importance of *History: The Last Things before the Last,* then, is that it not only offers a renewed consideration of Kracauer's often and unfairly maligned *Theory of Film* and a historiographic correction for *From Caligari to Hitler,* but also serves as a unique bridge between classical and modern German film theory. And just as powerfully, it pushes to its limits an entire tradition of classical thought on the practice of historical writing and knowing within a context that is decidedly modern.

An analysis of the simple surface manifestations of an epoch can contribute more to determining its place in the historical process than judgments of the epoch about itself. As expressions of the tendencies of a given time, these judgments cannot be considered valid testimonies about its overall situation. On the other hand the very unconscious nature of these surface manifestations allows for direct access to the underlying meaning of existing conditions. —Siegfried Kracauer, "The Mass Ornament" 67[5]

Film has enriched our field of perception with methods which can be illustrated by reference to those of Freudian theory. Fifty years ago, a slip of the tongue passed more or less unnoticed. Only exceptionally may such a slip have revealed dimensions of depth in a conversation which had seemed to be taking its course on the surface. Since *The Psychopathology of Everyday Life* things have changed. The book isolated and made analyzable things which had heretefore floated along unnoticed in the broad stream of perception. For the entire spectrum of optical, and now also acoustical, perception the film has brought about a similar deepening of apperception. . . .

Evidently, a different nature opens itself to the camera than to the naked eye—if only because an unconsciously penetrated space is substituted for a space consciously explored by man. . . . The camera introduces us to the optical unconscious in a similar way as psychoanalysis does to that of the drives. — Walter Benjamin, "The Work of Art in the Age of Mechanical Reproduction," in *Illuminations* 237–38

Film renders visible what we did not, or perhaps even could not, see before its advent. It effectively assists us in discovering the material world with its psycho-physical correspondences. We literally redeem this world from its dormant state, its state of virtual non-existence, by endeavoring to experience it through the camera. And we are free to experience it because we are fragmentized. The cinema can be defined as a medium particularly equipped to promote the redemption of physical reality. — Siegfried Kracauer, *Theory of Film* 300[6]

Social Hieroglyphs and the Optics of History   In his "Introduction to Siegfried Kracauer's 'The Mass Ornament,' " the late Karsten Witte observed that the link between Kracauer's early and late work "lies in his intention to decipher social tendencies revealed in ephemeral cultural phenomena."[7] Witte's arguments delineating the relationship between Kracauer's essays of the twenties and the later work on film and historiography are suggestive in their description of Kracauer's efforts to forge, in Foucault's terms, a "methodology of living comprehension" that could provide the basis for unlocking the specific form of historical knowledge communicated by the emblems of mass culture. Several themes introduced here hold specific interest for Kracauer's ideas on the image character of history and what they might mean for the figural. One of the central ideas in Kracauer's writings (to which I will return in a more detailed way) concerns the special epistemological status of mass cultural phenomena, a status that demands that they be cataloged and brought to the attention of an informed reading that can unlock their knowledge. In "The Mass Ornament," Kracauer observes that the culture of the mass, which is usually despised by traditional aesthetics, contains a measure of reality in the form of a social knowledge that is no longer accessible to communication through art or philosophy. Nor is it a communication of the masses to themselves: "Even though the masses bring it about," writes Kracauer, "they do not participate in conceiving the ornament" ("Mass Ornament" 69). The peculiar rationality of the mass ornament is that of the capitalist production process itself, which has occulted nature no less forcefully than the experience of community and national identity (*Volksgemeinschaft*). Both nature and personality, in Kracauer's argument, have been transformed as worked matter, patterned in the form of the commodity. In "The Mass Ornament," a privileged example of this transformation is the popularity of the Tiller Girls, a troupe of American dancers, usually without professional training, who performed intricate drill maneuvers in a style that Busby Berkeley later made popular in the American cinema. For example, in his 1937 essay "Girls and Crisis," Kracauer describes the Tiller Girls in the following manner:

> In that postwar era, in which *prosperity* appeared limitless and which could scarcely conceive of unemployment, the Girls were artificially manufactured in the USA and exported to Europe by the dozens. Not only were they products; at the same time they demonstrated the greatness of American production. I distinctly recall the appearance of such troupes in the season of their glory. When they formed an undulating snake, they radiantly illustrated the virtues of the conveyor belt; when they tapped their feet in fast tempo, it sounded like *business, business;* when they kicked their legs high with mathematical precision, they joyously affirmed the progress of rationalization; and when they kept repeating the same movements without ever interrupting their routine, one envisioned an uninterrupted chain of autos gliding from the factories into the world, and believed that the blessings of prosperity had no end.[8]

What the Tiller Girls represent is nothing less than a new form of aesthetic production in which the aggregation of human bodies has become the raw material and the experience of the mass the product. In this way, the "natural" human form is transformed into a social hieroglyph:

> The human figure used in this mass ornament has begun its *exodus* from the organic splendor and individual constituency (*Gestalthaftigkeit*) and entered the realm of anonymity into which it exteriorized itself when it stands in truth and when the knowledge radiating from its human source dissolves the contours of the visible natural form. Nature is deprived of its substance in the mass ornament, and this indicates the condition under which only those as-

pects of nature can assert themselves which do not resist illumina-
tion through reason. . . . The organic center is removed and the
remaining parts are composed according to laws yielding knowledge about truth, however temporally conditioned such knowledge
might be—and not according to the laws of nature. ("Mass Ornament" 73–74)

The deployment of the concept of nature here demonstrates that if
there is a fundamental idealism pervading Kracauer's thought, it resides not in the concept of "realism" but in the equation of humanity
with nature and a lost organic presence. Paradoxically, however, it
is only on the basis of a humanity divided against its integral being
that Kracauer defines reason according to the criterion of nonidentity. There is little doubt that the influence of Lukács's *Theory of the
Novel* and *History and Class Consciousness* is being felt here. Thus the
problem of "nature," which may cause potential confusions in understanding Kracauer's meaning, may productively be understood in relation to Lukács's ideas concerning "second nature" as the false, mythical
reality created by "man" though not understood by him because he has
lost sight of its historical origins.[9] In this manner, the obscured reason of capital finds itself *alienated,* given spatial form and substance,
in the directed, symmetrical patterning of human bodies. The calculated organization and Taylorization of the labor force, in which the
individuality of the worker has become subordinated to the total production process, thus finds its direct correlative in the choreography of
the Tiller Girls. The specific "truth" of aesthetic form is here decided
by the laws of capital. For Kracauer, this relation is not in the least
allegorical or metaphorical but is a measure of the "reality-content"
of capital itself, where the masses "who so spontaneously took to the
pattern in openly acknowledging the facts in their rough form, are superior to those intellectuals who despise it" ("Mass Ornament" 75).
Neither traditional art, whose ideal is the identity of nature and form,
nor idealist philosophy, which defines reason as the identity of thought
and being, can penetrate this relation because nature has been transformed and subjectivity has disappeared into the mass. In this manner,
Kracauer's work of the twenties can be understood as the beginning of
his search for new categories of thought that, as Karsten Witte notes,

took explicitly optical forms. Similarly, Miriam Hansen observes that in the same period, both Kracauer and Benjamin associate cinema with a fundamentally new form of reception under the name of *Zerstreuung,* "distraction." As a perceptual category intrinsic to cinematic expression, "distraction" was understood as a transformation of experience under capital that contained its own truth value that the categories of neither art nor philosophy, properly speaking, could recognize. "For Kracauer," writes Hansen, "the audience's abandoning themselves to 'distraction'—to 'pure externality,' to 'the discontinuous sequence of splendid sense impressions'—represents a mimetic process which reveals the 'true' structure of modern reality, thus acquiring a 'moral significance.'"[10]

This introduces the second major theme of Kracauer's work. Karsten Witte notes that for Kracauer the reality content of mass culture is given viscerally: "Spatial images (*Raumbilder*) are the dreams of society. Wherever the hieroglyphics of these images can be deciphered, one finds the basis of social reality."[11] The desire to comprehend the lived experience of a society dominated by capital, whose historically given forms of reason are both veiled and materially embodied in visual phenomena, increasingly commits Kracauer to phenomenology, *Lebensphilosophie,* and the lasting influence of Husserl, Simmel, and Dilthey. This philosophical orientation, which is still pervasive in the book on history, in no way commits Kracauer to an identity theory of knowledge, however. Instead close attention to the *Frankfurter Zeitung* essays confounds the tired film theory *doxa* of a theory of realism where Kracauer is accused of constructing a vaguely formulated identity between "physical reality," "camera reality," and "nature."

On this basis, a decisive shift of emphasis, which transforms the redemptive character of Kracauer's analyses, may be identified in his last work. The special emphasis on history and photography in late Kracauer is no longer motivated simply by the desire to rescue forgotten and despised elements of mass culture. Rather, what Kracauer comes to understand in *History: The Last Things before the Last* is that it is the form(s) of historical knowledge itself—which will include not only historiography proper but also photography and the *mémoire involontaire* of Proust—that he had been attempting to define and redeem. History and photography must now be understood as special categories of representing and knowing that are alone capable of exploring and comprehending those aspects of experience to which philosophy and art have become blind.

The montage of citations that begin this section now reveal their intricate relationship. For example, the reference to psychoanalysis in Benjamin is neither irrelevant nor incompatible with Kracauer's thought. In the book on history, he consistently refers to the representational characteristics of both photography and history as modes of *alienation,* as cognitive apparatuses that are able to name and thus to call virtually into existence phenomena that otherwise might be lost to thought. Social life is understood here as having an indeterminate, multiple, and fragmentary character that overwhelms individual perception and reduces it to unconscious thought; in a life administered by capital, reason and reality are necessarily nonidentical. By transposing and therefore unavoidably reducing the multiple experiences of daily life, photography and history are understood by Kracauer as complementary modalities because they are able to comprehend this reality by selectively giving it form and rendering it accessible and cognizable to a critical and self-reflective consciousness.

For Kracauer, history and photography comprise parallel projects. And in *The Last Things before the Last,* as in the 1927 essay on photography, he takes great pains to explain the former with reference to the latter. Similar to the way in which *Theory of Film* takes the form of detailing the multiple resources of cinematic expression, Kracauer's book on history takes the form of an open-ended critical account of the resources available to historical expression. But more important for Kracauer, both history and photography have the same object, what he calls "historical reality" in the first case and "physical reality" in the second. However, if "reality" is the common denominator between the two, it is reducible to neither an experience of nature nor an a priori objective state. In fact, Kracauer's hostility to simple empiricism is such that neither history nor photography should be understood as purely objective modes of representation. If they sustain a mimetic relation with their object, this relation is not one of identity but one of "similarity," "correspondence," or "affinity." The correspondences between history and photography are not to be rendered through their common relationship to nature, but with Husserl's *Lebenswelt,* an indispensable concept for Kracauer in that it names the world of everyday experience as materially constituted by the incalculable accumulation of events and situations precipitated by human praxis. According to Kracauer, the Lebenswelt is unknowable in many respects: "It is full of intrinsic contingencies which obstruct its calculability, its subsumption under the deterministic principle. . . . In addition, historical reality is virtually endless, issuing from a dark which is increasingly receding and extending into an open-ended future. And finally it is indeterminate as to meaning. Its characteristics conform to the materials of which it is woven" (*History* 45). Readers of Kracauer's *Theory of Film* will immediately recognize the "affinities" characteristic of photographic expression—fortuitousness, indeterminacy, endlessness, in short, the "flow of life"—and in fact, the second chapter of the history book, "The Historical Approach," remarkably parallels the section in *Theory of Film* on the "photographic approach" (*Theory* 12–23). However, to assert that the Lebenswelt is unknowable does not mean that it is unintelligible or unrepresentable. As Martin Jay points out, Kracauer argues that " 'Reality is . . . a construction,' consisting of a mosaic of different observations."[12] Comprised of a multiplicity of points of view and an indeterminable accumulation of images and artifacts, historical reality is insensible outside of what Kracauer calls the "intellectual universe," or more precisely the archive of historiographic concepts that hold those figures available to articulate the object of history by establishing the conditions of its intelligibility. In sum, what characterizes this intellectual universe that comprises the forms of "reality" proper to history and photography, and conditions their potential knowledges, is the accumulation of figures or concepts whose structure and forms of organization are permeated by the contingent and indeterminate quality of the Lebenswelt. If in Kracauer's view there is a mimetic relation between the Lebenswelt on the one hand and history or photography on the other, this relation is not one of unmediated expressivity. Rather, history and photography render the Lebenswelt intelligible through their structural correspondence or affinities with it.

Kracauer's notion of photography's "affinities" with physical reality is one of his most notorious ideas from the standpoint of modern film theory. To properly comprehend the relation he was attempting to express, and to understand how Kracauer himself rethought this relation in the history book, it is necessary to make a detour through Benjamin's study of German tragic drama, and to attempt to recast this idea in the light of Benjamin's understanding of mimesis as "nonsensuous similarity" (*unsinnliche Ähnlichkeit*).[13] In a critique of Kant set forth in the *Trauerspiel* study, Benjamin opposes scientific knowledge (*Erkenntnis*), in which the subject constitutes the world by imposing its own cognitive categories, with a philosophical experience of truth (*Erfahrung*) in which the role of the subject is the representation of ideas (*Darstellung der Ideen*) whose structure is objectively determined by the particularity of the phenomena examined. However, the function of cognitive categories or concepts—what Kant would call "regulative ideas"—is not elided here, but rather they now serve the intermediary function of "translating" particular empirically given phenomena into an ideational representation. Here Benjamin notes that "the phenomena, however, do not enter whole into the realm of the ideas, not in their raw empirical existence, mixed as it were with mere appearance (*Schein*), but they are redeemed alone in their elements. . . . In this partitioning of them, the phenomena stand under concepts. It is the concepts which carry out the unravelling of the phenomena into their elements."[14] For example, in "The Mass Ornament," Kracauer wishes to illuminate the fate of reason under capital. From the standpoint of traditional critical thought, however, the idea of reason is obdurate in both the aesthetic phenomena of the Tiller Girls and that of the transformation of nature under capital. For Kracauer, it is an occulted reason that is blind to its historical and ideological origins. Only by juxtaposing these two apparently divergent and unrelated phenomena can their profound similarity be exposed in the flash of a historical or dialectical image. This image is the mass ornament, which, like the latent image revealed in a developing photograph, gives representational form to the common structural principle superintending the transformation of both nature and the body: the particular form of "rationality" of the Taylor system that subjugates the organization of labor no less than the organization of mass aesthetic phenomena.

Thus the lesson of a careful reading of Kracauer's "The Mass Ornament" is its demonstration of the complexity of his understanding of the problems of mimetic representation. If history, photography, and the activity of *mémoire involontaire* demonstrate a special cognitive capacity inherent in the mimetic faculty, then this conceptualization of mimesis must be distinguished rigorously from a Platonic tradition on the one hand and, more important for historical understanding, the influence of Hegel on the other. Like his student Adorno, and his friend Benjamin, Kracauer vigorously rejected the Hegelian idea that the study of history guarantees the identification of reason with reality. Rather, as Susan Buck-Morss has observed, history should be understood as a discontinuous space, "unfolding within a multiplicity of divisions of human praxis through a dialectical process which was open-ended. History did not guarantee the identity of reason and reality. Rather, history unfolded in the spaces *between* subjects and objects, men and nature, whose very nonidentity was history's motor force" (*Origin of Negative Dialectic* 47). Indeed, Kracauer's arguments concerning "the mass ornament" demonstrate his conviction that the concept of reason cannot be understood in any universal way but is tied ineluctably to the specificity of a historical situation: it releases its knowledge only when penetrated by a historical optics, in fact, a dialectical or historical image whose basis is conceptual rather than "aesthetic."

This means that the photographer's selectivity is of a kind which is closer to empathy than to disengaged spontaneity. He resembles perhaps most of all the imaginative reader intent on studying and deciphering an elusive text. Like a reader, the photographer is steeped in the book of nature. . . . The photographer summons up his being, not to discharge it in autonomous creations but to dissolve it into the substances of the objects that close in on him. Once again, Proust is right: selectivity within this medium is inseparable from processes of alienation.—Siegfried Kracauer, *Theory of Film* 16 [15]

In other words: it is to writing and language that clairvoyance has, over the course of history, yielded its old powers.

So speed, that swiftness in reading or writing which can scarcely be separated from this process, would then become, as it were, the effort or gift of letting the mind participate in that measure of time in which similarities flash up fleetingly out of the stream of things only in order to become immediately engulfed again.—Walter Benjamin, "The Doctrine of the Similar" 68

The Antinomic Character of Time The "mass ornament" is a "historical image" (*geschichtliche Bilder*) in the precise sense that Adorno and Benjamin gave to the concept as an image that "illuminated contradictions rather than negating or sublating them; the procedure was one of mimetic representation rather than synthesis."[16] In *History: The Last Things before the Last,* this concept returns in the form of the image character of history as the means for comprehending and communicating the multiple forces at work in the Lebenswelt. To defend history as a specific field of critical inquiry, no less genuine in its identity than art or philosophy and in fact preferable in the kinds of knowledge available to it, Kracauer explores the conceptual equipment of historiography in its rendering of the Lebenswelt through a series of structural correspondences.

Kracauer's argument unfolds less as a systematic exploration of history than as a perambulation through the writings on historical writing, or the figures that make up the intellectual universe in which the subject of history has been comprehended. The first figure that Kracauer treats in detail is that of the "historian's journey," which defines the subject of historical knowing. The way to this concept is paved in Kracauer's book by a comparison between the "historical approach" and the "photographic approach," in which the writing of history is characterized as a mode of alienation where the historian functions as an extraterritorial attuned to both the "realist" and "formative" moments of this experience.

These terms, which play an integral part in *Theory of Film,* have an equally strong role in *History: The Last Things before the Last,* and it is necessary to understand their precise meaning. In the history book, Kracauer points to the coincidence that marks the birth of modern historiography at about the same time as that of photography. In 1824, less than two decades before the advent of the photograph, Ranke assaulted the prevailing moral and philosophical attitudes in the writing of history, proclaiming instead that its sole object is to show "how things actually were [*wie es eigentlich gewesen*]" (*History* 48–49). The emergence and subsequent popularization of photography seems to appear as the fulfillment of this realist tendency in its ability to map the natural world with a fidelity "equal to nature itself."[17] Among the genres of historical writing, the realist tendency resembles most closely the accomplishment of "technical histories" in which the greatest amount of detail is accumulated for the smallest period of time. In the best of instances, this type of history is redeemed by the figure of the *collector,* whose insistence that "no fact should go lost" nonetheless reveals a theological motif, "as if fact-oriented accounts breathed pity with the dead" (*History* 136).[18]

But Kracauer is profoundly suspicious of this tendency because it threatens the interpretive subjectivity of the historian. Referring the reader back to *Theory of Film,* Kracauer reconsiders his discussion of Marcel's visit to his grandmother in *Guermantes Way,* where Proust characterizes the experience of photography as "the product of complete alienation" (*Theory* 14–15). When Marcel visits his grandmother unannounced after many years, Proust describes Marcel's perception of her as mechanical, as that of a "photographer" or a "stranger," where the palimpsest of years of loving memories is stripped away to reveal a dejected old woman. Proust undoubtedly describes this perception to oppose it to the experience of mémoire involontaire.[19] Kracauer, however, sees a more subtle dialectic involved, in which the harsh light of photography is inseparable from aesthetic agency and the force of interpretation, such that the photographer, no less than the historian, becomes an "imaginative reader" whose formative, interpretive efforts are inseparable from the degree of knowledge that "historical reality" may yield. According to Kracauer, what mémoire involontaire reveals in its analogy to the experience of historical subjectivity is best described by the figure of the extraterritorial or exile—a fragmented subjectivity produced by a disrupted life history and producing a consciousness formed by the superimposition of discontinuous historical moments. "The exile's true mode of existence," writes Kracauer, "is that of a stranger. So he may look at his previous existence with the eyes of one 'who does not belong to the house.' . . . It is only in this state of self-effacement, or homelessness, that the historian can commune with the material of his concern" (*History* 83–84).

Historical knowing, then, is governed by a special dialectic where the realist moment involves a form of surrender in which the historian's subjectivity is negated by the massive and indeterminate flow of historical events; and in dialectical response, the aesthetic, formative moment governs the precipitation of order out of this material, which, shaped by historical contingency, maps out the pattern of the historian's narrative. In its most powerful manifestations, this dialectic will generate what Kracauer calls "the historical idea," which, like Burkhardt's image of the awakening of the individual in the Renaissance or Marx's distinction between base and superstructure, reveals unsuspected contexts and relationships of a relatively wide scope. The historical idea inaugurates a new terrain in which a wide variety of primary historical material distributes and organizes itself, illuminating previously unthought patterns of intelligibility. Moreover, as an example of what Kracauer calls "anteroom thinking," the historical idea is important because it fuses the particular and the general in a way unavailable to philosophical knowing:

> Historical ideas appear to be of lasting significance because they connect the particular with the general in an articulate and truly unique way. Any such connection being an uncertain venture, they resemble flashes illumining the night. This is why their emergence in the historian's mind has been termed a "historical sensation" and said to "communicate a shock to the entire system . . . the shock . . . of recognition." They are nodal points—points at which the concrete and the abstract really become one. Whenever this happens, the flow of indeterminate historical events is suddenly arrested and all that is then exposed to view is seen in the light of an image or conception which takes it out of the transient flow to relate it to one or another of the momentous problems and questions that are forever staring at us.[20]

The explanatory wealth of the historical idea derives from its superimposition of the two poles of historical activity—the transformation of the historian's subjectivity by its immersion in the particulate and primary material of history, and the formative, conceptual activity of historical writing and interpretation proper—that fuse together in a powerful monadic image. It is through the agency of conceptual figures such as the historical idea that historical intelligibility becomes possible, but only in the form of a nonhomogeneous or discontinuous structure regulated by their peculiar affinities with the Lebenswelt. For Kracauer, this nonhomogeneous structure distributes itself, like film, along spatial and temporal axes. In a similar analogy with film, Kracauer describes historical space by differentiating what he calls "macro" and "micro" histories. There is no doubt that these terms define particular genres of historical writing—from the epic narratives of Spengler to meticulously detailed technical histories—but for Kracauer their real importance lies elsewhere. Applying an optical metaphor, in which macro histories are described as views in "long shot" and micro histories are likened to "close-ups," Kracauer defines a "law of perspective" that governs the potential intelligibility of historical space according to the particular attenuation of the historian's gaze: "In the micro dimension, a more or less dense fabric of given data canalizes the historian's imagination, his interpretive designs. As the distance from the data increases, they become scattered, thin out. The evidence thus loses its binding power, inviting less committed subjectivity to take over" (*History* 123). In other words, the law of perspective regulates movement between the macro and micro dimensions according to a ratio that governs the relation of the historian's subjectivity to the potential intelligibility of history. The higher the level of generality at which the historian operates, the more the particularity and materiality of history evaporates and is taken over by the historian's imagination. On the other hand, the more he or she is immersed in historical detail, the greater the chance that the formative intelligence of the historian will be overwhelmed by the sheer accumulation and density of data.

If Kracauer's law of perspective maps the nonhomogeneous structure of historical "reality" in its longitudinal dimension as a function of a variable and discontinuous density, he is equally attentive to its latitudinal dimensions, its distribution into uneven and temporally disjunct strata. Here Kracauer defines a "law of levels" that predicts the effects of microevents when martialed from one level of generality to another: "According to the law of levels, the contexts established at each level are valid for that level but do not apply to findings at other levels; which is to say that there is no way of deriving the regularities of macro history . . . from the facts and interpretations provided by micro history" (*History* 134). Similarly, Kracauer agrees with Claude Lévi-Strauss's characterization of the temporal structure of history in the critique of Jean-Paul Sartre formulated in the conclusion to *The Savage Mind*. History has no identity as a totality but rather can be represented only as a series of shifting configurations where differing periods or classes of dates, or even different kinds of history (histories of art, economy, technology, social life, etc.), are each informed by their own intrinsic system of temporal reference. In other words, to say that each level presents its own intrinsic system of regularities means that it exhibits a relatively autonomous structure to which relevant microevents must adapt or be displaced.

The key to understanding this proposition lies in Kracauer's hostility toward a tradition in the philosophy of history that views time as a linear, irreversible, and homogeneous continuum. Particularly abhorrent to Kracauer is a Hegelian conception of historical totality offered by "present-interest" historians, best represented by the work of Benedetto Croce and R. G. Collingwood. Here Kracauer sees the necessary fragmentation of historical subjectivity reduced to the punctual moment of a vulgar historicism—an "a priori imagination," in Collingwood's terms, where the scholar's interest in history and access to it is strictly circumscribed by his or her cultural location. "Whenever philosophers speculate on the 'idea of history,'" says Kracauer, "Hegel's 'world spirit' pops up behind the bushes" (*History* 64). In this manner, the concept of periodization necessary for present-interest history reveals two irremediable flaws:

> It rests on the untenable premise that the flow of chronological time is the carrier of all history; and it flagrantly conflicts with a large body of experiences regarding the structure of the period. . . . Contrary to what Croce postulates, the typical period is not so much a unified entity with a spirit of its own as a precarious conglomerate of tendencies, aspirations, and activities which more often than not manifest themselves independently of one another. . . .
>
> [If] the period is a unit at all, it is a diffuse, fluid, and essentially intangible unit. . . .
>
> And here is the point I wish to drive home. If the historian's "historical and social environment" is not a fairly self-contained whole but a fragile compound of frequently inconsistent endeavors in flux, the assumption that it moulds his mind makes little sense. It does

make sense only in the contexts of a philosophy which, like Croce's, hypostasizes a period spirit, claims our dependence on it, and thus determines the mind's place in the historical process from above and without. (*History* 66–67)

This is why Kracauer insists on opposing the idea of totality with that of the historical idea. Although the latter falls short of philosophical knowing, it nonetheless achieves a level of generality able to articulate the disparate and indeterminate elements of history by revealing their inherent relatedness without reducing them to a punctual moment or a single common force or cause. What is most important about the "law of levels," then, is that it demonstrates for Kracauer the resistance of human history to natural history "in that it proves impervious to longitudinal historical laws—laws which by implication, mistake the historical process for a natural process. . . . [Natural history] necessarily yields laws which, by definition, not only unduly minimize the role of contingencies in history but, more important, preclude man's freedom of choice, his ability to create new situations. They acknowledge instead a sort of natural evolution, so as to make allowances for the idea of progress without having to break away from strict determinism" (*History* 33, 37). The identification of the order of human history with that of nature, which has its fullest expression in the organicist metaphors of Comte and the world Spirit of Hegel, is thus permeated by a theological ideal of progress that subsumes the contingent possibilities of human praxis to a linear and uniform temporal continuum.

Thus the period, as a kind of snapshot of the historical continuum, disintegrates before our eyes: "From a meaningful spatiotemporal unit it turns into a kind of meeting place for chance encounters—something like the waiting room of a railway station" (*History* 150). However, if the period is a phantom unit, is the intelligibility of history then renounced along with the punctual moment of its subject? For Kracauer, such an either/or statement is markedly insensitive to the contradictory schema of historical time in which the period must be understood as "an antinomic entity embodying in a condensed form . . . two irreconcilable time conceptions" (155). On the one hand, the relations between periods or identifiable events can only be understood as a succession of discontinuities or breaks that rapidly undermine any attempt at chronological understanding. On the other, Kracauer states that "the same configuration of events which because of its spontaneous emergence defies the historical process marks also a moment of chronological time and has therefore its legitimate place in it (156). Here Kracauer will favor the concept of "shaped times" formulated by George Kubler after Henri Focillon, where events in different classes or magnitudes of historical investigation may be understood as unfolding according to immanent temporal schemata, even if those schemata are themselves incommensurable.[21] In other words, what the concept of shaped times means for Kracauer is that the very assertion of a period or event implies some chronological understanding as being valid for that event.

But ultimately Kracauer demands a more radical solution for comprehending the antinomic character of historical time, one with definite implications for the subject of historical knowing. Kracauer, of course, is not bothered in the least by the assertion of the fragmentary, discontinuous, or contingent quality of experience, and indeed he submits that we are free to experience the redemption of physical reality by the camera because we ourselves are fragmentized. "The integrated personality no doubt belongs among the favorite superstitions of modern psychology" (*History* 148). Moreover, in Proust's *A la recherche du temps perdu,* Kracauer discovers a palimpsestic, subjective experience of time that perfectly corresponds to the fragmentary and discontinuous forms of historical knowing. For Kracauer, however, the ultimate subject of historical knowing, the one who could resolve the antinomic character of time and give history its true name, could only be the figure of Ahasuerus, the Wandering Jew:

> He indeed would know firsthand about the developments and transitions, for he alone in all history has had the unsought opportunity to experience the process of becoming and decaying itself. (How terrible he must look! To be sure, his face cannot have suffered from aging, but I imagine it to be many faces, each reflecting one of the periods which he traversed and all of them combining into ever new patterns, as he restlessly, and vainly, tries on his wanderings to reconstruct out of the times that shaped him the one time he is doomed to incarnate.) (*History* 157)

Whereas the curse of Ahasuerus is his immortality, the curse of the historian is his or her finitude, which, in order to render history as a space that is legible and therefore communicable, must bridge with nearly the speed of clairvoyance "the dialectics between the flow of time and the temporal sequences negating it" (*History* 158). Kracauer therefore returns to Proust to find a more practical model for sustaining a subject of historical knowing against the complex erosions of time. It is above all a sensitivity to that complexity that Kracauer admires: "Proust radically de-emphasizes chronology. With him, it appears, history is no process at all but a hodge-podge of kaleidoscopic changes—something like clouds that gather and disperse at random" (160). In Proust's novels, the sense of a flow of time is overwhelmed by the depiction of a seemingly discontinuous chain of events where simple causality is dissolved and the self-identity of the subject, as the focal point through which these events must be narrated, is successively overturned through the very accumulation and dispersion of narrative situations. In the seemingly random discharges of mémoire involontaire, time is atomized with complete indifference to chronological understanding, and each atom expands in scale to a "close-up" shot through with a "texture of reflections, analogies, reminiscences, etc., which indiscriminately refer to all the worlds [Marcel] . . . has been passing and altogether serve to disclose the essential meanings of the incident from which they radiate and towards which they converge" (161).

Even for Proustian narrative, the antinomic character of time is ultimately irresoluble; Proust can only adopt a provisional solution wherein temporal continuity is retrospectively established. By the end of the novel, Kracauer notes that the reader, who has previously been caught up in the "unaccountable zig-zag routes spreading over the whole scroll of the past," can now realize that a precise clockwork chronology has strung together the succession of Marcel's selves: "Proust succeeds in reinstating chronological time as a substantial medium only a posteriori; the story of his (or Marcel's) fragmentized life must have reached its terminus before it can reveal itself to him as a unified process" (*History* 161–63). But the punctual moment of this terminus is undecidable and must forever divide fiction from history. Lacking death as the signature of finitude, it must understand the ending it confers as the continuity of the being-written, or a continuous unfolding toward an apodictic moment. This aesthetic solution, where history is identified with the movement of writing, locates the fragile hope of understanding in a backward glance that can only be conferred at death, but which nonetheless is deferred onto narrative as the medium through which meaning can unfold as a continuum that does not threaten the subject producing it. The incommensurability of time can only be resolved in a fiction. "But," as Kracauer finally notes, "nothing of the sort applies to history. Neither has history an end nor is it amenable to aesthetic redemption. The antinomy at the core of time is insoluble. Perhaps the truth is that it can only be resolved at the end of Time. In a sense, Proust's personal solution foreshadows, or indeed signifies, this unthinkable end — the imaginary moment at which Ahasuerus, before disintegrating, may for the first time be able to look back on his wanderings through the periods" (163).

The soothsayers who found out from time what it had in store certainly did not experience time as either homogeneous or empty. Anyone who keeps this in mind will perhaps get an idea of how past times were experienced in remembrance — namely, in just the same way. We know that the Jews were prohibited from investigating the future. The Torah and the prayers instruct them in remembrance, however. This stripped the future of its magic, to which all those succumb who turn to the soothsayers for enlightenment. This does not imply, however, that for the Jews the future turned into homogeneous, empty time. For every second of time was the strait gate through which the Messiah might enter. — Walter Benjamin, "Theses on the Philosophy of History" 266

I have pointed out in *Theory of Film* that the photographic media help us overcome our abstractness by familiarizing us, for the first time as it were, with "this Earth which is our habitat" (Gabriel Marcel); they help us to think *through* things, not above them. Otherwise expressed, the photographic media make it much easier for us to incorporate the transient phenomena of the outer world, thereby redeeming them from oblivion. Something of this kind will also have to be said of history. — Siegfried Kracauer, *History* 192

Anteroom Thinking, or "The Last Things before the Last"   All the arguments presented so far with respect to Kracauer's views on history have coincided with the question of historical *intelligibility*. While this perspective is not exactly unfair to his thought, it is not surprising to note that Kracauer, both ontologist and melancholy materialist, would ultimately prefer to emphasize the *experience* of history, as well as photography, as the recognition of a form of knowledge that, until now, has rested unnamed "between the hazy expanses in which we form opinions and the high level areas harboring the products of man's most lofty aspirations (*History* 191). All of which is to say that Kracauer, either unwilling or unable to divorce, in Althusserian terms, the real object from the object-in-thought, both affirms and denies the ontological character of history and photography. Nor was he able to follow Adorno in observing a strict principle of nonidentity that would render history as a purely cognitive concept. This very undecidability forms the continuous thread of Kracauer's argument and finally becomes the basis on which history and photography are named as "intermediate" epistemic categories, or examples of what Kracauer will call "anteroom thinking":

> One may define the area of historical reality, like that of photographic reality, as an anteroom area. Both realities are of a kind which does not lend itself to being dealt with in a definite way. The peculiar material in these areas eludes the grasp of systematic thought; nor can it be shaped in the form of a work of art. Like the statements we make about physical reality with the aid of the camera, those which result from our preoccupation with historical reality may certainly attain to a level above mere opinion; but they do not convey, or reach out for ultimate truths, as do philosophy and art proper. They share their inherently provisional character with the material they record, explore, and penetrate. (*History* 191)

In *History: The Last Things before the Last,* this undecidability articulates itself across two interrelated problems — that of historicism, in which history must decide what portion of its knowledge derives from scientific thought, and the aesthetic dimension of historical writing, in which it must decide what portion of its "figures of thought" derives from (fictional) narrative. In this respect, it is interesting to compare the first chapter, where history is differentiated from the natural sciences, and the second to last, where the genre of "general history" is critiqued for borrowing too much from fiction such that artful continuities override the nonhomogeneous structure of history. By following this arc, one begins to understand that Kracauer finds in the criticisms of history's hybrid nature the very basis for its redemption. If history is to be defined as a form of genuine hermeneutic inquiry, with its own object and its own cognitive resources, it must make a detour through both science and literature without letting its path be determined by one or the other. Historical knowing must be defined in this specific intermediate area.

In the history book, the continuing influence of Wilhelm Dilthey initially allows Kracauer to steer his middle course. Rejecting Hegelian metaphysics no less forcefully than the attempt by Auguste Comte and Henry Thomas Buckle to elevate history to the status of natural science, Dilthey's distinguishing of history as *Geisteswissenschaften,* as an area distinct from *Naturwissenschaften,* enables the gambit that opens Kracauer's argument. Kracauer forcefully asserts that the possibilities of historical understanding are inseparable from its object — the Lebenswelt as the sphere of "historical reality." Kracauer's insistence on the nonidentity of history and nature need not be argued again here. But Kracauer asserts that like the natural sciences, "historical science" bases its knowledge on the observation of definable regularities in its object. Referring back to his own essays of the 1920s, Kracauer formulates a "principle of mental economy" that describes the Lebenswelt as a particular "zone of inertia" where the unpredictability of the individual will is subsumed within the identity of the mass.[22] The multiple activities that define human praxis are not wholly incalculable, and thus society may be understood as an entity that displays specific properties:

> Conspicuous among them is a peculiar quality of the materials from which it is built: they largely fall into that zone of inertia in which the mind resides absent-mindedly. Many of these materials, such as customs, rites, certain institutions, ever-recurrent routine activities, and the like, coincide in forming the background of our social existence. . . .

In sum, society is full of events which defy control because they happen to occur in the dimly lit region where mental intensity is reduced to zero. . . . The social universe with its near-stable customs and volatile opinions, its small groups and masses, would seem to fall under the rule of nature. In other words, it is possible and legitimate, to break down the phenomena that make up this universe into repeatable elements and analyze their interrelationships and interactions for regularities. (*History* 23–25)

Paradoxically, it is only because individual subjectivity may be dispersed within the rule of the mass, which acts according to its own temporal and causal schemata, that historical reality demonstrates regularities that may then become the object of historical knowing. This assertion, of course, has little novelty with respect to Kracauer's writings in particular and the literature of social theory in general. Moreover, having made the point, Kracauer does not insist on it, for the Lebenswelt simultaneously holds a radical potentiality: "History is the realm of contingencies, of new beginnings. All regularities discovered in it, or read into it, are of limited range" (*History* 31). In fact, in one of the few demonstrably political asides in the book, Kracauer equates the contingent quality of the Lebenswelt, its incalculability by any deterministic principle, with an ever renewable possibility of human freedom: "True, things may change under a unified global management of human affairs, but then the question arises to what extent can the living forces which produce the contingencies be subjected to worldwide control without either revolting or withering. If anarchy calls for order, order tends to beget anarchy" (45). The very forces that tend to paralyze social life, to reify it and give it the form of an object, are simultaneously, for Kracauer, the forces that energize it and generate in the Lebenswelt the constant possibility of unforeseen, even revolutionary, potentialities. By definition, then, historical reality confounds any attempt to describe it according to universals or to render it predictable through a principle of determination. This being so, the historian requires a principle of understanding that is itself contingent and that, in the course of its own narration of human events, avoids both the Scylla of abstract thought and the Charybdis of false concreteness. History is a "storytelling medium," Kracauer readily admits, no less so than natural science, which must tell the story of the geophysical origins of the planet, yet history still comprises narrative understanding of a special type. To explain, Kracauer recounts that on the day of the Kennedy assassination, people spontaneously formed groups in the street to mourn the event, to discuss it, and to rehearse its implications; in short, to render it intelligible. "No doubt," Kracauer writes, "a primitive instinct impelled them thus to evoke a past which had been the present a moment ago and to picture to themselves, and try to appraise, the full scope of what they—we—had thoughtlessly possessed and abruptly lost. In doing so, they followed a desire which is at the bottom of all history writing: they wanted to 'understand'" (43).

For Kracauer, this form of understanding has an explicit context given as Dilthey's offering of *Verstehen* as the specific form of comprehension of historical science, one that has nothing to do with scientific explanations and "exhausts itself in penetrating individual entities of, perhaps, untraceable origins" (*History* 44). The figure of Verstehen, in fact, without itself ever becoming an object of inquiry in Kracauer's book, is nonetheless its central organizing concept. For Kracauer, the concept of historical understanding is the shifting focal point (no chapter in particular is dedicated to it, no extensive argument is attached to it exclusively) where all the principal lines of thought in the book converge. The experience of Verstehen is permeated by the contingent quality of the Lebenswelt. It describes the floating, unlocalizable, extraterritorial subjectivity that must dedicate itself to two times and perambulate without a fixed abode. It refuses to dedicate itself exclusively to any singular intepretive schema or philosophical system, especially one that tends to identify history as a totality. And it participates in the particularity of daily life, taking from the more general and abstract spheres of thought only what it needs to render that experience intelligible: "[Historical explanations] cannot be dissolved or extended into statements about causal relationships, structural configurations, and the like. Nor do they easily admit of wider application. They are relatively self-contained; they result from, and respond to, unique encounters with opaque entities" (96). As examples of "anteroom thinking," both historical and photographic knowing fall under the category of Verstehen. In doing so they define an epistemological space "which borders on the world of daily life—the Lebenswelt—and extends to the confines of philosophy proper. In it, we usually concentrate not so much on the last things, as the last things before the last" (211). The specificity of historical understanding, then, is that it situates itself just short of "last things"—the universalizing truth claims of philosophy or art—while addressing itself to the particularity of experience in a way that resists immersion in that "zone of inertia where mental activity is reduced to zero."

But in rallying to the defense of historical understanding, Kracauer does not claim to have resolved the problems of historicism and to have identified thereby the quantity of knowledge that belongs to history: "Once historicity is recognized as part and parcel of the human condition, the problem arises as to how to reconcile the ensuing relativity of knowledge with the quest of reason for significant truths of general validity" (*History* 196). Here the problem of historical knowing must confront an impasse that divides, in Kracauer's terms, "transcendental" and "immanentist" epistemologies. The transcendental view, which comprises theological and metaphysical arguments inherited from Hegel, must assume the existence of timeless truths, values, or norms; that is, some principle of reason through which history finds itself identified. Kracauer's hostility to, and critique of, this problematic need not be reemphasized. The "immanentist" position, whose genealogy descends from Dilthey through Heidegger and Gadamer, presents a somewhat trickier problem. Here the acceptance of historicity as a basic premise excludes recourse to timeless truths or ontological arguments. Each time will decide its own perspective on the problem of truth. But despite his greater sympathies with this position, Kracauer voices extreme suspicion. Modern hermeneutics, with its assumption of the relativity of truth and its justifications for assuming that "each 'truth' is the last word within its own concrete situation and that the different perspectives form a hierarchy in the total historical process," finds that it "must 'absolutize' history in order to retrieve the absolute from it" (198). In Kracauer's view, when its dialectical dance is concluded, the anti-ontological position resembles nothing less than an ontology where history becomes a "success story," or "a stuffy closed system which, in accordance with Hegel's dictum, '*What is real is rational,*' shuts out the lost causes, the unrealized possibilities."[23] There is little doubt that in staging this critique, Kracauer finds himself in complete accord with Benjamin's thesis that "there is no document of civilization which is not at the same time a document of barbarism. And just as such a document is not free of barbarism, barbarism taints also the manner in which it was transmitted from one owner to another" (Benjamin, "Theses," 258).

Here the full consequences of Kracauer's insistence on the redemptive character of history and photography are best understood. If history and photography define areas of epistemological activity that fall outside the claims of philosophical and artistic activity, this acknowledgment constitutes not the problem but the solution. "With the acceptance of this insight," he argues, "the ground is prepared for a theoretical acknowledgment of the nameless possibilities that may be assumed to exist, and to wait for recognition, in the interstices of the extant doctrines of high generality. . . . [If] the truths in the interstices cannot be won by way of deduction from an established conception or principle, they may well arise out of absorption in configurations of particulars" (*History* 215). Kracauer's lesson is that history and photography themselves might have rested as nameless and unredeemed possibilities if a critique could not be forwarded that resisted the exclusivity of philosophical and aesthetic definitions. As examples of anteroom thinking, historical and photographic "knowing" are to be valued for their ambiguity, their resistance to closure, and their elusiveness with respect to systematic thought. For Kracauer, the last things, art and philosophy, should be approached with a degree of suspicion. By virtue of their generality, systematicity, and abstractness, both philosophical and aesthetic truths tend to adopt a radical character: "They favor either-or decisions, develop a penchant for exclusiveness, and have a way of freezing into dogmas" (214). More important, they are blind to the experience of everyday life and will always fail in their attempts to come to grips with the antinomic character of time and the nonhomogeneous structure of reality that only history and photography can articulate by virtue of their correspondences to it.

Consider, then, the poetic coincidence that left Kracauer's work on history, though nearly complete, unfinished at the time of his death. With the insight that the nonhomogeneous structure of the "intellectual universe" tends to dispose with philosophical certainties, he nonetheless seemed compelled to define and redefine the potential conditions of knowledge, to continually reenter the province of philosophy in order to gaze back at history or the cinema. Kracauer's solutions to the problems of historical knowing are not revolutionary, and the powerful critique of philosophical knowing that his writings seem to imply is not meant to either reject or "deconstruct" the province of philosophy or the necessity of an ontological grounding of knowledge per se. In the end, this led him to accept a radical compromise. With full awareness that death alone is the sanction of everything that the storyteller can tell, Kracauer decided to accept the duplicitous character of philosophical truth. Caught between the transcendental and immanentist positions, he finally argues that "neither can the timeless be stripped of the vestiges of temporality, nor does the temporal wholly engulf the timeless. Rather, we are forced to assume that the two aspects of truths exist side by side, relating to each other in ways which I believe to be theoretically undefinable" (*History* 200). This "side-by-side" principle thus becomes the final figure of thought in Kracauer's reflections on history. Here the possibility of knowledge takes place only in the form of a calculated risk. The presumption of ontological principles becomes, for Kracauer, gambles in Kafka's sense of the term: "They meaningfully enter the scene on (unpredictable) occasions and then presumably fulfill vital functions" (200).

Kracauer thought of this side-by-side principle neither as a stumbling block nor as a deus ex machina for the principle of reason. Rather, this refusal to decide between the absolutes of philosophy and the gamble of anteroom thinking defines for him a kind of existential freedom that he understood allegorically in Kafka's depiction of the relationship between Sancho Panza and Don Quixote. The fragmentary notes that serve as the concluding chapter of *History: The Last Things before the Last* are thus brought to closure through the following citation from Kafka's *Parables and Paradoxes*:

> Without making any boast of it Sancho Panza succeeded in the course of years, by devouring a great number of romances of chivalry and adventure in the evening and night hours, in so diverting from him his demon, whom he later called Don Quixote, that his demon thereupon set out in perfect freedom on the maddest exploits, which, however, for the lack of a preordained object, which

should have been Sancho Panza himself, harmed nobody. A free man, Sancho Panza philosophically followed Don Quixote on his crusades, perhaps out of a sense of responsibility, and had of them a great and edifying entertainment to the end.[24]

There is little doubt, then, that for Kracauer, anteroom thinking defines a utopian moment in which the compromise knowledges of history and photography constitute a possible freedom that escapes the oblivion of lived experience without freezing into the damnation of systematic thought and universal truth. Hence the melancholy aspect of Kracauer's thought, which accepts the camera as a force of alienation, and the discourse of the historian as that of the exile, as the price for occupying the anteroom separating the immediacy of lived experience and the timelessness of philosophical knowing.

I began this chapter by comparing Kracauer's theory of history with Foucault's. But only by turning now to Deleuze, and Deleuze's own special reading of Foucault, can the force of the figural as historical image be clarified in its special relationship with cinema. This is a meeting between two different, though related, conceptualizations of time in relation to space. Here Kracauer's version of the antinomic character of time in its incommensurability with space (both in terms of spatial expression and in the chronological rendering of time) encounters Deleuze's time-image as Event and eternal return. In both cases, however, the figural expression of time in relation to space offers a new Idea of historical "sense" that anticipates a new position for the historical subject.

6. A GENEALOGY OF TIME

Non pas passer les universaux à la râpe de l'histoire, mais faire passer l'histoire au fil d'une pensée qui refuse les universaux. Quelle histoire alors?—Michel Foucault, note written 7 January 1979, in *Dits et écrits*, vol. 1

If cinema does not die a violent death, it retains the power of a beginning.—Gilles Deleuze, preface to the English edition of *Cinema 2: The Time-Image*

Two Stories of 1968 *First story of 1968.* In *Ce que je crois,* Maurice Clavel reports, "When I disembarked at the gare de Lyon in Paris on the third of May, I bought the newspapers, and, reading the headlines reporting the first student riot, said calmly to my wife, 'Isn't it strange, that's it, here we are . . .' 'Where?' she asked me. 'In the middle of Foucault. . . .' For finally, didn't *The Order of Things* herald this great geological fracturing of our humanist culture that emerged in May 1968?" [1]

Second story of 1968. On the same day, a young critic writing for *Cahiers du cinéma*—having just seen Alain Resnais's *Je t'aime, je t'aime*—emerges from a theater in the Latin Quarter and is swept up in the force of history as students and police clash among barricades and burning cars. What rapport can there be between fiction and reality, he thinks afterward? What is the historical significance of this film, perhaps Resnais's most disorienting meditation on time, apparently so distant from any political thought? What can cinema mean for this apocalyptic present marked by the collective belief that the passing of time is a carnivalesque Event—in fact, a break in time between past and future where the future is open to an infinite set of possibilities, anything is possible, and change is inevitable?

The filiations between these two stories are deeper than they appear at first glance. Could Resnais's most abstract meditation on time and memory relate forcefully to the historical eruption of May and June 1968 in France? This idea is no less odd than the first reaction of Maurice Clavel: immediately to isolate French poststructuralism as one of the primary causes of the student and worker protests.

As in the previous chapter, here film and the philosophy of history confront each other yet again, although with different philosophical stakes, in asking: What is history, or perhaps historical thought, through visual culture? To answer this question, we must not only examine the relationship between film and audiovisual culture in general but also ask with Foucault: Which history, then? The immediate impact of modern French media and art is to mark the emergence of a visual culture distinctly different from that of the prewar period, one of whose qualities is the redefinition of how time and thought are expressed through audiovisual culture. Indeed, to state my thesis directly, after 1958 there emerges in French audiovisual culture a new philosophy of history in images that is indelibly associated with Nietzsche's presence in French poststructuralist thought. Here we find a strange reversal, first signaled in Deleuze's writings on cinema.[2] Although visual media are usually considered as arts of space, in modern French visual culture, space is, in strikingly diverse ways, "invested" by time. In their new Nietzschean elaboration, space and time are refigured: space becomes an Event defined by the force of time as becoming and virtuality. Space no longer occupies a single time but is instead crossed by multiple lines of descent (so many alternative paths and deviations in the line of time either barred, forgotten, or barely dreamed) and launches into the future as an undetermined set of possibilities. This is yet another way of reading the figural, not only as a transformation in the field of audiovisuality, but also as a historical image.

Two Audiovisual Regimes: The Movement-Image and Time-Image

Michel Foucault and Gilles Deleuze are the two figures most closely associated with the French turn to Nietzsche in the 1960s.[3] Foucault remarked only infrequently on the cinema and indeed is often considered a historian of "discourse" rather than of visual culture. In his book on Foucault, Deleuze takes the opposite tack. For Deleuze, Foucault is a philosopher of the visible as well as the discursive. Indeed, Deleuze suggests, Foucault's description of epistemic shifts is marked by the emplacement of audiovisual regimes: changing articulations of the visible with respect to the expressible—modes of seeing and ways of saying—that organize knowledge, power, and subjectivity in distinct historical eras.

This philosophical consideration of history as the emplacement and displacement of audiovisual regimes also informs Deleuze's two-volume theory of film, *Cinema 1: The Movement-Image* and *Cinema 2: The Time-Image.* One consequence of these books is to present a case for the primacy of cinema in the emergence and organization of twentieth-century visual culture. Deleuze argues that the history of cinema as an audiovisual form is marked by a tectonic shift. The displacement of the movement-image by the time-image involves a turn both in the order of signs, requiring two different semiotics, and in the image of thought characterizing the philosophical orientation of the two regimes. The movement-image is characterized by a Hegelian logic, that is, a dialectical organization of images and signs in an organic representation marked qualitatively by a will to truth. Alternatively, the time-image presumes a Nietzschean aesthetic whose images and signs are organized by "fabulation," a falsifying narration defined not by representation but by simulacra whose qualities are "powers of the false": the *indiscernibility* of the real and the imaginary in the image; a temporal (dis)ordering of narration presenting differences in the present that are *inexplicable,* and alternative versions of the past whose truth or falseness are *undecidable;* and, as a result, a transformation in the problem of judgment, of deciding the necessity or contingency of possible or probable interpretations where *incompossible* worlds proliferate as incongruous presents and not necessarily true pasts. These are two different images of thought where the Hegelian will to truth, which identifies the orderly unfolding of history with reason, is challenged by a Nietzschean critique of values that asks not "What is true?" but rather "Who wants the truth, and what do they will in wanting it?"[4]

The movement-image and the time-image thus present two broad regimes of images and signs. Indeed, the emergence of the latter from the former traces a slow but definite shift in the nature of visual culture wherein the aesthetic innovations of the French New Wave and contemporary cinema in France resonate with other experiments in French audiovisual culture and the arts. Deleuze's second volume is especially useful for defining the exemplarity of French film and audiovisual culture since 1958. However, I also want to make a larger argument concerning the nature of Deleuze's philosophical analysis. The transition described from *The Movement-Image* to *The Time-Image* also effects a more general displacement in the philosophy of history, indeed a shifting relation between history and thought marked by confrontations in the postwar *episteme* between existentialism—with its Hegelian conception of history and politics—and the poststructuralism of Deleuze and Foucault, with their Nietzschean and genealogical concepts of history and thought. This new historical sense equally informs the reconsideration of time and change in contemporary French visual culture.

It may seem odd to ask the question of history of Deleuze, since he insisted that his two books do not offer a "history of cinema."[5] Certainly they are the product of philosophical activity and not historical research in any sense of the term. Deleuze has every right to emphasize that what the two books offer is a taxonomy of signs and their logics as well as an elaboration of concepts, and are thus primarily works of philosophy.

At the same time, however, the two books present many features of a historical work. They are organized across a broad temporal division: a historical break divides the time-image, which appears largely in the period following World War II, from the movement-image that precedes it. Indeed, Deleuze even presents a historical context for this break. Prewar societies were sustained by organic ideologies (democracy or socialism) that functioned as universals defined by a notion of history as progress. The movement-image is marked by the coherence of sensorimotor situations: perceptions derive from coherent and meaningful images of the world and extend into actions capable of transforming the world; events are linked in meaningful ways organized by origins and ends; opposition and conflict are resolvable through actions and are amenable to coherent solutions; individuals act as the agents of history; and finally the individual stands, *pars pro toto,* for the collective and thus expresses the will of a people.[6]

In the movement-image, then, the protagonists' actions drive a chronological narrative marked by the dialectical unfolding of effects from causes, reactions from actions, according to a logic of "rational intervals"—the beginning of an image or sequence unfolds in continuity from the ones that precede it. An image of organic unity forms as images are linked or extended according to principles of association and contiguity, and associated images are integrated into a conceptual whole and differentiated into more extensive sets. This is a chronological or empirical conception where time can only be presented indirectly as continuous segmentations of space whose parts are commensurate with the whole of the film. Deleuze calls this process "an open totality in movement" that gives rise to a model of the True as totalization, an ideal world perfectly commensurate and analogous with both its referent and the subject who comprehends it. This notion of chronological time conforms precisely with a linear and teleological conception of history.

The time-image emerges from Italian neorealism and comes to fruition in the French New Wave. The narrative innovations of neorealism, the New Wave, or New German Cinema all derive from the experience of physical, social, and psychological reconstruction of societies devastated during the second World War. This experience defines a set of characteristics that make possible the emergence of direct images of time. As images of emptied and wasted spaces surged in everyday life, postwar cinema discovered "a dispersive and lacunary reality" that motivated ambiguous and undeciphered images (*Movement-Image* 212). Especially in the French New Wave, narration is freed from sensorimotor situations and any teleological orientation. Lines of action become lines of flight whose points of departure and arrival are arbitrary or undetermined: journeys to and from Paris and the provinces (Chabrol's *Le beau serge* or *Les cousins* [1958]); errant trajectories in the city whose value is more ethical or analytical than spatial (Rohmer's *Moral Tales* or Truffaut's Antoine Doinel trilogy); investigations whose object is obscure and whose ends are inconclusive (Rivette's *Paris nous appartient* [1961]). But perhaps the purest example of what Deleuze calls the *forme-balade* is found in films such as Truffaut's *Tirez-sur le pianiste* (1960) or Godard's *À bout de souffle* (1959) or *Pierrot le fou* (1965). Here classical narration yields to unpredictable lines of flight: an accumulation of disparate urban landscapes and dis-

junct geographies connected only by the dual sense of the French word
évasion, both flight from the law and play or leisure.

The protagonists of New Wave films thus define a nomadism where
the characters of the time-image wander errantly and observe in
emptied and disconnected spaces; linear actions dissolve into aleatory
strolls that organize elliptical narratives guided predominantly by
chance.[7] In so doing they represent a kind of postmodern historical
subjectivity—the faltering belief in totality, either from the point of
view of the great organic ideologies or from a belief in the image as anything other than a partial and contingent description of reality. Because
the linking of images is no longer motivated by actions, space changes
in nature, becoming a series of disconnected "any-spaces-whatever"
organized by a logic of "irrational intervals" or "interstices" that no
longer form a part of any sequence either as the end of one or the beginning of another. Because it is autonomous and irreducible, the irrational interval gives rise to a transcendental or direct image of time as
aberrant or false movement. It is not spatial, nor does it form part of an
image. Rather, as a direct image of time, the interstice presents a force
that unhinges images and sounds into disconnected series and epi-
sodic sequences that can no longer form an organic image of the whole.
Another hallmark of the figural, this geometry of the time-image is not
totalizable as an image of Truth. Acts of seeing and hearing replace the
linking of images by motivated actions and the exertion of will; pure
description replaces referential anchoring. In this manner, new kinds
of images and signs appear where "making-false [*faire-faux*] becomes
the sign of a new realism, in opposition to the making true of the old"
(*Movement-Image* 213). The movement-image presents time indirectly
as the unfolding of a causally motivated space, a truthful image that
subsumes the reality it represents as a return of the Same. But with the
direct image of time—elliptical events marked only by chance connections, undeciphered and ambiguous images producing events in their
unique duration—there also appear new values. As I will argue later,
this is a Nietzschean conception of time and history marked by the
logic of eternal recurrence.

Finally, Deleuze argues in the preface to *The Movement-Image* that
the cinema has a place in both the history of art and the history of philosophy. In each case, this relates to conceptual innovation in cinematic

practice that Deleuze examines through his taxonomy of images and signs. Although these classifications are largely philosophical—based on Henri Bergson's *Matter and Memory* and, especially in the first volume, the semiotic of Charles Sanders Peirce—the fundamental division of the time-image from the movement-image is art historical. Mapping a century-long transformation in our cultural modes of envisioning and representing, Deleuze adopts Wilhelm Worringer's distinction between organic and crystalline regimes to characterize the qualitative differences between the movement-image and time-image.[8] However, when Deleuze refers to the organic movement-image as "classic" and the crystalline time-image as "modern," this means neither that the latter flows from the former as natural progression or teleology nor that the modern form necessarily opposes the classic as negation or critique. Instead, this transition represents a distinct, if gradual, transformation in the nature of belief and the possibilities of thought. If the modern cinema offers a *direct* presentation of time, the emergence of this time-image is not a necessary consequence of the evolution of the movement-image. For Deleuze, the history of cinema is in no way a progression toward an ever more perfect representation of time. Rather, the relation between time and thought is imagined differently in the postwar period, as represented in the signs produced by the time-image and by changes in the image of thought occurring in postwar science, art, and philosophy. And here history returns to philosophy, since what is at stake is a shift in our image of thought, that is, "the image of what thought gives itself of what it means to think, to make use of thought, to find one's bearings in thought."[9]

One could map postwar filmmaking in France as the emergence of the crystalline regime of the time-image as a new perspective on the history of film style. But I want to argue instead that Deleuze presents us with two "histories" or, more precisely, two distinct and incommensurable logics for thinking historically *through* images and signs. If Deleuze demurs from characterizing the content of his books as "history," they nonetheless present a shift in the way history is thought, and indeed may suggest that we reconsider the very idea of history as a philosophical concept and as a force expressed through audiovisual culture. In French film since 1958, there appears a new orientation of the visible with respect to the expressible—of image and sound as well as movement and time—that defines a new conceptual relation with questions of history, memory, and politics while marking the emergence of a new form of subjectivity, one of whose consequences may have been to ignite the historical desire expressed in May 1968.

The exemplarity of the time-image in contemporary French cinema thus becomes the occasion to examine three new premises for reading the figural: that reading Deleuze and Foucault together is a way of comprehending what a cinematic history of concepts means in contrast to a dialectical conception of history; that the movement-image and time-image are historical in the sense of presenting two distinct audiovisual regimes, which may be distinguished by, among other criteria, the passage from a Hegelian philosophy of history to a Nietzschean or genealogical historical thought; and that French cinema since 1958 may be characterized by the concept of genealogy elaborated by Foucault in his reading of Nietzsche.

I believe the ultimate goal of the human sciences to be not to constitute, but to dissolve man.—Claude Lévi-Strauss, *The Savage Mind*

The Ends of the Dialectic and the Return of History: Hegel & Nietzsche When Deleuze remarks that his film books are not history, it is necessary to ask: What does "history" mean in this context? To understand the Nietzschean dimension of French cinema as a genealogy of time, we must examine how and under what conditions a philosophical discourse on Nietzsche emerged and circulated in French intellectual culture, and how it transformed notions of the historical subject.

In a 1967 interview with Raymond Bellour, Foucault remarked that in the 1950s and 1960s the discipline of history was the object of a curious "sacralization" by the French Left. Many intellectuals observed a respectful distance to history as a way of reconciling their research and writing with their political consciences. Under the cross of history, this attitude became "a prayer to the gods of just causes."[10] To question the identity of history with reason, or to exhume the Hegelian foundations of historical knowing through a genealogical critique, was unthinkable because it would expose the historical contingency of the political rationality associated with the particular Marxism of the French Communist Party. "In the eyes of certain people," Foucault explained, the discipline of history constituted the last refuge of the dialectical order: in history one could save the kingdom of rational contradiction. Thus many intellectuals maintain—for two reasons and against any *vraisemblance*—a conception of history organized on the model of the story (*récit*) of the great sweep of events taken up in a hierarchy of determinations. Individuals are seized in the interior of this totality which is beyond them and plays in them, and of which they are at the same time, perhaps, the unconscious authors. To the point where this history, a project of both the individual and the totality, has for certain people become untouchable. For this would be to attack the grand cause of revolution by refusing such forms said to be historical. (*Dit et écrits* 585–86)

Indeed, paraphrasing Nietzsche's "On the Uses and Disadvantages of History," one might say that in the immediate postwar period, the French suffered from the "disease of history" as defined by a Hegelian tradition associated with phenomenology and existentialism.

In this interview, Foucault implicitly addresses a number of conflicts that arose as existentialism, structuralism, and poststructuralism vied for intellectual dominance in postwar France. This intellectual history underscores a number of concepts that circulated in art practice and theory, as well as film and film theory, with respect to the nature of representation, signification, and the place of the subject. And in these conflicts, a shift in the represented logic of history may be traced as well.

The leading philosophers of the existentialist period—Jean-Paul Sartre and Maurice Merleau-Ponty—derived their philosophical positions from the phenomenology of Husserl and Heidegger as well as Marx's writings on political economy. Without question, however, the predominant philosophical influence of the immediate postwar period was Hegel. Therefore, to offer the figure of Nietzsche as central to the thinking of history in the postwar period is not self-evident. But, it must be said, this is equally the case for Hegel. Before World War II, French academic philosophy considered Hegel a Romantic whose ideas were long put to rest by more scientific approaches to philosophy. However, in the immediate postwar period, a Hegelianized Marxism rapidly became the dominant discourse for students of philosophy in

Foucault's and Deleuze's generation. The renewed prestige of Hegel in France was due principally to two figures: Aléxandre Kojève and Jean Hyppolite. From 1933 to 1939, Kojève's lectures on Hegel's *Phenomenology of the Spirit* at the Ecole Pratique des Hautes Etudes marked many of the principal figures in the next generation of French philosophy, including Raymond Aron, Maurice Merleau-Ponty, Raymond Queneau, Georges Bataille, Pierre Klossowski, and Jacques Lacan. At about the same time, Hyppolite was working on the first French translations of Hegel's *Phenomenology,* which appeared in two volumes, in 1939 and 1941. The greater influence of Kojève's lectures was delayed until 1947, when they were finally published as *Introduction à la lecture de Hegel: Leçons sur la phénoménologie d l'esprit,* in a version edited by Raymond Queneau from his lecture notes. In the same year, Hyppolite defended and published his thesis on Hegel, *Genèse et structure de la "Phénoménologie de l'esprit" de Hegel.* This influential book was quickly followed by studies of Hegel's logic and philosophy of history, as well as a series of studies on Marx and Hegel.[11] As a professor first at the prestigious Lycée Henri-IV, and then at the Sorbonne and the Collège de France, Hyppolite's teaching exerted an enormous influence on a whole generation of French philosophers—including Michel Foucault, Gilles Deleuze, Louis Althusser, and Jacques Derrida—all of whom would nevertheless eventually produce important critiques of Hegel.

The closeness of French Hegelianism to both existentialism and Marxism was something explicitly recognized and commented on by both Hyppolite and Merleau-Ponty. Indeed, it would be difficult to say whether it was the "rediscovery" of Marx's 1844 Paris manuscripts and the general postwar prestige of Marxist philosophy that encouraged the interest in Hegel, or whether it was the predominance of Hegel that opened a new context for Marxist thought in France. In any case, in the heyday of existentialism and phenomenology, Hegel had achieved a powerful though curious place in the history of philosophy—at once the apogee of classical thought and the origin of modern Continental philosophy. For Hyppolite, the genealogy of modern philosophy through Feuerbach, Kierkegaard, Nietzsche, and Marx could be read as original responses to specific confrontations with Hegel's thought. For Merleau-Ponty, the silence regarding Hegel in the first half of the twentieth century was an ignoble forgetting of Hegel's influence such that the most urgent project of modern philosophy was to reconnect those ungrateful doctrines to their Hegelian origins. The preeminence of Hegel in the immediate postwar period is amply represented, then, in Merleau-Ponty's comment in *Sense and Non-Sense* that "all the great philosophical ideas of the past century had their beginnings in Hegel: the philosophies of Marx and Nietzsche, phenomenology, German existentialism, and psychoanalysis; it was he who started the attempt to explore the irrational and integrate it into an expanded reason which remains the task of our century" (63).

By the middle of the 1960s, however, history's largely Hegelian project seemed more and more *démodé* as linguistics, sociology, and ethnology abandoned dialectical concepts for the synchronic analysis of "structures." Indeed, despite his own vexed relationship with structuralism, the phenomenal and completely unexpected success of *The Order of Things* in spring 1966 placed Foucault's work in the foreground of the cultural conflict between existentialism and structuralism, above all with its more often than not misunderstood pronouncements on "the death of man." A more directed challenge to existentialism appeared in another oft-quoted remark: "Marxism is in the thought of the 19th century life like a fish in water," implying, of course, that in the mid–twentieth century, the dialectic was a whale beached on the same sand where the face of "man" was dissolving in the ocean.

For all its complexity, structuralism's critique of phenomenology and existentialism targeted two fundamental concepts: the subject and history. Although the publication of Claude Lévi-Strauss's *Structural Anthropology* in 1958 should be considered as the opening volley of structuralism's critique of existentialism, perhaps the more important touchstone was the conclusion to *The Savage Mind* (1962), which attacked Sartre's philosophy as a "contemporary mythology." Explicitly targeting Sartre's *Critique of Dialectical Reason* (1960), Lévi-Strauss presented structuralism's most powerful critique of existential Marxism's Hegelianized version of the subject, above all as an agent in history. (In a 1966 interview, Foucault was even less kind, stating that "*The Critique of Dialectical Reason* is the magnificent and pathetic attempt of a 19th century man to think the 20th century. In this sense, Sartre is the last Hegelian, and I would say even, the last Marxist.")[12]

The originality of Lévi-Strauss's argument was to present the structure of myth as a thought without subject. Like the other key figures of structuralism, Lévi-Strauss was inspired by the semiology of Ferdinand de Saussure, who, instead of following the traditional methods of historical philology, chose to study the problem of linguistic meaning in the systematic structure of language itself. In reconstructing the system of language (langue), semiology studies not the isolated elements of language or individual speech acts (parole) but rather the patterned system of differences constituting their structure independent of any actual act of speaking. In this manner, "Linguistics thus presents us with a dialectical and totalizing entity but one outside (or beneath) consciousness and will. Language, an unreflecting totalization, is human reason which has its reasons and of which man knows nothing" (*Savage Mind* 252).[13] Here structuralism and existential Marxism confront each other with competing concepts of totality, one that is dialectical and temporal, resulting from human praxis, the other that is spatial and relational or systemic. For structuralism, the dialectic mounts an illusion of the Cogito as a figure of universal rationality. By focusing on systemic invariants and the level of langue while setting aside the more ephemeral evolution of daily and individual speech, only synchronic analysis establishes a scientific and social theory of language. In "A quoi reconnaît-on le structuralisme?" Deleuze characterized this concept as a kind of virtual totality, a transcendental topology defined by the symbolic rather than the transcendental humanism of Sartre's dialectic. Here the self-present agency of the phenomenological subject dissolves into an anonymous logic of signification where consciousness becomes little more than a surface effect and history is defined not by human agency and conflict but by displacements in systems of thought that are both collective and anonymous.

In Lévi-Strauss's argument, then, Sartre mystifies history according to criteria that differentiate temporal and spatial thinking. In existential Marxism, the temporal dimension of dialectical reason is granted a special status on the presumption that it defines the human Cogito. But the difference between ethnology and philosophy in this respect is not so great. Whereas the historian reconstitutes an image of past societies as they conceived themselves in their own present, the ethnographer reconstructs the historical stages that precede actually existing societies in time. Like the semiologist, the ethnographer produces synchronic or atemporal slices of space, snapshots, as it were, of a temporal evolution. But the deeper problem returns to a Hegelian privileging of "temporal" or dialectical versus spatial thinking, above all in how Sartre disparages the peoples of "primitive" societies as being "without history." "And so we end up," writes Lévi-Strauss, "in the paradox of a system which invokes the criterion of historical consciousness to distinguish the 'primitive' from the 'civilized' but—contrary to its claim—is itself ahistorical. It offers not a concrete image of history but an abstract schema of men making history of such a kind that it can manifest itself in the trend of their lives as a synchronic totality. Its relation to history is therefore the same as that of primitives to the eternal past: in Sartre's system, history plays exactly the part of myth" (*Savage Mind* 254). Therefore it is necessary to challenge the identification of History with the unfolding of Reason, above all when it imposes on us "the unavowed aim of making historicity the last refuge of a transcendental humanism: as if men could regain the illusion of liberty on the plane of the 'we' merely by giving up the 'I's that are too obviously wanting in consistency" (262).

It is in this manner that Lévi-Strauss, Lacan, and Althusser all drew on the methodology of Saussurean linguistics for their critical investigations of the human sciences: anthropology, psychoanalysis, and political economy. Where the existentialists privileged the concept of human action in history, structuralism emphasized the synchronic analysis of "structures" independent of human agency—myth, the logic of the signifier, and history as "absent cause." And where existentialism privileged the philosophical analysis of consciousness as the central fact of human existence, structuralism was characterized by its "antihumanism," its decentering of the subject as a function of social structures. Foucault referred to this as a passion of "concept and system" in contradistinction to the existentialist passion for "life and existence."[14] Where Sartre's project was to recover meaning from a world that the bourgeoisie had rendered absurd, the lesson of structuralism was to demonstrate a displacement in the concept of meaning itself. Therefore when Lacan argues that the unconscious is structured like a language, a shift occurs where it is no longer the subject who speaks or acts, but rather the anonymous system of language that speaks through the subject, or what Foucault identified as an anonymous thought or knowledge without subject that is found in modern literature as much as the theories of structuralism.

The rereadings of Freud and Marx by Lacan and Althusser, as well as Heidegger's magisterial if idiosyncratic recovery of Nietzsche, set the conditions for poststructuralism to emerge as a distinctly philosophical response to the structuralist privileging of the human sciences. Nietzsche was certainly never entirely absent from French thought, having circulated through the literary and cultural avant-garde in the works of Georges Bataille, Pierre Klossowski, Albert Camus, André Malraux, and Maurice Blanchot, among others. But this was largely a subterranean and marginal presence. As Alan D. Schrift notes, in postwar philosophical circles, Nietzsche's place was decisively subordinate to that of the "three Hs": Hegel, Husserl, and Heidegger (*Nietzsche's French Legacy* 3). The stage was set for the "new Nietzscheanism" with the publication of Deleuze's *Nietzsche and Philosophy* in 1962, a book whose profound influence on French philosophy has yet to be fully accounted for. Subsequently two important colloquiums on Nietzsche, the first organized by Deleuze at Royaumont in July 1964 and the second occurring at Cerisy-La-Salle in July 1972, framed a number of other important events, including the translation and publication of Nietzsche's complete works under Deleuze and Foucault's editorship and the appearance of a number of important studies on or influenced by Nietzsche.[15]

One of the curious consequences of the rise of structuralism, with its emphasis on reasserting the methodological rigors of the social sciences, was to undercut the enormous prestige of philosophy in the postwar period. Indeed, Lévi-Strauss's critique of Sartre was symptomatic of a more general attack by the social sciences on the standing of philosophy in the humanities. Therefore, one way to identify the difference of poststructuralism — in the work of Deleuze, Foucault, or Derrida — is through its reassertion of the powers of philosophy with respect to the problems and concepts posed by structuralism. The passage through Nietzsche, then, was important for two reasons. First, in the institutional framework of, as Deleuze put it, a "generation ruined by the history of philosophy," Nietzsche's status as a marginal philosopher in France opened a line of flight for young philosophers fatigued by the rationalist and Hegelian traditions of academic philosophy.[16] One may think it ironic, then, that Foucault should succeed to Jean Hyppolite's chair at the Collège de France in 1970. But Foucault's homages to Hyppolite make clear that while the new Nietzscheanism appeared as a philosophical critique of Hegel, its historical response to the "Hegel generation" was not one of dialectical opposition or conflict but rather the search for alternative styles of reading and critique sensitive to the formidable powers of the dialectic. In *The Order of Discourse,* his inaugural lecture at the Collège de France, Foucault remarked:

> Our entire epoch, whether through logic or epistemology, through Marx or through Nietzsche, tries to escape from Hegel. . . . But to really escape from Hegel means appreciating what it costs to break with him; to know up to what point, insidiously perhaps, that Hegel is close to us; and to know, in what allows us to think against Hegel, that which is still Hegelian; and, in our recourse against him, to measure what may yet be a ruse wherein he opposes us, waiting immobile, elsewhere. Now, if there are more than one among us who owe Jean Hyppolite a debt, it is because he tirelessly followed, for us and ahead of us, the path diverging from Hegel, which takes distance from him, and through which we find ourselves brought back to him, but otherwise, with the necessity of leaving him again.[17]

To free oneself from the dialectic meant transforming the terrain of philosophical concepts, not superseding philosophy in a new dialectical gesture or a different form of totality. For poststructuralism, then, Hyppolite was less the master Hegelian than the innovator of a different approach to the history of philosophical thought, one that recognized "in each system — no matter how complete it seems — what overflows it, exceeds it, and puts it in a relation of both exchange and default with respect to philosophy itself."[18] Foucault and others saw in Hyppolite a philosophical style that defined the principal problems and approaches of the postwar period, including a number of questions that would define the new Nietzscheanism of the 1960s; namely, how to think the relation between violence and discourse, or between logic and existence, and that philosophical thinking is a practical necessity "that is a way of putting non-philosophy to work while always residing close to it, there where it is tied to existence" (Foucault, "Hyppolite" 785).

The difference of the "new Nietzscheanism" was marked not only by a different conceptualization of philosophical style and discourse but also in the way that philosophy reconsidered its own relation to history and the philosophy of history. Lévi-Strauss's attack on Sartre signaled a real confrontation, indeed an opposition, between structuralism and a Hegelianized existentialism. This conflict was marked both temporally, as a story where one discourse supersedes another, and spatially as the discourse of the "human sciences" drew its borders against philosophy. Alternatively the historical relation of the new Nietzscheanism to existentialism *and* structuralism is different from the opposition of structuralism to existentialism. It is strongly marked neither by a period nor by a consistent terrain of concepts, nor did Nietzsche's thought function as an authenticating origin in the same way as the names of Hegel and Marx, Freud or Saussure. What Nietzsche enabled was not only a new style of philosophizing but also a new conceptualization of history in relation to discourse and the powers of discourse that was cunning and subtle enough to evade the traps of dialectic.

And herein lies the second fundamental reason for the turn to Nietzsche. The passage through Nietzsche presented a way of retaining the structuralist emphasis on an anonymous thought without subject while rethinking problems of agency and history. Schrift notes that one consequence of the turn to Nietzsche, in Foucault, for example, was to reexamine how questions of agency could be addressed without returning to phenomenology's emphasis on the centrality of human consciousness. "That is to say," Schrift writes, "where the structuralists responded to existentialism's privileging of consciousness and history by eliminating them both, the poststructuralists took from structuralism insights concerning the working of linguistic and systemic forces and returned with insights to reinvoke the question of the subject in terms of a notion of constituted-constitutive-constituting agency situated and operating within a complex network of socio-historical and intersubjective relations" (*Nietzsche's French Legacy* 5–6). Thus the turn to Nietzsche reinvented the relation between history and agency in four ways: by rearticulating the relation between language, power, and desire; by transforming the problem of meaning so as to undermine any claim to universality; by opposing binary oppositions with a logic of differential meaning; and by conceiving the subject as a complex site crossed by discursive, libidinal, and social forces that both constrained and enabled the possibilities of agency. In this manner, a new conceptualization of history and the subject appeared in the Nietzscheanism of Deleuze, Foucault, Derrida, Klossowski, Hélène Cixous, and Sarah Kofman, although with very different manifestations in each. The renewed interest in Nietzsche had multiple dimensions, then, and was less a "return" in the sense of Lacan's return to Freud, or Althusser's rereading of Marx, than the opening of a new territory of concepts along multiple lines of descent: a critique of the will to truth, an interpretation of the complex connections between knowledge and power, and a new attention to questions of style and rhetoric in philosophical discourse.

Genealogy, Countermemory, Event   Contrary to the usual way of representing poststructuralism, the turn to Nietzsche was a way of reasserting the force of history occluded by structuralism, and in so doing, reassessing what history means in relation to force, memory, or time. Deleuze is right to insist that his theory does not present a history of cinema. But the logic of the time-image itself can be revaluated in the Nietzschean sense as the emergence of a historical *dispositif* that presupposes not only a rearticulation of time in relation to space but also the expression of a new "historical sense" and the anticipation of a new historical subject. I want to continue, then, with some indications of how Deleuze's Nietzschean aesthetic of the time-image resonates with Foucault's discussion of genealogy.

The sixties and seventies in France were an extraordinary period of cinematic experimentation and cross-fertilization with literature, art, critical theory, and philosophy as represented most clearly in the films of Alain Resnais, Jean-Luc Godard, Alain Robbe-Grillet, and Marguerite Duras. Moreover, after the phenomenal success of *The Order of Things* in 1966 — and the subsequent influence of publications such as "Nietzsche, Genealogy, History" — Foucault's radical reconceptualization of the historical project became increasingly influential in both film theory and practice. In the 1970s, for example, *Cahiers du cinéma* began to reassess the problem of history by publishing its collective analyses of *Young Mr. Lincoln, Hangmen Also Die,* and *La Marseillaise,* as well as Jean-Louis Comolli's series of essays on technology and ideology and discussions of Foucault's ideas concerning popular memory as countermemory.[19]

At about the same time, a new kind of historical filmmaking emerged in the work of Comolli, René Allio, and others. Some of these films such as Allio's *Moi, Pierre Rivière . . .* (1976) and Hervé Guibert's project for filming *Herculine Barbin, dite Alexina B* (1979) were directly influenced by Foucault's research. Of course, a number of films of the 1960s anticipated a genealogical examination of history and a rethinking of time — above all Alain Resnais's *Nuit et brouillard* (1955), *Hiroshima mon amour* (1959), *Muriel* (1963), and *La guerre est finie* (1966), as well as a number of films by Chris Marker, and by Jean-Marie Straub and Danièlle Huillet. However, it was the release of Marcel Ophul's *Le chagrin et la pitié* in 1971 — as well as *Les camisards* (René Allio, 1970) and *Le sauveur* (Michel Mardore, 1970) — that launched a decade of films that explicitly took on problems of historical representation, knowing, and memory more or less in the context of Foucault and the new history.[20]

The question remains open, however, of why contemporary French cinema should have been, and in many respects continues to be, a privileged site for a meditation on time. Even in Deleuze's account, the time-image has avatars in many different countries and different periods of film history. Yet French filmmakers, and the history of contemporary French cinema, form a definitive crest line throughout *The Time-Image* in the experiments with time and subjectivity expressed, each in different ways, in the work of Jean Renoir, Max Ophuls, Luis Buñuel, Robert Bresson, Alain Resnais, Jean Rouch, Marguerite Duras, Alain Robbe-Grillet, Jacques Rivette, Jean-Luc Godard, Eric Rohmer, Jean-Marie Straub and Danièlle Huillet, Philippe Garrel, and others.

A deeper exercise in intellectual and aesthetic history needs to explain the conditions that enabled this genealogical current to pass through philosophy and history to film and back again. My argument here, however, is that only in France was this experimentation *philo-*

sophically possible. From *The Order of Things* to *Cinema 2: The Time-Image,* there runs a Nietzschean thread that passes between philosophy, film theory, and film practice as an extraordinary examination of time and history both in philosophy and in cinema. To follow this thread through the different domains of French art and thought, then, we must ask the following question: How can time be the basis for historical knowing? Hegel's dialectical conception of the relation between reason and history and Nietzsche's genealogy as a critique of values, above all those marked by the will to truth, give very different responses to this question.

In Foucault's and Deleuze's accounts, only through difference can we think historically—that is, in relation to time and time's definition of subjectivity. In "Theatrum Philosophicum," Foucault's appreciation of Deleuze's philosophy of time in *Difference and Repetition* and *Logic of Sense,* he explains that there have been three great attempts in philosophy to think the event, all of which have failed: neopositivism, phenomenology, and the philosophy of history. In each case difference is foreclosed by the figure of the circle, or what Foucault calls the "ill-conceived principle of return" ("Theatrum" 165, 76).[21] The philosophy of history, for example, defines events as existence in time, but only on the condition that they are spatialized and submitted to a centered and hierarchical order. The philosophy of history encloses the event in a circular time where, according to Foucault, "it treats the present as a figure framed by the future and past. The present is the future in another time whose very form is already being drawn; and it is a past to come which preserves the identity of the present's content" (176, 83). The philosophy of history is founded, like the movement-image, on an empirical conception of time: a chronological ordering of events in space and a volumetric expansion of the whole that are drawn together in a circular figure of dialectical commensurability. From the present to the past, and from the present to the future, time can only be represented as the return of the Same in a spatial image of analogical adequation.

In "Nietzsche, Genealogy, History," Foucault opposes the philosophy of history with what Nietzsche called "effective history."[22] To effect must be taken in its most literal sense—to do or to take action. Rather than being a meditation on history's monuments, *effective* history seeks to take action *in* and *for* the present through the analysis of continuing and emerging regimes of forces. Genealogy does not take refuge in the absolute, for effective history is without constants and, in this manner, requires a new form of "historical sense." In "On the Uses and Disadvantages of History for Life," Nietzsche uses the term *historicher Sinn,* which can be translated as meaning or sense. Nietzsche develops this concept with a strategic ambiguity. Foucault makes the case, however, that genealogy requires a new "sense" incorporating all the connotations of the term: meaning, logic, perception or perspective, instinct, sensibility, reason. For the historical subject, it is nothing less than a new positionality within history and historical knowing.

For history to be effective, and to construct this new positionality, genealogy opposes itself to the search for both origins and ends. This does not mean that genealogy counters history as an alternative, and therefore a truer or deeper, philosophy. Rather, it opposes "the metahistorical deployment of ideal significations and indefinite teleologies" ("Nietzsche" 140). To search for origins is to try to recover "what has already been" in an image exactly adequate to itself. Nietzsche condemned the concept of origin (*Ursprung*) as a search for the ideal form behind appearances: a static and ideal meaning ordered by a time signifiable in space that freezes historical thought in "an attempt to capture the exact essence of things, their purest possibilities, and their carefully protected identities, because this search assumes the existence of immobile forms that precede the external world of accident and succession" (142). In this respect, the philosophy of history, like the indirect image of time as space, belongs to what Deleuze called the Platonic order of representation.

The search for origins is complemented by a teleological movement. By drawing a circle that passes between two points—a beginning and an end—things are given form on a territory where time and space are frozen in an idealized dialectical image. Confined to a space ordered by teleology, historical knowing demands judgment as a transcendent and "suprahistorical" perspective, universal because it is timeless, that Nietzsche associates with both Plato and Hegel. This is an empyrean perspective where the historian stands outside and above time, as it were. Here the function of history is to reduce the heterogeneity of time in a closed totality. This implies a finality where all of history is rendered as representable and explainable, as if on a smooth and reflective surface in which we recognize only ourselves and, at the same time, are reconciled to all the displacements or dislocations of the past, no matter how unjust. This "historians' history," according to Foucault, thus "finds its support outside of time and pretends to base its judgments on an apocalyptic objectivity" ("Nietzsche" 152). The search for origins is marked, like the organic narration of the movement-image, by a specific value—the will to truth. It seeks to confirm itself in an image of Truth as the selfsame, or repetition as resolution rather than differentiation.

This is why, in its critique of origins and the circular form of time, genealogy recasts history as discontinuity; the highest task of effective history is to introduce discontinuity into time. This involves a redefinition of time as a nonlinearity with neither origin nor finality—what Nietzsche called *Entstehung*, or emergence, wherein history is considered as "the very body of becoming" ("Nietzsche" 144). By the same token, teleology is replaced by *Herkunft*, or provenance, which uncovers, within the apparently unique aspect of a concept or character, the proliferation of events from which they descend. Without meaning accorded proactively by an origin or retroactively by an end, history ceases to be spatial and representational. Instead it concerns time and the Event: what Deleuze called the *virtual* as the myriad unheard or unacted-on possibilities that reside in the interval of every passing present. Genealogy does not return in time to reestablish a continuity broken by forgetting; it does not show the past as an ideal form animating an ever-present secret that would be the ground for a concept or character, there from the beginning. "To follow the complex web of provenance," Foucault writes, "is to hold what happened in its proper dispersion: to identify the accidents, the minute deviations—or conversely, the complete reversals—the errors, the false appraisals, and the faulty calculations that gave birth to those things that continue to have value for us; it is to discover that at the root of what we know and who we are, there is neither truth nor being, but the exteriority of an accident" (146, *141*).

Therefore effective history liberates us from universal history because it knows that the quality of becoming offers the following possibility: that the forces of history are not directed by destiny, nor do they know timeless regulative mechanisms. History is defined, rather, by the aleatory singularity of events where struggle takes place in chance encounters. The historians' history reconciles us to the injustices of the past in confirming our belief that the present moment results inescapably from iron necessity and good intentions. Alternatively, historical sense reintroduces becoming to all that one thought immortal in humanity and, in this way, only "confirms our existence among countless lost events, without a landmark or point of reference" ("Nietzsche" 154–55). Historical knowing does not mean "to find again" and certainly not "to find ourselves." Rather, history "effects" in the degree that it "introduces discontinuity into our very being" (154).

In this way, historical knowing must itself be subjected to a genealogical critique. Rather than posing an image of Truth in the transcendent subject who judges, genealogy looks for discontinuities in the forms of knowledge and their patterns of descent, both in the concepts of history and in the values that inform them. Rather than pretending to be objective, or that history follows natural laws, effective history diagnoses and evaluates, affirms or critiques, setting in play a will to power that challenges current values with its own. According to Foucault, the search for the ideal form behind appearances in the Platonic theory of representation, and the dialectical will to truth of the Hegelian philosophy of history, is an invention of the dominant classes (*classes dirigeantes*) who seek to foreclose understanding of the multiple and contingent (in)determinations that mark every event. Genealogy, alternatively, understands that the historical beginning of things is not marked by an identity frozen at the point of origin; rather, it is the disparate—the discord of multiple and undetermined counter-possibilities—that claims the attention of the genealogist.

The dialectical perspective is suprahistorical; it freezes time in a spatial image as a totality and, paradoxically, forecloses time from history in an act of judgment. Thus it will never understand or express change except by erecting monuments to the past. In this respect, the logic of the movement-image is entirely commensurate with the dialectical or Hegelian conception of history. With its empirical conception of time as a linear and chronological force, the movement-image projects an image of (historical) thought marked by dialectical opposition and conflict ending in teleology—an indirect image of time given as a spatial whole. And in a grand dialectical gesture, the movement-image projects its own history in just the same way. In *The Movement-Image*, the evolution of the indirect image of time unfolds, in Deleuze's account, in an image of history as progress—the gradual and teleological perfection of a logic of signs and an image of thought that reaches its culmination and limit in the late films of Alfred Hitchcock.[23] By bringing the movement-image to its logical conclusion, and also in suggesting a "beyond" the movement-image, Hitchcock's films paradoxically signal in cinema both the "end of history" and the emergence of genealogy.

The history of the movement-image is the movement of a great dialectical synthesis wherein the indirect image of time functions as a universalizing logic that encompasses and subsumes all the forms of difference articulated within it. There are, of course, industrial and economic reasons for this universality; namely, Hollywood's aesthetic and economic domination of world cinema. But curiously, for Deleuze, even if the montage forms of Soviet cinema and the great European experimental film movements of the 1920s differ in kind from Hollywood cinema by challenging its characterization of movement and time based on action and causality, logically they do not differ in nature. All are variations animated by the same "world spirit" as it were, or rather, in Deleuze's terms, an "image of thought" that comprises an organic representation and an indirect image of time.

Alternatively, the time-image and the movement-image are separated by fundamental discontinuities that no dialectic can master. Whereas the movement-image is universal, the time-image is rare even in the postwar period. Thus discontinuity is not negativity in the Hegelian sense, nor is the time-image a critique or overcoming of the movement-image. Its logical nature is based fundamentally on discontinuity, but there is no definitive break between the time-image and the movement-image that can be measured along a linear and chronological time line. Between the two regimes there is a fundamental slippage where the presentation of time changes as the meaning of time shifts with respect to historical understanding. Only the movement-image has a History, as it were; it demands that we look for its origin to understand its gradual progression in a teleology. But the time-image demands instead a genealogy. It neither displaces the movement-image nor marks its end. Rather, we must look for the time-image, in French cinema as elsewhere, as multiple lines of descent that have a fluctuating appearance in time.

The two images of time, indirect and direct, thus have a curious relationship in the history of cinema. The movement-image may logically have completed its evolution or accomplished its teleological unfolding in the postwar period, but it does not "end" there; in fact, it retains more than ever the force of universality promoted by the economic hegemony of Hollywood and multinational entertainment corporations. Looking at certain of the more adventurous contemporary directors, or the discontinuous images of music videos, we can understand how the movement-image has accommodated the time-image—while nonetheless marginalizing and limiting it—and thus perpetuates a certain image of thought and conceptualization of the whole. In many respects, the logic of the movement-image persists as strongly as ever, although in a postmodern frame as pastiche and hybrid or schizophrenic style. The new French stylists of the *cinéma du look*—Luc Besson, Jean-Jacques Beneix, Léos Carax, and even Matthieu Kassovitz—are as good examples as any.

Alternatively there are strong intimations of the time-image in films by Jean Renoir and Max Ophuls that both follow *and* precede the end of World War II. The time-image does not follow on the "end" of the movement-image; rather, it appears intermittently in the classic period as an ever-possible and eternally recurring force. Time as virtuality persists as a reserve within history—the potentiality of lines of variation and unanticipated innovations within the space of history. Its genealogy threads through the movement-image in a discontinuous and "untimely" fashion, "that is to say," as Nietzsche wrote, "acting counter to our time and thereby acting on our time and, let us hope, for the benefit of a time to come." [24] In fact, what it is, is time as force and eternal recurrence—the metaphysical foundation of a countermemory ever renewable in creative expression. The dialectical and teleological unfolding of the movement-image in space, and the emergence of the direct image of time in the autonomous or irrational interval, thus coexist in a complex and contradictory play of forces.

Characterized by an open totality in movement, only the movement-image has a "history" in the sense of reaching that teleological point or retrospective synthesis where a final sense or logical culmination is achieved. Whereas the movement-image is marked by the logic of an organic representation and a universal dialectical unity, the time-image promotes another logic that — in its own discreet, subterranean, and cunning fashion — threads through even the first fifty years of cinema before throwing the movement-image into crisis in Italy and France. If the time-image is not "historical," this means that we should not look for its meaning in either origins or ends. Because it is fundamentally nonlinear and nonchronological, the time-image is not renderable as a history of progress or as a progression, nor is it subject to a spatial representation. It is what happens between spaces, between events, a fissuring of space by time as the eternal recurrence of chance and possibility. And this is why even if in Deleuze's rather dire and often elitist perspective, the cinema is dying from a quantitative and qualitative mediocrity, it always preserves the power of a new becoming and a new beginning.

Therefore only the movement-image "evolves"; the time-image "recurs." Their concept of history is different because they present two different conceptions of time, two different relationships with the whole, and a qualitative difference in the expression of change. The fundamental discontinuity resides in the heart of time itself. The movement-image presents time as Cronos — time as repetition of the same; history as a circle. But if time is presented "directly" in modern French cinema, this is rather Aïon — not a succession of presents but recurrence as a labyrinthine branching of time. In "Theatrum Philosophicum," Foucault embraces Deleuze's concept of time for genealogy, describing it as "a splitting quicker than thought and narrower than any instant. It causes the same present to arise — on both sides of this indefinitely splitting arrow — as always existing, as indefinitely present, and as indefinite future. It is important to understand that this does not imply a succession of present instances that derive from a continuous flux and that, as a result of their plenitude, allow us to perceive the thickness of the past and the outline of a future in which they in turn become the past. Rather, it is the straight line of the future that repeatedly cuts the smallest width of the present, that indefinitely recuts it starting from itself." This is how Foucault characterizes Deleuze's provocative and original rethinking of the concept of eternal recurrence, for "what repeats itself is time; and the present—split by this arrow of the future that carries it forward by always causing it to swerve from one side to the other—this present endlessly recurs. It recurs as singular difference; what never recurs is the analogous, the similar, and the identical" ("Theatrum" 193–95, 97).[25] The time-image recurs rather than "evolves" because it is incommensurable with the empirical conception of time where past, present, and future are ordered as chronological succession. Time no longer resolves itself in the image of a circle that subsequently grows in volume and depth; this is history as teleology. Rather, the thinking of history becomes a synthesis of time where every passing present introduces chance as a line of variation—a nomadic becoming—that liberates us from the tyranny of both a fixed memory of the past and an already determined future. Defined by Nietzsche as eternal recurrence, time as Aïon is rather a virtuality "in" the present. It divides the passing present, so that time is never identical to itself but rather falls back into the past as multiple lines of descent and launches into the future as an undetermined set of possibilities.

Where the movement-image is organic, following the concept of time as succession or Cronos, the montage form of the time-image presents this fundamental discontinuity in time as false or aberrant movements. Marked by recurrence rather than repetition, the irrational interval ensures the incommensurability of interval and whole. Because the interval is a dissociative force, succession gives way to *series*. Images are strung together as heterogeneous spaces that are incommensurable one with the other. Seriality thus defines the montage form of the time-image. But in so doing, the value of the interval changes and unleashes new powers.

Consider *Ici et ailleurs* (Godard-Gorin-Miéville 1975). The opening of the film shows well the forms of discontinuity characteristic of the time-image. There are no credits. In fact, there is no real "beginning" to the film, whose origins are equally indistinct and in question. Godard's voice simply appears over black leader:

En 1970, ce film s'appelait *Victoire*.
En 1974, il s'appele *Ici et ailleurs,*
et ailleurs,
et. . . .[26]

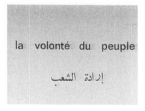

Ici et ailleurs (Godard-Gorin-Miéville, 1975).

This narration continues over two images: First, videotext on black background:

mon

ton

son image

And then a filmed image of the word "ET" apparently carved out of Styrofoam. Miéville repeats the same text over four images: a fedayeen man showing a woman how to aim a rifle; a French family watching television; a group of fedayeen in the desert; and then a black title on white background that states, in both French and Arabic, "The will of the people."

Subsequently the images divide into four intercalated series. First there is documentary footage of the Palestinian fedayeen shot in February and July 1970 in Jordan and Lebanon by Godard and Gorin's Dziga Vertov Group, which was to have been part of a film entitled *Victoire.* Then there are images constructed in 1974: diegetic material involving a French family, their everyday life, their relations with the media, and the father's search for work; didactic studio performances that include the "diegetic" actors; and finally nondiegetic inserts of various types (interpolated videotext, intertitles and placards, images processed by video mixer, black leader, filmed televisions, slide viewers, and sound mixers, etc.). The film freely intermixes different materi-

Ici et ailleurs (Godard-Gorin-Miéville, 1975).

als of expression and styles of presentation (documentary, fictional, didactic) so as to maximize the difference between series. This effect of discontinuity and heterogeneity is produced, as it were, by the "ET" that circulates between Godard's voice and the image, passing into Miéville's voice, and indeed *between* all the images as an irrational interval. In series, the interval divides rather than associates, thus attaining a new value. "[In] Godard's method," writes Deleuze, "it is not a question of association. Given one image, another image has to be chosen which will induce an interstice *between* the two. This is not an operation of association, but of differentiation ... given one potential, another one has to be chosen, not any whatever, but in such a way that a difference of potential is established between the two, which will be production of a third or of something new" (*Time-Image* 179–80).

Throughout the film, "here and elsewhere" functions as a concept that organizes a disparate set of spaces (Jordan-France, film-video, image-sound) and times (1970, 1974) that in their strategic repetitions continually differ one from the other as incommensurable series. The series of images, and images and sounds, can neither be unified in a transcendent perspective nor reconciled into a whole that will confer a retroactive sense on the history, indeed histories, that the film presents. 1970 *and* 1974: the film holds the two times together in their incommensurability. The documentary images can neither repeat nor adequately represent the strategies and politics of the fedayeen in 1970, nor do they sustain a coherent memory of, much less restore to life, a movement all but destroyed by the betrayal of Black September — the massacre at Amman of the fedayeen by Jordanian troops. No action unifies the images. No historical meaning can be recovered by linking 1970 Jordan to 1974 France in a chronological and continuous time. Each time Godard and Miéville return to the Palestinian images ("EN REPENSANT A CELA," states a recurrent video intertitle), the film branches into yet more complex series, each of which reflexively questions the capacity of images and sounds to master the past by incorporating it as a present image. Each repetition of the "original" documentary images yields a differentiation and complexification of sense that falsifies preceding series. The formal organization of the first film, as well as the political perspective of the Dziga Vertov Group, are continually questioned along with the nature of their identification with the conflict and their methods for filming it. Images repeat in discontinuous series; sounds and voices interrogate the self-evidence of given images, gradually revealing artifices in their construction and suggesting ever more complex and subtle variations in how they should be read, reinterpreted, and juxtaposed with other images and sounds. The film unfolds as a genealogical critique not of the Middle East conflict but of its historical representations both in the mass media and in the interval that separates the unfinished *Victoire* from the ever provisional *Ici et ailleurs* as two divergent perspectives on the problems of making a political film. Instead of a "truthful" representation, Godard and Miéville seem to suggest, we need a pedagogy of the image that critically evaluates its relations with time and history. In this way, the recurrence in series of *Victoire* within *Ici et ailleurs* implicitly takes place as a Nietzschean critique and revaluation of the earlier film's theory of direct revolutionary action modeled on a Hegelianized existential Marxism.

One might say that this is a film about a failed project — including the 1970 film on the Palestinians, the Dziga Vertov Group as a media collective, and indeed the revolutionary aspirations of May 1968. Perhaps it is better to say that it is a film about the "ill-conceived principle of return," and an exercise in effective history that unleashes new powers of the image and a new form of historical sense in the then present of 1974. We live in a society where images and sounds are made to be consumed, yet whose infernal repetitions across film, television, print, and radio, rather, consume us. "Little by little," the sound track recounts, "we are replaced by uninterrupted chains of images enslaving one another, each image has its place, like each of us at our place in a chain of events where we have lost all power." This is a psychological automaton where the image functions as a substitute for thinking and a vehicle for the accumulation of pseudoevents in a false totality that crowds out the myriad alternatives and countermemories that a genealogical history might liberate for us.

Yet in their incommensurability, the images of *Ici et ailleurs* return in ever more differentiated series that interrogate the mass media's crowding out of both the memory and actuality of revolutionary struggle. While no image or sound will ever be an adequate or "truthful" representation of this struggle, the irrational interval nonetheless sustains a principle of recurrence where the struggle for Palestinian self-determination enters into series with a number of other singular points distributed throughout the film—the French Revolution (1789), the Soviet Revolution (1917), the Popular Front in France (1936), and the popular uprisings of 1968—which are made to circulate across the media-saturated present of 1974 France. It does not matter that these are all "failed" revolutions that the film cannot add up in a restored totality. For what is at stake is not return but recurrence—the force of time as change—where the interstice sustains new values and a new form of historical sense. *Ici et ailleurs* becomes "effective" history by introducing discontinuity into time in the form of the interstice. Rational connections present spatial intervals—the indirect image of time as a succession of sets or segmentations of space. But irrational intervals are not spatial, nor are they images in the usual sense. They open onto what is outside space yet immanent to it: the anteriority of time to space as virtuality, becoming, the fact of returning for that which differs. This force opens a line of variation in any image, sign, idea, or concept that attempts to express it. If time is given to us here as a perception, this is not an analogical image in space but rather time as virtuality or Event— a reserve within history of ever-renewable and unanticipated lines of variation "acting counter to our time and thereby acting on our time, let us hope, for the benefit of a time to come." In other words, when time is rendered as incommensurable with space in the interstice, a vast territory of potentialities opens in every present that passes. Through events, virtuality unfolds as an unlimited reserve of future acts, each of which is equally possible in itself, yet incompossible with all the others. Thus the event "is pure immanence of what is not actualized or of what remains indifferent to actualization, since its reality does not depend upon it. The event is immaterial, incorporeal, unlivable: pure *reserve*. . . . It is no longer time that exists between two instants; it is the event that is a meanwhile [*un entre-temps*]: the meanwhile is not part of the eternal, but neither is it part of time—it belongs to becoming." [27] Events are immanent to every moment of time's passing yet remain both outside and in between the passage of time. Between each measure of time there is an infinite movement, so many possible worlds and immanent modes of existence, that we must recover from time's passing.

The direct image of time, then, is a paradoxical construction. Rather than a historical image of thought, it gives us "thought without image." [28] Here we find one of the deepest and most profound potentialities of the figural. The irrational interval offers a nonspatial perception—not space but force, the force of time as change, interrupting repetition with difference and parceling succession into series. There is movement in the image, of course, which is given as an actual perception in space. But the differential relations "between" images and sounds are furrowed by a pure virtuality: the force of time as eternal recurrence. Time is always outside the image; it recedes from the image toward an absolute horizon, since it is incommensurable with space. The "will to falsehood" of the direct time-image draws all its powers from this quality of incommensurability: indiscernibility of the real and the imaginary in the image; inexplicability of narrative events; undecidability of relative perspectives on the same event, both in the present and in the relation of present and past; and, finally, the incompossibility of narrative worlds, which proliferate as incongruous presents and not necessarily true pasts.

Foucault's adoption of Nietzsche's concepts of Entstehung (emergence) and Herkunft (descent) are equally marked by Deleuze's analysis of time as eternal recurrence, as the foregoing citation from

"Theatrum Philosophicum" makes clear. This is why the time-image requires genealogy rather than History and how the time-image projects a new concept of historical sense. In Hegel's phenomenology and philosophy of history, the dialectic does not liberate the different; on the contrary, it guarantees that difference will always be recaptured by unity and totality. The dialectical sovereignty of the same lets the different be only under the law of the negative as a moment of nonbeing. In dialectical contradiction, we find not the subversiveness of the Other but a secret work for the benefit of the identical and return of the Same.

But the time-image reveals in cinema a new thinking of difference, indeed a new thought of time, as event and series, that liberates difference from the logical system where it is mastered by opposition, negation, and contradiction. In other words, one quality of the direct image of time is to free difference from the dialectic, which informs all philosophies of representation and indeed the philosophy of history. In this way, modern French cinema answers the call made by the turn to Nietzsche in French philosophy of the 1960s. From the image of thought to a thought without image, the time-image liberates historical sense from the historical image of thought as the body of becoming. Here Foucault's genealogy and Deleuze's time-image coincide in a common project: to reject resemblance in representation, to free difference from the dialectic, and to free the subject from judgment and the will to truth.

There is no better way of characterizing the qualities of the figural as a historical image. And in this way, the time-image deploys for us a countermemory that may free identity from the circle of universal history. In "Nietzsche, Genealogy, History," Foucault outlines three dimensions of historical sense that confront the concepts of universal history: oppose an idea of history as reminiscence or recognition with a parodic use of history; oppose history as continuity or tradition by showing the dissociative quality of identity; and finally oppose the will to truth in history with the powers of the false. In each case, Foucault asks that another form of time be deployed in history: a countermemory that detours the will to truth promoted by the metaphysical and anthropological models of history. In all three lines of descent, modern French cinema presents neither the "death of the subject" nor the "end of history." Rather, as in the philosophy of Foucault and Deleuze, there is a reconceptualization of the historical subject and the Event as a "critical ontology of the present." As Alan Schrift notes, "insofar as the subject position delivered to us by modernity is not an ontological necessity, other subject positions and possibilities of knowledge will be historically possible in terms of the contingencies of the present moment. . . . Foucault's genealogy of the subject provides a theoretical articulation of this account of multiple subject positioning insofar as it frames the subject not as a substance but as a form, a form, moreover, that is not always identical to itself" (57). This is not only a discontinuity in time that disrupts understanding the Event in terms of origin, unity, and finality but also a discontinuity that divides the subject internally, who thus becomes open to change, multiplicity, and is marked as much by chance or contingency as by necessity and determination. For Deleuze, philosophy and art become experimentation — an opening and exploration of new territories and lines of variation in our current modes of existence and our spaces of desire and sociality. In Foucault, this is the overcoming of a will to truth where the "purpose of history, guided by genealogy, is not to discover the roots of our identity, but to commit itself to its dissipation" ("Nietzsche" 162). Here Being finds no shelter from the force of time as change. Time forever divides the subject from itself, introducing an interstice or "irrational interval" in the subject, who is now crossed by difference and nonidentity. Divided by time as eternal recurrence, the historical subject expresses an affirmation that "new thought is possible; thought is again possible" (Foucault, "Theatrum" 196). Expressed equally in the Nietzschean dimension of French cinema and historical thought, one can easily imagine this phrase as graffiti from May 1968.

7. AN UNCERTAIN UTOPIA—DIGITAL CULTURE

An Image of Technological Abundance Do you want to watch the movie you want, the minute you want? Learn special things from faraway places? Pay a toll without slowing down or receive a phone call on your television set? Would you like to carry your medical history in your wallet? You will! This technological promise was made by American Telephone and Telegraph (AT&T) in a print and television advertising campaign broadcast in the United States throughout 1993 and 1994. In a series of seven thirty-second spots, comprising twenty-one miniscenarios, AT&T stages a technological desire that it promises to fulfill in the near future. The scenography of these spots offers a utopian vision of science fiction becoming science fact as education, entertainment, medicine, communication, and transportation are positively transformed by the technological reorganization of social time and space.

No doubt these ads present an impressive array of products: software, smart cards, cellular and mobile communications, networked communications and product vending, videophones, and desktop videoconferencing for education, telemedicine, and small businesses.[1] There is one catch. Although all of these technologies existed in nascent forms, none of the products displayed in these images were available for consumer purchase in 1994, and many still are not in 2001. Of course, there is no spectator naive enough to believe they will ever see these products in the form presented by AT&T. As the scenography of these images makes clear, this campaign is an exercise in science fiction. In an effort to remodel its corporate image, AT&T presents a careful mixture of products already present in embryo (phones with data links and computer screens are available at many American airports and now even on airplanes) or in development (handheld cellular personal digital assistants) with products and services we will undoubtedly not see for many years.[2] The real objective of this campaign is evidently not to sell existing products or services but to inspire the desire for a different world, in fact, a utopian world based on technological innovation that will be brought into existence not by individuals working for social change and equality but by the invention and marketing of capitalist "third-wave" companies. It is a seductive vision meant to convince us that capitalism, for centuries the source of so many of the world's social problems and inequities, can still be the solution, if we only let it again transform itself historically by unleashing the productive capacity of digital communications technologies.

This utopian projection has a remarkable diegetic consistency across the twenty-one miniscenarios presented by AT&T. All take place in an undefined future sometime between the late nineties and the first decade of the twenty-first century. The most salient characteristic of this utopia is that of an advanced communications technology—incorporating voice, text, and video data—perfectly integrated with all the activities and locales of everyday life (home, shopping mall, car, train, doctor's office, airport, beach, mountains, library, classroom, small businesses).

Equally striking is the social uniformity of the characters represented. This is a multiracial world where everyone is between eighteen and thirty-four years old and attractive. The apparent racial harmony is preserved, no doubt, by a lack of scarcity and uniform levels of wealth and education. No one is poor in this world, yet no one is really rich. All seem to be comfortably middle class, making the dual point that with the levels of productivity enabled by the emerging communications technologies, these products and services will be in the price range for all, and all these products and services will become increasingly necessary and ubiquitous, indeed transparent, to the execution of everyday life. The power of this utopian representation is to present the future as a recognizable extension of the present, a possible world emerging from our present circumstances, if only our consumer desire can be focused on "buying it," and therefore liberating the capital to produce it.

Here all of capitalism's inequities of class, money, power, and access to information have disappeared in an image of technological abundance. Everyone understands, of course, that the attainment of this ideal of social equality is the most fanciful aspect of this science fiction. Yet it is a world that most of us *would* desire, almost as much as we *want* the imaginary products displayed along with the qualitative change they promise in our everyday life: security, comfort, and convenience; unlimited and unconstrained mobility; entertainment on demand; unrestricted and instantaneous access to information regardless of our physical location; a recovery of time through increased productivity; the elimination of a felt qualitative distinction between work and leisure; and transparent and instantaneous communication, regardless of distance and barriers of language, that enhances collaborative work in education, business, and medicine.

Like every utopian discourse, AT&T's future world is most convincing to the extent that the future it projects is anchored in the familiarity of the present. But the temporality of these images is yet more complex. They say less about the future than they do about the present. In this way, these ads render transparent a long and brutal historical transformation that has already been taking place for some time wherein an industrial and disciplinary society yields to a cybernetic society of control, and a modernist culture of representation is displaced by an increasingly digital and "audiovisual" culture.[3]

In "Reading the Figural" I developed some concepts for understanding how the nature of representation, signification, and the social organization of human collectivities in time and space is changing with the appearance of new forms of digital communications. When I began writing that chapter in the spring of 1988, the technologies I referred to—for example, digitized video in multimedia publications or electronic publishing on the Internet—were either not commercially available or else not widely used by people in the humanities. Now they all are. This is an index of the speed of technological change and commercialization that today confronts critics who want to understand the social changes occurring in telecommunications, entertainment, and educational media. Perhaps the science fictions presented by AT&T are not that far off after all. We have again, within very a short time, been outdistanced by the economic and technological transformations now taking place. Now more than ever we live in a cybernetic or digital culture where a tectonic shift of the visible in relation to the expressible has changed relations of knowledge no less than the diagrammatic configuration of forces constituting power.

A Digression on Postmodernism Digital culture is an important, and global, aspect of contemporary everyday life that, in developed countries, is being defined as an emergent technology-driven culture. One vision of this culture is presented by the corporations such as AT&T, Intel, IBM, and Microsoft that will profit by marketing its technologies and patterns of consumption. The dreams appealed to in this technological utopia are apparent. But what forces and relations of power are also emerging? If our contemporary digital culture is something distinct, if we are beginning to inhabit a fundamentally new historical epoch with its own image of power, conceptualization of force, and sense of history, how do we describe it?

In the past ten to fifteen years, cultural studies have most often characterized this epoch as the "postmodern" or the cultural logic of late capitalism as defined by a qualitative shift in representation, the nature of subjectivity, and a new relation to historical time and consciousness.[4] With respect to this historical image, we might ask to what degree this apparently new historical epoch can be characterized as "postmodern." Indeed, most critical work on digital culture has been presented under the heading of "postmodernism" in cultural studies. For the moment, I prefer the more prosaic "digital culture" or perhaps Deleuze's compelling, if disturbing, phrase "control societies."[5] The idea of postmodernism is central to the definition of cultural studies, and one of the ways in which the field's interdisciplinarity has been defined. I have the same feeling for the term "postmodernism," however, as I do for "late capitalism." Unfortunately, the only thing "late" about capitalism is that it has rather inconveniently failed to disappear on schedule. Instead it has shown an alarmingly powerful capacity for adaptation, evolution, and growth in new historical circumstances, which is one of the more disturbing lessons for socialist critics of digital culture. This does not mean that capitalist political economy and culture are unchallengeable. But the term "late capitalism," as it circulates today, often represents an intellectual impasse and a failure of historical imagination. Considered dialectically, it expresses, on one hand, a powerful

From the *New York Times Sunday Magazine*, 1993.

observation represented in Ernst Mandel's magisterial work: we are on the threshold of a new era. Economic, political, and cultural forms are undergoing a global transformation. On the other, the term is laced with a regressive modernist nostalgia: that Marx's theory of history certifies the eventual end of capitalism and the emergence of global socialism.

Embedded in the term "postmodernism" is a similarly contradictory historical consciousness, the recognition of something new without the commensurate ability to imagine contemporary culture as separate from an earlier modernist culture. A 1993 cover for the *New York Times Sunday Magazine* comments humorously on this dilemma.

In this image, Hanna-Barbera's comic figures of prehistory, the Flintstones, are shown taken aback by the appearance of the futuristic Jetsons hailing them by videophone. The idea of postmodernism offers a similar kind of historical shock. Either we stand with the Jetsons in the contemporary without being able to give it a name, or we remain with the Flintstones, imagining the future from an infinitely prolonged past.

There is a discomfiting circularity in the term "postmodernism," an unconscious repetition of the past and a lack of will to invent the future, that can be symptomatic of a certain kind of interdisciplinary cultural studies. However, if we don't invent the future, AT&T will. Where Fredric Jameson rightly criticized the evaporation of a historical consciousness in the 1980s, the 1990s have been marked by the dominance of a new form of historical imagination influenced by Alvin Toffler's notion of technological "waves," an ideology most forcefully promulgated in the pages of *Wired*.[6] A thinly disguised apology for unregulated markets, in this perspective, the dominant value is knowing how to be *with* the historical currents driven by technological innovation. In this scenario, individuals are helpless to change the "waves" of history; instead one must anticipate their future flows and "surf" them.

This suggests a new conception of force that, as Deleuze points out, is characteristic of control societies. Industrial or disciplinary societies are based on an energetic and mechanistic conception of movement, effort, and resistance. Bodies apply pressure or are themselves the origin of movement, and the machines that replace physical functions are based on this principle. But in control societies, force withdraws from substance, becoming more gaseous or liquid. Where the idea of waves or currents becomes the dominant conception of force, relations of force involve knowing how to insert oneself in a preexisting current, characteristic of the popularity of sports such as windsurfing or hang gliding. "How to be taken up in the movement of a great wave," Deleuze writes, "a column of ascending air, 'to happen within' instead of making an effort—this is fundamental."[7] This is a passive relation to force, relenting to the new "invisible hand" where success rides on surrendering oneself to historical forces and where individuals absolve themselves from both responsibility and accountability for the social and ecological devastation resulting from the new capitalism.

In its cybernetic conception, this idea of force is further refined as virtual action at a distance. The withdrawal of the body and a physical presence in space means that individuals feel less and less accountable for their actions and speech acts, since they confront one another less and less in relations of reciprocity unified in both space and time. Similarly, the actions and practices of individuals and collectivities are no longer felt as producing the forces of history. Rather, history is experienced as a tide or tsunami whose energy derives from immense and invisible forces of technological change that are too complex and too enormous for individuals to fathom fully. In this historical perspective, "agency" means that one no longer invents, but rather capitalizes on the existing current. The most one can do is anticipate and attempt to navigate the rapid flows and directions of technological change. Hence the inflated salaries of futurists, the new weathermen of the third wave.

But history has not ended, pace Francis Fukiyama, though new forms of capitalism are emerging. And there is a chance that socialist theory can still elaborate strategies for resisting third-wave capitalism while recuperating alternative utopian elements useful for remodeling digital culture according to a progressive politics. We must deal with the fact that history does not end by learning to think historically about the ever-changing society we are in the midst of creating. The task of a contestatory cultural criticism, then, is to interrupt this repetition of the past in the present, to dismantle critically whatever concepts impede us from understanding the contemporary while inventing a new set of critical tools derived from an empirical engagement with the culture in which we live. In so doing, we both redeem and invent new modes of existence.

I use "empiricism" in Deleuze's sense of the term. Here empiricism refers neither to the teleological progress of human thought nor to the apprehension of an otherwise secret knowledge residing naturally though silently in the heart of things. Instead the complex and contradictory possibilities for either hegemony, resistance, or contestation are considered as the paradoxical operation of a power that is simultaneously not visible and not hidden. "We only need to know how to read," Deleuze argues, "however difficult it may prove to be. The secret exists only to be betrayed, or to betray itself. Each age articulates perfectly the most cynical element of its politics . . . to the point where transgression has little merit" (*Foucault* 54). Following Foucault,

Deleuze's point is that relations of power are perfectly self-evident. Nevertheless we need to create concepts that can make those relations intelligible.

Three Questions concerning Digital Culture   In an earlier version of this chapter, "Audiovisual Culture and Interdisciplinary Knowledge," I argued that three fundamental questions need to be asked to understand digital culture critically. I still believe in the heuristic value of these questions, even if our critical responses to them may have to change as digital culture evolves. First, how is the nature of representation and communication changing with respect to the digital creation, manipulation, and distribution of signs? Second, how is the form of the commodity changing along with its determinations of the space and time of the market, and the nature and value of exchange? And finally, how is our experience of collectivity changing, or, in Deleuze and Guattari's terminology, how are our "collective arrangements" in social time and space being restructured by the new communicational architectures of digital culture?

The Insubstantial Image. Through a number of striking images, the public discourse of AT&T and other high-tech companies welcomes us to a graphical, multimedia universe, thus introducing my first question: *How is the nature of representation and communication changing with respect to the digital creation, manipulation, and distribution of signs?* How are the properties of semiotic objects changing? And how may the act of reading change with these global shifts in the semiotic environment? In short, how is the nature of discourse, or what counts as discursive, being transformed by the new audiovisual regimes of digital culture?

As I argue in chapter 2, the emergence of a digital culture implies a shift in the semiotic environment, that is, the way a culture is defined by the signs it produces and the forms of communication it relies on. One consistent theme in both the mass-marketing of information technology and academic studies of digital culture suggests that the culture of the book is being "remediated," if not replaced, by one of hypermedia or the multimedia image where the linear form of writing and the act of reading are becoming increasingly graphical, temporal, and nonlinear.[8] The digital creation, recording, manipulation, and transmission of signs is producing a new audiovisual regime in the technological and semiotic convergence of film, video, computer imaging, and word processing that in turn encourages the intermixing of visual, verbal, written, musical, and sonic forms. This is most apparent in the appearance of new media: the CD-ROM and the new forms of distributed publication appearing on the World Wide Web, although as Jay Bolter and Richard Grusin have pointed out, older print media are also transforming themselves through adaptation to the graphic forms and logics of new media.

The most important phenomenon here is the displacement of analog recording, manipulation, and transmission by the digital. Equivalence in space is no longer the measure of representation. Rather, all representational forms (moving and still images, writing, sound) are leveled to the algorithmic manipulation of binary code. All space becomes an abstract computational space.[9] As analog forms of representation disappear, the criterion of resemblance is displaced by similitude. As I argued more fully in chapter 2, the idea of resemblance belongs to the era of representation. In resemblance, meaning derives from the authority of the original, an authenticating model that orders and ranks all the copies that can be derived from it. Alternatively, Foucault defines similitude as an ordering of signs where designation or reference has lost its centrality. In digital culture, the distinction between original and copy has lost its relevance.

Resemblance is also linked to affirmation. For Foucault, spatial semblance in representation yields meaning, implicitly or explicitly, in the form of a linguistic statement. Similitude changes this structure of reference and signification. It is no longer the image that illustrates and the sentence that comments. Rather, visuality and expression become transversal, producing a variety of hybrid forms. The distinction between linguistic and plastic representations, and along with it, the distinction between spatial and temporal arts, is also losing relevance. The border between a plastic space that organizes semblance, and linguistic expression that articulates difference, is disappearing. Expression is no longer reserved for linguistic activity that organizes "signs" and therefore meaning across difference; the field of the visible, as the silent representation of things, has become increasingly heterogeneous and complex. The visible, traversed by difference, becomes increasingly discursive, and consequently the linguistic, given volume and color, becomes increasingly graphical. Formerly, discourse was considered a linguistic activity; now it is a multimedia activity. Forms of expression and reading can no longer be considered as simply spatial or temporal, or distinguished by simultaneity and succession. Rather, digital culture presents us with mixed, layered, and heterogeneous audiovisual images unfolding in a nonlinear space and time.

This disconnection of the image from the criterion of spatial coherence is fundamental to our contemporary cultural sense of "virtuality" and the social relations it defines in our interactions with the new media and computer-mediated communications. Compared to the analogical arts—which are always instantiated in a fixed, Euclidean space—the digital arts seem abstract, ephemeral, and without substance. Digital representation is defined as "virtual" owing to its desubstantialization: the disappearance of a visible and tactile support for both image and text. At the same time, the powers of transformation in representation are radically augmented, thus motivating a shift in aesthetic function whose consequences are most clear in the changing status of photography's formerly privileged place as a "truthful" representation.[10] Because there is no act of closure for a data file, regardless of its output medium, it is open to modification at any time. Mutant versions proliferate rapidly and endlessly, and the work is open to continual appropriation, recontextualization, and creative transformation and deformation in ways that analogical and autographic arts are not. "So we must abandon the traditional conception of an art world populated by stable enduring, finished works," writes William Mitchell, "and replace it with one that recognizes continual mutation and proliferation of variants. . . . Notions of individual authorial responsibility for image content, authorial determination of meaning, and authorial prestige are correspondingly diminished" (*Reconfigured Eye* 52).

The unraveling of spatial coherence through desubstantialization affects as well the qualities of the territories we inhabit, whether physically or mentally. Increasingly, virtuality describes the elimination of a felt sense of space and distance as we interact in computer networks through the nonlinear forms of navigation appropriate to hypermedia. By the same token, the increasing velocity of information and the global reach of the electronic image world have made us all too aware of the gravity of our bodies—their slowness, fragility, and diminutive size, their vulnerability to time and force. Thus what most widely defines the contemporary cultural meaning of the virtual is an (illusory) sense of a becoming immaterial, not only of discourse but also of the body in its communicational exchanges, leading to a phenomenon that has been called "cyborg envy."

Here what the avatars of the "virtual" fundamentally misrecognize is the question of materiality in relation to technology. (When you think of vr, this is pretty funny considering the cumbersomeness of helmets and gloves, and the notoriously vertiginous results produced in the slow response of even the quickest computers to head-tracking mechanisms.) Paradoxically, with respect to electronic and digital imaging, what disappears is not the materiality of the support: analog video requires the magnetic alignment of iron particles on tape; the encoding of digital information requires the etching of magnetic information on disk. Rather, what is important is the transformation of the orientation of the eye, and its anchoring in the body, with respect to a semiotic support. To reprise Deleuze's terms discussed in chapter 2, this is a transformation of correlative as well as collateral, or discursive, relations. The example of virtual reality is less clear in this respect than the more quotidian experience of computer-mediated communications or searching the World Wide Web. The experience of networked communications encourages a transformation of perspective where the orientation and extensiveness of the body in space ceases to be the "gold standard" of our mental navigation in space. Nor can we sustain a clear internal map of geographic orientation as in telephony—our displacements in space are too rapid as we click from site to site. Instead we require ever more complex technological interfaces to translate digital information back to a more familiar human scale, and to map the nonlinear global pathways we have covered without leaving our chairs.

The new technologies require conceptual as much as visual navigation of the spaces they produce, which does not, however, make them any less material. What is required is a cognitive orientation that relies less and less on the visible, or perhaps connects to the visible and the expressible in new ways. The virtual is a transformation of the materiality of representation — defined not by invisibility per se, and certainly not by immateriality, but by a technological transformation of the lived materiality of human communication, which is informed by the velocities, automation, and geographically distributed nature of communication across and through computer networks. What is worked now is the space of communication — a composing of bodies and information in space-time regardless of distance in the architecture of global computer networks. Although these architectures are invisible from the point of view of the user, they are no less material for that. It is not that representation has become more and more immaterial and insubstantial. Rather, the eye and hand have gradually withdrawn their powers and relinquished them to machines — the very definition of automation — and in this way, the concept of the interface comes to define, both figuratively and literally, the machinic connectivity of digital culture.

Of course, once writing is defined as a symbolic trace in a receptive material, signs are perforce transmitted through a technological interface. The book is an interface no less than a wax tablet or a woodcut print. But from the woodcut to the computer, we have come to require technological systems of greater and greater complexity to translate representations into visible and sonic arrangements our bodies are capable of perceiving. It is not that one is more or less machinic than the other. All define a téchnē supporting historical regimes of signs and defining relations between signs and force in given societies.

Where Information Becomes Property and Time a Commodity. Discursive systems are a primary means of binding individuals into collectivities — a discursive machine organizing individuals through networks of sign exchange. Market relations affect no less forcefully the networks of social exchange in which the activities of everyday life are carried out whether individually or collectively. Thus the concepts of virtuality and the interface also inform my second question: *How is the form of the commodity changing along with its determinations of the space and time of the market and*

the nature and value of exchange? In what ways will our new powers to communicate be controlled and commodified? What techniques of documentation and surveillance will emerge with these technologies?

The shift to a "cybernetic" capitalism is characterized by a desubstantialization of commodities no less than that of signs.[11] The new commodities are losing their physicality and weight. The manufacture of physical objects such as cars and appliances is being augmented by the new globally managed commodities — data (access to information and entertainment) and services (largely convenience measured as the creation of "free" time). Like the proliferation of automobiles in the postwar period, however, with their concomitant transformation of social time and space, as information becomes increasingly commodified, it rapidly becomes a necessity rather than a luxury. Access to the Internet will soon become no less essential to the quotidian transactions of daily life than it already is for the global movements of international stock markets and commodity exchanges, which take advantage of the untrammeled speed and borderless nature of information for their own particular forms of arbitrage.

In this respect, among the more subtle yet striking features of the AT&T ads is the prominence of AT&T's copyright notice and trademark along with a representation of how the measured elapse of time is fundamental to the showcased technologies. AT&T does not hide its economic motivation. Rather, its images figure, in various ways, how information becomes property and how time itself is being transformed as a commodity.

Commercial broadcasting and telephony were the first innovators here. For example, with pay-per-view television, you purchase two hours of access rather than "a" movie; the pricing of Internet access tends to follow a similar model. Alternatively, advertisers pay for airtime whose value increases or decreases in relation to the number of receiving households that can be measured statistically. (In this respect, the public, or access to a certain idea of the public, is a commodity as well.)

Without access, there is no interface to digital culture — one cannot be included in its social networks or forms of exchange whether for good or ill. The question of access is therefore one of the principal political questions of digital culture. Not only does the concept of access unlock the multiple ways in which information is being commodified; it also demonstrates that there is no communication, or exchange of signs, in digital culture that is not now marked in some way by the forms of commodity exchange. This involves not only the marketing of connectivity to information networks and the knowledge of how to use them effectively but also the collection and sale of the personal information culled from data transactions for the purposes of direct marketing and other less subtle forms of social control. As access to personal information becomes ever more valuable to direct marketers, data itself becomes increasingly commodified, and this tendency permeates the process of digital communication itself along with its new forms of interactivity. "Information wants to be free" is a founding principle of "hacker ethics," but now it usually comes at a hidden cost, the trading of personal data for access whether the user is conscious of the trade-off or not, or even aware of being potentially subject to a continuous "dataveillance."[12]

Notions of identity are similarly transformed. Just as the image has become disconnected from criteria of spatial coherence, so in digital culture is personhood no longer sustained by a substantial identity under direct personal and bodily control, but rather by the statistical variables defining your "data image." The formulation and control of data images is fundamental to the exercise of power in control societies, since they define access to credit, as well as to social rights, resources, and privileges deriving from one's economic position and national identity. The desubstantialization of identity is often celebrated in digital culture. To the extent that on-line personae are no longer anchored in bodily or social markers of race and gender, individuals seem to be able to freely invent "data images" at will. But there is still an unequal division of power in that the data images that count—for access to credit, medical insurance, voting and residency rights, ownership of property, and so forth—are still culled, collated, and controlled by a few large corporations and marketing organizations. The right to control one's data image—outside of social and entertainment contexts—has yet to be obtained in the current political struggles over citizenship in cyberspace.[13] This changes the context of judging the utopian claims made for the permutability of identity in cyberspace, but neither should it diminish our critical appreciation of the desire to invent new lines of flight and forms of becoming out of virtual personae and communities.

The other side of the question of access to the new communications networks is the disappearance of a "free" or measureless time as access becomes easier and more continuous. The value of access to information is determined not by spatial quantity (weight, volume, or number); rather, it is measured by units of time. Alternatively, the value of services is measured by the time they "create." The idea of "free" time as a commodity has a paradoxical status, then, since it assumes that time has a value that is quantifiable and tenderable in a system of exchange. (This is doubtless true as time becomes an ever rarer commodity.) Content or data has no value, in a sense, save for its capacity to keep the client on-line with the clock ticking.

Once quantified, time is fragmented, becoming divisible into smaller and smaller usable bits. Here again the sale of access and the control of access by technology pose interesting problems. The new communications interfaces transform not only the nature of representation but also the temporality of social exchanges between the sender and receiver. The genealogy that passes, on the one hand, through the answering machine to fax to E-mail, and on the other from the beeper to the cellular phone, reveals a paradoxical attitude to questions of temporal access in this respect. The former ensure the instantaneity of the message while maintaining asynchrony between the sender and receiver. Because the sender is never sure *when* the addressee has actually *read* the message, the addressee guards his or her time in a private reserve and controls the time of response. However, the increasing preponderance of cellular devices shows a countervailing desire never to be out of contact. The tension between these different but related communications devices reveals a new social disequilibrium between the desire for continuous accessibility and the need for uninterrupted time. As the AT&T ads chillingly illustrate, the consequence of this disequilibrium is the erosion of the distinction between work and leisure. As a recent ad from Apple puts it, "Now you can access your office from wherever you happen to be. Bummer." Why is it that we are sold on the idea of a continuous access that reaches ever more deeply into "free" moments? Within the very concept of asynchrony, an idea of social struggle is embedded. The creation of "free" time by

Now you can access your office from anywhere you happen to be. Bummer.

cellular networks is largely the augmentation of the new digital economy's capacity to extort increased productivity from individuals, and the popularity of store-and-forward systems from answering machines to E-mail resides largely in the disjunction between sender and receiver where the former can be confident of the delivery of the message and the latter maintains control over accessibility and the time of response. Asynchronous communications restore an illusion of control to the individual, whose time is more clearly managed by those who demand that more of it be devoted to work.

The control of communication networks is undergoing a constant process of economic privatization, concentration, and centralization while points of reception proliferate exponentially: the office, the home, the car, the mall, even the beach. While we are promised instantaneous and synchronous communications, nevertheless control of communications remains with those who control the networks, and the ordering of time is most often determined by the demand of the new economy to extract increasing levels of productivity from individuals by requiring continuous access to their time. Sure you can fax at the beach. But this also demonstrates how the widening of access means not more information but the transformation of leisure time into labor time. In addition, reciprocity is more often defined not by instantaneity but rather by managing the temporal delay between receiving a request and responding to it. (Here a dystopian future is all too easily imagined where individuals are driven to bargain their time as commodity futures in order to balance the conflicting demands of increasing work and disappearing leisure.)

Machinic and Collective Arrangements. Given these transformations in the global economy, and in the structure of discourse, how is our image and experience of collectivity changing along with the ordering of social time and space? *What image of collective life is proposed by the new communications technologies?* Our urgent critical task is to understand how relations of power are being transformed, to formulate strategies of resistance equal to the task of challenging them, and to recognize the new modes of existence being invented as the expression of alternative utopian longings that may result in new forms of collectivity. This involves not only understanding our new "machinic arrangements" (*agencements machiniques*), in Deleuze and Guattari's sense of the term, but also asking what new forms of collectivity or "collective arrangements" (*agencements collectifs*) are emerging and what historical image of power organizes them.

The notorious difficulties of translating Deleuze and Guattari's use of the term *agencement* (whether machinic or collective, for they are related conceptually) must be preserved here.[14] In its most fundamental definition, an agencement is "machinic" in that it continually articulates, connects, or constructs in the pursuit of desire. Desire itself is machinic in that it seeks to *produce:* collectivities, organizations, territories; in short, "assemblages" or arrangements, groupings, and ensembles. Desire neither seeks nor attaches itself to objects, whether real or imaginary. Rather, it establishes relations—let us say, for the moment, *social* relations, of time and of space—that are inherently collective, though external to the elements arranged. The simplest way to understand why this is so is to recognize that agencements express both actions and states. The passive sense of the English translation, "arrangements," expresses only one dimension of the concept that in French fluctuates between active and passive modes: on one hand, an active force of becoming or a will expressed equally *by* and *through* individuals; on the other, the individuation or coalescing of a form or abstract machine. Thus agencement encompasses both active and passive forces, action and organization. It is possible to take the idea of "machinic arrangements" literally, especially in a digital culture where flows of information between machines are as consequential as flows of information between people, and where the signals transmitted between people are increasingly mediated by machines. But in a deeper sense, the machinic refers to what produces and in this sense is always expressive of an agency, in fact, a will to power, that is ever seeking out new connections. Machinic arrangements are equally the elaboration of a social network in the multiplicity of connections passing between and through bodies (whether organic or technological), and therefore they are inherently collective. These are both connections that I make, and which are made through me as my body is caught up in lines of force and greater multiplicities.

Thus the machinic refers neither primarily nor exclusively to technology in the limited sense, even though, in a cybernetic society of control, technology comes more and more to define the social architectures in which we live and communicate. Machinic relations are social relations or networks expressing force and organizing desire. An *assemblage machinique* is thus a collective organism characterized by a particular will to power and conceptualization of force. Force and desire are two sides of this "agencing." Just as agency has its two sides — I act as the point or origin of force, and forces act through me by catching me up as the singular point in a larger network or organism — so do machinic "assemblages." This is a model of power based on two constantly interacting temporal forces that operate at different rhythms: that which slows and stratifies, reifies, spatializes and forms; and that which becomes, the creation of the unforeseen, the undetermined, and the proliferation of creative lines of flight. The stratification or sedimentation of desire and force in space is territorialization; this is what

Deleuze and Guattari call abstract machines or power as a diagrammatic force. But it is also expressive of a becoming in time, the proliferation of lines of flight and deterritorializations of desire in new branchings and connections of unforeseen social relations.

As we become more and more "machinic," it is easy to decry, and not without some justification, how a technological power exercised *through* us limits our bodily powers and powers of thought, as well as our relations with others. But there is another side to this agencement: namely, the unforeseen relations we fashion out of these new relations of force that may augment our bodily and mental powers and enhance our relations with others. If this were not the case, we could not recognize either the inchoate utopian voices speaking in even the most banal artifacts of mass culture, including the images produced by AT&T, or the counterutopias expressed in areas of contemporary culture resistant to, and less territorialized by, the mass media and commodified forms of communication. The machinic is also a desiring relation, a will to becoming, that seeks out ever more complex connections to augment our bodily and mental powers. The question is thus, how do we recognize and redeem this desire in the construction of new arrangements that oppose the abstract machine of capitalism? This is a question not only of decoding the forms of experience expressed by the new social hieroglyphics of simulation and hypermedia but also of evaluating the new modes of existence appearing as the forces unleashed by cybernetic capitalism reorganize and reconfigure the lived spatiality and temporality of everyday life.

This means evaluating not only discursive phenomena—what appears on our television screens and computer monitors—but also the architectural spaces we inhabit, whether they are physical or virtual. Foucault suggests that we can map or diagram the social architecture of power by asking: How is space divided? How is time ordered? What strategies of composing bodies in space-time are deployed? If there is indeed a social architecture of space and time structured by the transmission of information, then what kinds of communicational structures do we inhabit in the collective arrangements of both wired and wireless networks?

Here the long history of "wired" communications—telegraphy, telephony, and now the Internet—is as or more significant than that of broadcast entertainment, radio and television. Fundamental to this history is the elaboration of an image of power where the geographic expansion of networks and potential points of contact is directly related to a serialization of space and a fragmentation of time. Within this history, the concept of machinic arrangements expresses a struggle where the parcelization of space and time either falls into sedimentary strata — the formal relations of power — or is refashioned and reorganized into new relations expressive of unforeseen desires and unrecognized forces. The evolution and expansion of telecommunications networks have transformed the spatial and temporal parameters of collective experience such that a formally organic public space is becoming increasingly serialized and dispersed. Alternatively, as even the AT&T ads suggest, perhaps a new image of liberation is also emerging, a new nomadism of the cellular network wherein the possibility of communication is disjoined from fixed geographic points in space.

However, this global shift in digital communications also inaugurates the new strategies of power that characterize control societies. Deleuze situates the emergence of this new social form in the genealogy of power elaborated in the later works of Michel Foucault, starting with *Discipline and Punish.* Here the gradual transition from sovereign to disciplinary societies is characterized not only by new articulations of the visible with respect to the expressible but also by a new conceptualization of force expressed through *processus machiniques,* "technological processes," implying a transition between two very different diagrams of power. The disciplinary model of industrial capitalism relied on a panoptic model. Here the subject was caught up in a regime of visibility whose condition of possibility is a physical architecture that segments bodies in space. Control societies organize power through the invisible or virtual architectures of computer networks and telecommunications. As I have discussed, the model of control is that of a virtual "dataveillance" wherein all identity is comprised of "data images," rather than the implied surveillance of physical bodies. In the cellular environment of network communication, bodies are mobile rather than fixed. Indeed, unconstrained mobility, of either bodies or flows of information, is the measure of "freedom" in control societies. But mediated by computer networks, all movements and actions leave behind an electronic trace subject to documentation and electronic registration. Like criminals tagged with electronic collars, our every action in electronic networks is traced and recorded. We may move at the speed of light, but like snails, our trail follows wherever we go. In this way, control societies are developing the alarming capacity of resolving lines of flight, no matter how numerous or quick, into maps of power. For Siegfried Kracauer, the social hieroglyphics of modern culture had visible forms, well represented by the historical images of photography and film. But the immanent forces that organize collective life in contemporary culture are virtual. Their legibility relies less on a "visual" image than on the action of an interface that can resolve information in a useful and controllable form. This interface is conceptual as much as technological, and thus, more than ever, it requires a critical philosophy of technology to unlock its historical image and to make legible the strategies of resistance and lines of flight that are created within it.

The initial form of the network as a social space was determined by broadcast distribution, which produced a serialization of social space with the household as its minimal unit. Here the public was defined as a molecular organization of private space, a random distribution of static or moving bodies divided in space but potentially unified in time. However, in the years elapsed since *1984*, it is now the distribution cloud, rather than the Panopticon, that best maps the deployment of power in digital culture. This serialization of space implies, on the one hand, the elimination of space defined as distance and, on the other, the proliferation of disparate points with no relation to one another save their link to a common network. As cellular networks and the Internet overtake broadcasting as the dominant interface informing our collective arrangements, the nature of serialization also changes. This change is intimately linked to the desubstantialization of identity and its transformation as data. On one hand, both reception and transmission become detached from any particular geographic point. On the other, social identity is increasingly replaced by the accumulation of passwords and codes that define location and access.

This process of serialization has also effected a qualitative transformation of time, as I have discussed. The heyday of broadcast television was the last figuration of the collective as a mass: the serialization of space into millions of monads that were nonetheless united in a temporal whole. Time had a sort of spatial unity guaranteed both by the

reach of broadcasting and by its uni-
lateral force. This mass image has now
been fragmented not only by the proliferation of channels and micromarkets
through cable and satellite distribution
but also by the cellular network model,
which turns every monad into a trans-
mitter as well as a receiver. And each
monad is its own micromarket.

It is striking, then, how AT&T insists on marketing the social ideal of
"organic" space characteristic of earlier
forms of community. Here communication is defined ideally as a temporal
reciprocity across disunified or disparate
spaces. In actual practice, this form of
"interactivity" is often highly mediated,
asynchronous, and reified. In the mini-
scenario touting a lesson in jazz through
distance learning, notice how the precise series of matched-angle cuts, and
the professor's hand pointing right, give
the impression of spatial as well as verbal communication with the student in
Oakland. In this way, a collective space
divided and fragmented by distance is
rendered as organic through the mediation of technology. Moreover, this particular form of serialization is softened
by invoking old media as renovated in
the context of new media: now you *can*
talk back to your television! No matter
that there is hardly the chance this student will ever have personal contact with
his teacher. Or the fact that the teacher's
"productivity" is maximized by enlarg-
ing his class at the price of increasing

distance from his students. (Little doubt that the additional profit from radically increased enrollments does not return to his salary.) In this way, AT&T emphasizes the elimination of distance, rather than separation in space, as the utopian sign that one can overcome the forms of alienation occurring with the new capitalism. The awful image of the parent who tucks her baby in by videophone thus becomes the sign of a technological solution, rather than the origin of a new form of alienation wherein the increased demands for work erode the most intimate forms of social contact. Serialization produces a fading of tactility, a kind of informational disembodiment in the circulation of signs, that AT&T attempts to describe as an augmentation, rather than a diminution, of experience. "Personal information management" — faxing, electronic mail, answering devices — means subtracting the personal from information. Thus the spatiotemporal architecture of telecommunications can be formulated as molecular proliferation of points of consumption; relaying of points through centralized nodes of control and exchange; and control time by managing asynchrony, or the delay between message and response.

With broadcast distribution, the "public space" of communication became increasingly indistinguishable from a "market space." Again, broadcasting was the historical innovator. An old cliché still rings true: television does not sell products to people, it sells a market to advertisers; and increasingly, the same may be said for the World Wide Web and other forms of communication on the Internet. The question then becomes how to determine the exchange value of the public, who are no longer considered as a "mass" but rather as ever-permutable assemblages of data. By the same token, considering the public as a commodity deprives the body politic of agency by converting it into a virtual — and therefore quantifiable, measurable, and numerically manipulable — space of consumption. The strategies of those who market and those who govern are becoming indistinguishable. Both rely on the same statistical and demographic models to define and differentiate target consumers, correlating them numerically with given units of time while defining "public opinion" through polls and random sampling.

The disappearance of "organic" community is one way of measuring the forms of reification and alienation in electronic culture. But nostalgia for this form of locality, which is after all long gone in many respects, should not blind us to the utopian appeal of "virtual communities." One can also talk about virtuality as the conquering of substance by ideas, an organism separated in space and time but united in the mutual elaboration of a common, if often conflicted, conceptual space that Pierre Lévy has characterized as a "universality without totality."[15] The virtual communities defined by news groups, chat rooms, IRC channels, and multiuser domains are communities whose unity is defined by a shared set of ideas, perspectives, and cultural or subcultural identities regardless of the geographic distribution or distance between their constituent members. Indeed, the nonpresence of the body in networked communications—in which markers of gender, race, nationality, and class are not only indiscernible but continuously permutable—lends itself to this idea of communications communities bound by ideas, shared interests, and the capacity for communication, rather than national, ethnic, or sexual allegiances. At the same time, these virtual communities are more fragile, ephemeral, and volatile than physical communities defined by geographic allegiances; and the nonpresence of the body, in which the other appears only as ephemeral text or a shadowy avatar whose geographic location is indiscernible, often leads users to believe that they will not be rendered accountable for the ethical consequences of their opinions and discursive acts.[16]

In sum, social control no longer entails the disciplinary model of catching the subject up in a continuous regime of visible surveillance by an invisible though actual interlocutor. Rather, the cybernetic model of control works through the subtle and continuous extraction of data in each exchange of information, which models virtual identity according to the interests of the market: the potentiality of desire for a product, the capacity for exercising credit, and the probability of being able to pay. Moreover, through the automation of data extraction and collation, the visibility and accountability of those who exercise power disappears into virtual space, no less than the identity of the consumer disappears into a data image. In this respect, one of the most interesting debates occurring today is whether the Internet will continue to be developed as a public space of electronic communication, or whether it will be commodified as an "information superhighway." By the same token, one of the most interesting questions now confronting us involves the definition of what Howard Rheingold calls "virtual communities" on the net.[17] Will these communities have free or commercialized access to information? That is, will information continue to become a commodity regulated by a system of exchange?

An Impossible Ideal of Power The figuration of utopia in the artifacts of contemporary technoculture is uncertain because the relation of the future to the present is indeterminate and thus presents itself as a site of political struggle. The images presented in cybernetic capitalism's promotion of new communications technologies are not necessarily duplicitous or false. As Siegfried Kracauer argued already in the 1920s, collectivities organize around and through mass images because they recognize, no matter how imperfectly, the alienated expression of a genuine social knowledge and an authentic desire for change. In some respects, the AT&T ads may indeed express a longing for forms of community and modes of existence already potentialized by our new (cybernetic) machinic arrangements, but whose existence is threatened by the desire to commodify and control the new forms of communication and the collectivities they inspire. Thus a contestatory criticism should be attentive not only to the negative consequences of contemporary technoculture but also to the alternative utopian desires, no matter how silent or contradictory, expressed there.

The point of mapping the techniques of power and procedures of expression in digital culture, then, is to make clearer the possibilities of critique and strategies of contestation. A progressive critique of digital culture requires thinking historically, that is, in relation to time. We must create ways of mapping the functioning of power and strategies of resistance in ways that are attentive to the volatility, ambivalence, and contradictoriness of the social transformations now taking place. AT&T presents us with one image of utopia, but it is an uncertain utopia indeed. Uncertain because the rapid commodification of the new communication technologies confronts us with real paradoxes. The force of utopia resides in defining desire as multiplicity—a proliferation of possible worlds alternative to the one we now inhabit. But these worlds do not emerge from the same desire, nor can desire itself be characterized as singular, homogeneous, and without contradiction. Future-oriented desires are ambivalent and polyvalent by nature:

they can be pulled in different and often contradictory political and social directions. In fact, they are "incompossible worlds," in Leibniz's sense of the term, that represent different and often agonistic ethical dimensions, each of which is equally possible in itself, yet exclusive of the others. This means that there are no false utopias; capitalism and socialism cannot be opposed in this way. Incompossible worlds are innumerable variations of the future virtually present in the moment we now inhabit. The deepest sense of the "virtual," then, is the potentiality of the actual. This is the expression of an Event in Deleuze's sense of the term, which in every passing moment holds in reserve the multiplicity of undetermined forces that ensure future trajectories as throws of the dice, rather than the linear unfolding of a dialectic of power or the ineluctable movement of historical waves.[18]

Understanding what virtualities reside in the forces unleashed by cybernetic arrangements may well mean unlocking how technological concepts translate into new categories of social experience, or how a machine logic or architecture may insinuate itself into the relations of power that flow through us and connect us one to another. Even "scientific" concepts remain external to the technologies in which they are functionalized, and in this way they express sets of powers or potentialities that can flow in contrary directions. The evolution of the Internet transmission protocols provides a relatively simple example for understanding this problem.[19] From the beginning of its history, a concept of "information potlatch" was built into the infrastructure of the Internet as a principle of information reciprocity between interconnected terminals and routers that assumed for each amount of information demanded and given, an equal amount would be returned to the networked community. This was a key principle of the "hacker ethic," underwriting the principles of freeware and shareware, that was built into the conceptual design of distributed, packet-switched networks. This principle derived from the best ideals of communities that were both scientific and countercultural. One of the great paradoxes of the Internet, then, was how an intrinsically open, decentralized, and nonhierarchical network was allowed to flourish within the secretive and closed world of military research. The whole history of cybernetics, in fact, is marked by the struggle to define how the nature of power is augmented and transformed by computer-mediated communications: as unrestricted or restricted flows? Thus the most insidious consequence of the increasing commodification of the network has been the displacement of this ideal of free and transparent communication by surreptitious data mining and invasions of data privacy. An ethical principle of reciprocity has been perverted and replaced by another version of exchange marked by the logic of commodities and a new capitalist division of labor. In this respect, the social and political issues relating to electronic privacy and encryption have become increasingly vexed. Here the cypherpunk vision of omnipresent virtual surveillance deepens in its (perhaps justified!) paranoia in direct ratio with the reorganization of the network by the forms of commodity exchange. My main point, however, is that the implementation of even "purely" technological concepts presents us with complex sites of social struggle and myriad choices whose historical outcomes have political consequences.

I should also add that the figure of utopia is not reserved exclusively for communities wishing to build an alternative to capitalism, and the calls of utopia can respond to any number of ethical perspectives that can, in various degrees, be mutually exclusive, and that enable different series of powers. The logic of utopia holds within itself a principle of undecidability that makes it reversible through political or cultural recontextualization if not anchored by strong ethical claims. Anyone who has seen AT&T's ad campaign will have noticed how their production designers project an image of utopia by explicitly adopting the dystopian futurist designs of *Blade Runner.* This shows precisely the curious social tension that informs these ads. AT&T markets its image of the future by capitalizing on the cult popularity of a technology-oriented film. This reference, however, immediately recalls a disturbing virtual image: *Blade Runner*'s vision of an ecologically devastated planet whose society is divided into economic extremes based on access to technology, and where the distinction between what is human and what is artificial is rapidly disappearing. This is the reverse side of William Gibson's oft-cited complaint of how techno-utopians have completely missed the deep political ironies of his cyberpunk trilogy. AT&T has reverse engineered its shiny utopian future from the darker pages of cyberpunk. But in so doing it has not purged its political un-

conscious, which takes the form of a repressed dystopian image that persists as a kind of virtual image, a counterutopia that may return in the form of a critique of cybernetic capitalism.

The fantasies of digital culture promulgated by AT&T, IBM, Intel, and Microsoft in the mass media are easy to deconstruct and thus to dismiss. But we should not look away too quickly, for the figuration of utopia in contemporary technoculture expresses a complex, if by no means clear, site of political struggle. No doubt these corporations wish to promote an idea of a cybernetic capitalism as what Slavoj Žižek has called a "hegemonic universal" whose "values" are formulated as an ineluctable (if pleasurable) world-historical force. Here the utopia of capitalism is represented as the universal expression of a social good that can only come about through a "friction-free" capitalism where the global proliferation of free markets is equated with the virtualization of commodities in the worldwide reach of digital communications networks. This is not the simple imposition of a new model of power by those who represent the political and economic interests of what has been called the "multinational entertainment state." Rather, ideology has no force if it cannot recognize and solicit popular desires representing new forms of community. "In other words," writes Žižek, "each hegemonic universality has to incorporate *at least two* particular contents, the authentic popular content as well as its distortion by the relations of domination and exploitation."[20] This is another way of thinking about the "political unconscious," in Jameson's felicitous phrase, of contemporary technoculture, and in this way we can see exactly why Deleuze writes that "the secret exists only to betray itself." For the "truth" of these ads resides not in the recognition that they "misrepresent" themselves but rather in that they express quite directly, if in a distorted form, popular desires and values already apparent in the new machinic arrangements of digital culture. This distortion is a cynical attempt not only to capitalize and market new technologies but also to exploit them in such a way as to maintain and extend the cultural logic of contemporary capitalism, whose values may be challenged by the potentiality of the new forms of communications. The marketing of the "new" is what in fact impedes the invention of new forms of community as defined by Howard Rheingold and others.

There is a deep risk in fearing that the penetration of society by digital culture will be total and complete, and that the appearance of new strategies of virtual surveillance and automated social control are inevitable and unchallengeable. The history of technology has shown repeatedly that this is never the case. A contestatory cultural criticism needs to be attentive to nuances in the consumption and use of these new technologies, both for good and ill, and alert to the possibilities for creatively subverting them and turning them to more democratic ends. I would like to conclude by suggesting several ways of looking at how the appearance of a digital culture is still open to political and intellectual challenge and redirection.

Unlike panoptic or disciplinary societies, which are visible regimes constituted by actual architectures, control societies are virtual regimes in a networked environment whose power is effected through a continuous control and instantaneous communication in open milieus. The expansion of this invisible architecture, the global communications network, is simultaneously the expression of an (impossible) ideal of power exercised on a "closed" world. Paul Edwards has examined the history and social theory of this closed-world discourse, which has so marked the military and governments of developed countries since World War II. The closed world is defined by a military utopia of the automated functioning of power through the casting of a global net of surveillance capable of instantaneous and automated response to perceived aggression—an ideal totalitarian space of command and control.[21] But what has most forcefully marked the history of constructing a cybernetic system of communication, command, and control of the global military environment are its continual, and sometimes catastrophic, failures.

This is an important historical lesson, for technology fails, and the probability of technology failing increases relative to its complexity, as Murphy's Law dictates. The use of technology always requires specialized knowledge. On one hand, this will surely slow the advance of markets for the new media and new technologies. On the other, we should be critically alert to how new class divisions emerge on the basis of technological knowledge. Furthermore, what is true of the complexity of technology is equally true of the complexity of economic organizations and the juridical apparatuses that support them. Cybernetic capitalism is no less replete with structural contradictions than industrial capitalism, as the 1998 collapse of international currency markets in Southeast Asia, and then Brazil, has made painfully clear. In this respect, I hope we can look forward to more critical, historical analyses of the international political economy of digital culture.

In addition, successful commodification requires the prior existence or creation of a compelling desire or need. This is the whole point of the AT&T ads, as well as the current media obsession with multimedia computing. The historical situation is still very fluid and inchoate. Not only will a great many of these products fail to attract a market, but there is also time for the public to redefine how these technologies will be used, indeed to redefine what a "public" will mean in a digital culture. Both old and new forms of political action, legislation, and lobbying should be brought to bear here. An interesting example of what can be done is represented in the efforts of organizations in the United States such as the Electronic Frontier Foundation, the Electronic Privacy Information Center, and the Center for Democracy and Technology to protect the Internet from commercialization, to assure the rights of individuals to maintain controls over their personal information and "data images," and to extend constitutional protections to network communications. Once time and access to information are commodified, all the power imbalances, class inequities, and forms of alienation typical of capitalism will appear as well. This is yet another area where critical study of the political economy of digital culture is urgent.

Simultaneously, we must treat with irony every attempt to define cyberspace as a political territory detached from any national sovereignty or whose rules are somehow different from those of the "real world."[22] The solution is not to declare the independence of cyberspace as some kind of virtual sovereign realm, for it is not the State per se that inhibits the liberatory and critical potential of the new communications technologies but rather the forces of cybernetic capitalism, which are themselves global and increasingly supercharged by these selfsame technologies. This is why Žižek cagily critiques how libertarian politics mistake the abstract universality of capitalism for that of the nation-state: "This . . . demonization of the state is thoroughly ambiguous, since it is predominantly appropriated by right-wing populist discourse and/or market liberalism: its main targets are the state interventions which try to maintain a kind of minimal social balance and security. . . . So, while cyberspace ideologists can dream about the next evolutionary step in which we will no longer be mechanically interacting 'Cartesian' individuals, in which each 'person' will cut his or her substantial link to his individual body and conceive of itself as part of the new holistic Mind which lives and acts through him or her, what is obfuscated in such a direct 'naturalization' of the World Wide Web or market is the set of power relations—of political decisions, of institutional conditions—which 'organisms' like the Internet (or the market or capitalism . . .) need in order to thrive" (36–37). In this way, it is easy to see that the political unconscious of most libertarian manifestos on the politics of the Internet (as appearing in the pages of *Wired,* for example) is, precisely, politics! The libertarian targeting of the State thus sublates the abstract universality of capitalism as the real political problem, when in point of fact we need a different kind of institutional politics—in fact, socialist—to articulate and encourage the more inventive and popular collective arrangements of digital culture. Thus each time *Wired* publishes another slavish profile of a free marketing cybernaut next to complaints about legislative inhibitions on electronic free speech, one wants to cry out: "It's capitalism, stupid!"

Finally, for every new strategy of power that emerges, there also always emerges a countervailing culture of resistance. The question, then, is how to reintroduce some friction into "friction-free" capitalism. There has already been some interest, both in the popular press and in cultural studies, in examining the counterculture of computing wherein the structure of digital arts and communications is subject to what the Situationists called cultural *détournement*.[23] The ethics and tactics of the "digital underground" are exemplary in this respect: culture jammers, guerrilla media, cyberpunk culture, warez or software pirates, hackers, and phone phreaks all provide rich material for examining the creative possibilities that already exist for resisting, redesigning, and critiquing digital culture.[24] Here the idea of "hacker ethics"—defined by theft of service and proprietary information, open access to knowledge, unrestricted dialogue within communities of like interest regardless of geographic location—provides one conceptual foundation for discussing the liberatory potential of packet-switched networks and the qualitative transformation of communication and community they presuppose. The struggle against capitalism is often inchoate in these communities, but it is nonetheless a struggle against the control of information, the commodification of communication, and the capitalist exploitation of the networked economy.

AT&T presents us with the two sides of utopia—the dream of the individual's absolute control over information is also the nightmare of total surveillance and the reification of private experience. These technologies serve to define, regulate, observe, and document human collectivities. They also allow access to more information and new possibilities of communication that are already finding expression as the "minor" voices of our new machinic arrangements. Only a contestatory critical thinking can map the relations of power and strategies of resistance emerging in digital culture and turn them to socialist values.

NOTES

1. Presenting the Figural

1 All translations are my own unless otherwise indicated.

2 See in particular Metz's essays translated as *Film Language*.

3 See, for example, Lyotard, "Dialectique, index, forme," in *Discours, figure*, 27–52. I should emphasize again that Lyotard's originality lies in situating the work of Benveniste, and indeed the Saussurean enterprise of structural linguistics, in a genealogy with Hegel's phenomenology. Lyotard is referring here to a passage at the end of section A.1 ("Sense-Certainty, This, and Meaning") of Hegel's *Phenomenology*. See Hegel, *Phänomenologie des Geistes*, 88.

4 This spacing at the heart of discourse relies on three important distinctions: negation, negativeness, and negativity. Lyotard distinguishes them as follows: "The negation of the grammarian or the logician, which can be seen in negative statements; the discontinuity of the structuralist and the linguist, hidden in the language-system (*langue*), which keeps the terms of the language separated and by respecting invariances, integrates them into a whole; finally hidden in the utterance (*parole*) there is the lack recognized by the logician and analyst, the lack that runs through discourse and gives it its referential power. Hence: syntactical negation, structural negativeness, intentional negativity." From Mary Lydon's translation, published in *Theatre Journal* as "Fiscourse, Digure: The Utopia behind the Scenes of Phantasy," 343. Also see Lyotard, *Discours, figure*, 121.

5 See also Mary Lydon's translation of this chapter, "The Dream-Work Does Not Think," published in *Oxford Literary Review*.

6 This chapter has also been translated as "The Connivances of Desire with the Figural" in *Driftworks*. The relevant passage is on page 61.

7 See Freud's oft-cited essay "The Unconscious," 159–216.

8 See Freud, *The Standard Edition*, vol. 5, p. 611.

9 In Mary Lydon's translation, "Fiscourse, Digure," 334.

10 Ibid., 354.

11 Ibid., 357.

12 Cited in *Discours, figure*, 224 n. 32, from Félix Klee, ed., *P. Klee par lui-même et par son fils F. Klee*, 116; my translation from the French.

13 Interior citation from Klee, *Das bildnerische Denken*, 454.

14 This is something very different, and more radical, than a denigration of vision or a critique of "ocularcentrism," as Martin Jay would have in an otherwise very fine book, *Downcast Eyes*.

15 For a superb overview of both the changes and continuities of Lyotard's arguments concerning art and politics, see David Carroll's *Paraesthetics,* especially chapters 2 and 7.

16   Lyotard, "Answering the Question: What Is Postmodernism?" In *The Postmodern Condition,* 79.

17   Lyotard, "The Sublime and the Avant-Garde," 43. I will refer here to the text as originally published in *Artforum* in Lisa Liebmann's translation. The emended French version was published in a collection of Lyotard's essays called *L'inhumain.*

18   The two central texts are "Presenting the Unpresentable: The Sublime" (1982) and "The Sublime and the Avant-Garde" (1983). These were followed by a deeper account of Kant's third Critique, the 1991 *Leçons sur l'Analytique du sublime.*

19   In "Presenting the Unpresentable: The Sublime," Lyotard suggests that painting finds its philosophical vocation when liberated from representation by photography: "Painting became a philosophical activity: previously defined rules governing the formation of pictorial images were not enunciated and applied automatically. Rather painting's rule became the re-evaluation of those pictorial rules, as philosophy re-evaluates philosophical syntax" (65).

20   In "Presenting the Unpresentable," globalization projects the idea of community in yet another direction: "In the current state of techno-science and accumulated capital in the developed world, community identity requires no spiritual allegiance, nor does it demand a grand shared ideology, but it crystallizes instead through the mediation of the total sum of goods and services, which are being exchanged at a prodigious rate. At the edge of the twenty-first century, the search for knowledge, technology, and capital is evident in the very structure of our languages. The traditional function of the state has shifted: it need no longer incarnate the idea of community, and tends instead to identify with its infinite potential to generate data, know-how, and wealth" (66–67). Of course, what comes after postmodernism is a grand shared ideology, perhaps the grandest: globalization, or one world dominated by the forms of exchange unleashed by unbridled free markets.

21   Also see the concluding chapter of my *Gilles Deleuze's Time Machine.*

22   Eisenstein, "Perspectives," 36.

23   These arguments, which seemed to have obsessed the writing on aesthetics produced in the eighteenth century, devolve from a fundamental misunderstanding of the *Ars Poetica.* I would use this observation to further my claim that what is really at stake is a desire to define and protect speech as the mirror of thought and the site of rational expression. Cf. Richard Rorty's *Philosophy and the Mirror of Nature.*

24   For two of the best overviews of this question, see Ernst Cassirer's *The Philosophy of the Enlightenment* and David E. Wellbery's *Lessing's "Laocoön": Semiotics and Aesthetics in the Age of Reason.*

25 See *October 77* (summer 1996): 25.

26 See Binckley, "Refiguring Culture" and "Camera Fantasia."

27 Barthes, *Camera Lucida,* 80.

28 This, of course, is Nelson Goodman's terminology from *Languages of Art.* I am also indebted to William Mitchell's reading of Goodman in relation to problems of photography. See Mitchell, *The Reconfigured Eye,* chapter 3.

29 See Benjamin, "Das Kunstwerk im Zeitalter seiner technischen Reproduzierbarkeit," sec. 11, in *Illuminationen;* translated as "The Work of Art in the Age of Mechanical Reproduction."

30 See Walker's essay "Through the Looking Glass," 444. John Walker was the founder of Autodesk, one of the pioneers in computer-aided design and early innovators of virtual reality technologies. For an alternative perspective, see Sandy Stone's essay, "Will the Real Body Please Stand Up"?

31 On the ideology of digital culture as a new form of idealism, see Slavoj Žižek's essays "Multiculturalism, or The Cultural Logic of Multinational Capitalism" and "Cyberspace, or The Unbearable Closure of Being."

2. Reading the Figural

1 In the current situation, critical theory ignores at its peril the importance of economic analysis, since information and entertainment are becoming increasingly dominant as globally managed commodities. Over the past ten years, the links between the global expansion of media economies, the increasing "cooperation" between public institutions and private corporations, and the commercialization of the most intimate forms of electronic communication have become ever larger and more interconnected. In short, an international information economy is evolving simultaneously on the most global and most personal scales. Without doubt, the powerful new technologies of electronic communication and image processing will be developed and distributed only in forms whose exchange value can be calculated precisely, and those forms will determine ideological effects. (The public appearance of the Internet, and since 1990 the World Wide Web, charges these problems with renewed urgency.) Jay Olgilvy, adviser to the London Stock Exchange, isn't kidding when he states that a Nobel Prize is waiting for the person who defines the economics of information. See Stewart Brand, *The Media Lab,* especially 229–49. For another important account of this problem with respect to the debate on postmodernism, see Jennifer Wicke, "The Perfume of Information."

2 I follow Umberto Eco in identifying two traditions in the study of signification — that of semiology descending from Ferdinand de Saussure and that of semiotics descending from Charles Sanders Peirce. In my view, the semiotic tradition has proved to be both less compromised by a linguistic bias and more flexible in describing historical mutations in the ordering of signs. An interesting reading of

Peirce, which informs my argument here, is found in Gilles Deleuze's two books on cinema, *The Movement-Image* and *The Time-Image*. Also see my book *Gilles Deleuze's Time Machine*, especially chapter 3.

3   In an early draft of this chapter, I referred to the current period as "late" capitalism. This term is rhetorically unfortunate, even though it has enabled some striking analyses by Marxist economists. The only thing "late" about capitalism is that it long ago failed to collapse on schedule. As Fredric Jameson suggests, perhaps the term "postmodernism" best describes the current state of political economy with respect to the spatial and temporal ordering of experience. (See his *Postmodernism, or The Cultural Logic of Late Capitalism*.) This is the only definition of the term that I am inclined to accept. Later in this chapter, I refer to Foucault's division of the Modern from the Classic era on the basis of their theories of signs and representation. Here "Modernism" refers to a *philosophical* epoch, originating in the eighteenth century, which still largely defines professional philosophy as it is practiced today.

4   It is not coincidental that I draw so heavily on the conceptual language of "chaos," or the modeling of nonlinear systems. A good account of the philosophical implications of this developing thought in mathematics and physics can be found in Ilya Prigogine and Isabelle Stengers, *Order Out of Chaos*. Also see Claire Parnet's 1985 interview with Deleuze published in *Negotiations* as "Mediators."

5   Much of my argument concerning the originality of Deleuze's reading of Foucault derives from the way that English translations of Foucault's work have tended to suppress his sensitivity to problems of space. Foucault himself is equally at fault, however, in the choice he made while struggling to create a new set of concepts to articulate relations between the "visible" and the "expressible." The problem of the énoncé is a good case in point. Foucault's translators should be forgiven for choosing to express this term as "statement," for while arguing against any linguistic conceptualization of the term, Foucault nonetheless selected a highly charged word with a long history in linguistic thought and analytic philosophy. In contrast, Deleuze emphasizes restoring a sense of Foucault's development of the énoncé as a spatial figure. However, even Deleuze stops short of questioning the status of the énoncé as an oral or written statement as opposed to the "visible" as the potential field of emergence of "observables." For these reasons, I have chosen the rather banal expedient of translating *énonçable* as "expressible," since even the English language has not banished the painter, the photographer, the videographer, or the hypermedia and Web designer from the field of expression. Through this strategy, I hope nonetheless to demonstrate the power and range of "expressions" in Foucault's description of what counts as an énoncé. I would like to thank Dana Polan for drawing my

attention to the interest of Deleuze's reading of Foucault in this respect. See Polan's review of *Foucault*, "Powers of Vision, Visions of Power."

6 If Foucault and Deleuze cast themselves as radical "empiricists," one must nonetheless stress the originality of their use of the term. Their empiricism refers neither to a teleological progress of human thought nor to the apprehension of an otherwise secret knowledge residing naturally though silently at the heart of things. Rather, it stages the paradox of the énoncé as simultaneously "not visible and not hidden." The énoncé partakes of a radical positivity even if the gaze does not recognize it. In this respect, Deleuze believes that Foucault gives primacy to the expressible. In each historical formation, the expressible serves as a "dominant," not in the sense of controlling or defining the visible but as the measure of its autonomy. Énoncés are thus considered to be determinant with respect to knowledge. They render "things" as visible or observable, and they "cause to be seen," even if what they render visible is something other than what they themselves intend to express. As a critical concept, what the diagram produces is a map of the practices of knowledge, or a blueprint for the matrix that generates énoncés in a space defined between the visible and the expressible. "We need only know how to read," writes Deleuze, "however difficult that may prove to be. The secret exists only in order to be betrayed, or to betray itself. Each age articulates perfectly the most cynical element of its politics, or the rawest element of its sexuality, to the point where transgression has little merit. Each age says [énonce] everything it can according to the conditions laid down for its statements [énoncés]" (*Foucault*, 54).

7 See in particular "Defining the Statement," in Foucault, *Archaeology*, 79–87. Deleuze's commentary, which makes a somewhat different emphasis, is found in the first chapter of *Foucault*, 1–22.

8 Arguing against the "prestige" of writing in order to return the analysis of speech to its proper place in linguistics, Saussure says, "le mot écrit se mêle si intimement au mot parlé dont il est image, qu'il finit par usurper le rôle principal; on en vient à donner autant et plus d'importance à la représentation du signe vocal qu'à ce signe lui-même. C'est comme si l'on croyait que, pour connaître quelqu'un, il vaut mieux regarder sa photographie que son visage" (*Cours* 45). Curiously, the English translation omits this reference.

9 Modernism should be considered as the last stage of referentiality in the arts: nonobjective painting insisted on abstraction as the expressiveness of the artist's spiritual or mental states; abstract expressionism must refer to an authentic existential action. Self-reference is nonetheless reference, and both movements devolve from a long tradition of Romanticism. It is here that the economic, aesthetic, and philosophical definitions of modernity coincide perfectly. As Foucault insists, the Modern age is the age of "man." As cultural documents of the

Modern age, the more art ceased to resemble an external world, the more it referred to the inner world of "the artist." And no extreme of abstraction or lack
of deictic markers will make modern art (and most postmodern art) any less
an art of the subject, understood as a self-identical, freely creative origin.

3. The Figure and the Text

1 Following Philippe Sollers's essay "Niveaux semantiques d'un texte moderne,"
   I differentiate throughout this chapter between two conceptualizations of writing—one that constitutes an empirical object whose relations are established by
   logocentric thought; the other that is inflected by Derrida's philosophy:

   > By *writing*, two registers must be rigorously distinguished:
   > —first, and here the word is applied without quotation marks, writing
   > as it is currently known: that which is effectively written, that is, the pho-
   > netic writing in use in our culture that corresponds to a representation of
   > speech. . . .
   > —second, and here the word appears with quotation marks ("writing"),
   > one portrays the effect of opening language—its articulation, its scansion, its
   > overdetermination, its *spacing*—such that there would seem to be an archi-
   > writing [*pre-écriture*] within writing, a trace anterior to the distinction sig-
   > nifier/signified, an immobilization of the graphic within speech. (Sollers 317;
   > my translation)

2 The more recent work of Raymond Bellour extends and complicates the question of movement and intelligibility, not only in the context of media theory
   but also in relation to video and new media as well as film. See, for example,
   his collections *L'Entre-images, L'Entre-images, 2,* and other essays of the 1990s.
   One inspiration for the redirection of Bellour's work and others is how the
   concept of movement has fundamentally been transformed by Gilles Deleuze's
   books *Cinema 1: The Movement-Image* and *Cinema 2: The Time-Image.* I analyze
   Deleuze's arguments in greater depth in my book *Gilles Deleuze's Time Machine.*
   For a more extensive analysis of the contributions of Bellour, Metz, and Kuntzel
   to a theory of reading, see the last chapter of my *The Difficulty of Difference.*

3 That the photographic image confounds intelligibility by escaping writing, or
   perhaps more precisely linguistic sense, is the most constant theme uniting
   Barthes's otherwise diverse writings on photography. In "The Photographic
   Message" (1961), for example, Barthes associates photography with a "traumatic" suspension of language, or a blocking of meaning, as the potential site
   of a "pure" denotation that functions as a small preserve of "reality" untouched
   by ideological meanings. In later essays such as "The Third Meaning" (1970),
   this becomes an "obtuse meaning" that eludes both linguistic articulation and
   the cultural and ideological meanings fixed by connotation. Characterized not

by signification but by *signifiance,* here the signifier always runs ahead of meaning and cannot be anchored by a fixed denotation or limited connotation. The photographic image always produces multiple and indeterminate meanings. In this manner, Barthes values *signifiance* as being both pleasurable and political—in resisting meaning, it always exceeds and confounds ideological norms of reading or interpretation. And at the same time, it produces ever-renewable, pleasurable meanings. In his last book, *Camera Lucida,* the concept of the *punctum* implies a retreat from the social into a preserve of purely personal meanings. In each of these examples, the image is opposed to speech as both nondiscursive and irrational. Similarly, film is opposed to photography because it restores through factors of movement both articulation or coding to the image as well as a syntagmatic organization. It is for these reasons that Barthes's otherwise fascinating accounts of photography are completely unable to recognize the figural force of cinematographic "writing."

4 See in particular Derrida's essay, "Freud and the Scene of Writing," 207.

5 For a deeper account of this problem, see my book *The Difficulty of Difference,* especially the last three chapters.

6 See especially Benveniste, "Sémiologie de la langue," in *Problèmes de linguistique générale,* vol. 2.

7 See especially Eisenstein, "The Dramaturgy of Film Form" and "The Fourth Dimension of Cinema," in *Selected Works,* vol. 1, *Writings, 1922–34,* 161–94.

8 See, for example, Ropars's essays "The Overture of *October*" and "The Overture of *October,* Part II."

9 Jakobson, "Closing Statement: Linguistics and Poetics," 358. I am grateful to Dana Polan for verifying the place of Jakobsonian poetics in Ropars's other essays. For another account of this problem, see his " 'Desire Shifts the Difference': Figural Poetics and Figural Politics in the Film Theory of Marie-Claire Ropars-Wuilleumier."

10 For a related and more extensive critique of "semiotic modernism" and a deeper account of the theory of critical reading I propose, see my book *The Crisis of Political Modernism,* especially the concluding chapter and the preface to the second edition.

11 For an alternative reading of Ropars's theory, see Peter Brunette and David Wills's *Screen/Play,* especially pages 128–34.

4. The Ends of the Aesthetic

1 Responses were printed on the *New York Times'* Op-Ed page, 6 February 1990, A28.

2 Williams, *Keywords,* 28. For a concise account of *aisthesis* see F. E. Peters's *Greek Philosophical Terms,* 8–15. This problem has been addressed recently in important and different ways in David Wellbery, *Lessing's "Laocoön": Semiotics and*

Aesthetics in the Age of Reason; Terry Eagleton, *The Ideology of the Aesthetic;* Howard Caygill, *Art of Judgment;* and John Guillory, *Cultural Capital.*

3   This problem continues to confront the social history of art. A philosophical understanding of these ideas would benefit greatly from a detailed historical account of the transformation of art markets in the eighteenth and nineteenth centuries linked to changing ideas on the social identity and meaning of artworks. I speculate that the idea of autonomous art's freedom from exchange value appears in the eighteenth century as the culmination of a long process during which the roots of modern capitalism also appear. This process witnesses the development of artistic forms and practices that increasingly detach the art object from special social, religious, and political contexts, allowing them to circulate in the form of commodities. A key event in this emergence is undoubtedly the creation of the Louvre in 1792 as a state treasure-house for art, where the state not only manages the market value of its assets but also, through its mission for popular education, contributes to a transformation of the social meanings accruing to artworks as well as the condition of their reception. The French Revolution thus completes a process by which art is detached economically and ideologically from the context of patronage by church and court, coming increasingly under the dominance of the bourgeoisie and state-managed capital economies. Similarly, in the nineteenth century, the doctrine of *l'art pour l'art* arises with the diminution of the power of the Academy and the increasing domination of the art market by the Salons, and then art dealers. In this manner, the emergence of the aesthetic in the eighteenth and nineteenth centuries is intimately linked both to problems of epistemology (deciding cognitive relations between subject and object) and to the theory of signs (the problem of representation, how signs differ from each other and in their mediate relation to knowledge).

4   The former first appeared in book form as "Parergon" in *La vérité en peinture,* 21–168. I will cite mostly from Craig Owens's translation of pages 41–94, which appeared as "The Parergon" in *October* 9 (summer 1979): 3–40. An alternative translation by Geoff Bennington and Ian McCleod has appeared in *The Truth in Painting,* 34–82. "Economimesis" was initially published in Sylviane Agacinski et al., *Mimesis des articulations.* I will cite from R. Klein's translation that appeared in *Diacritics* 11 (1981): 3–25.

5   Further on, Derrida writes: "For my impatient critics, if they insist on seeing the thing itself: every analytic of aesthetic judgment presupposes that we can rigorously distinguish between the intrinsic and the extrinsic. Aesthetic judgment *must* concern intrinsic beauty and not the around and about. It is therefore necessary to know—this is the fundamental presupposition, the foundation—how to define the intrinsic, the framed, and what to exclude as frame *and* beyond the frame. We are thus *already* at the unlocatable center of the problem. And since,

when we ask, 'What is a frame?', Kant responds, 'It is a *parergon,* a composite of inside and outside, but a composite which is not an amalgam of half-and-half, an outside which is called inside the inside to constitute it as inside.' And when he gives us examples of the *parergon,* besides the frame, drapery, and columns, we say to ourselves that there are indeed 'considerable difficulties,' and that the choice of examples, as well as their association, is not self-evident" ("Parergon," 26–27).

6 Owens uses J. C. Meredith's 1928 translation of the *Critique of Judgment,* 85. In his translation of "Economimesis," R. Klein uses the 1892 translation by J. H. Bernard (New York: Hafner Press, 1951). When in my text Derrida cites Kant, readers can assume that I am following Owens's and Klein's choices. On occasion I will also use Werner S. Pluhar's translation. I have compared all translations to the *Kritik der Urteilskraft* published by Suhrkamp Taschenbuch Verlag, 1974.

7 Thus in Derrida's reading of Kant, "Mercenary art belongs to art only by analogy. And if one follows this play of analogy, mercenary productivity also resembles that of bees: lack of freedom, a determined purpose or finality, utility, finitude of the code, fixity of the program without reason and without the play of the imagination. The craftsman, the worker, like the bee, does not play. And indeed the hierarchical opposition of liberal art and mercenary art is that of play and work. 'We regard the first as if it could only prove purposive as play, i.e. as occupation that is pleasant in itself. But the second is regarded as work, i.e. as occupation which is unpleasant (a trouble) in itself and which is only attractive on account of its effect (for example salary) and which can consequently only be imposed on us by constraint (*zwangmässig*)' [§ 43]" ("Economimesis" 5).

8 As Derrida further explains, "Nature furnishes rules to the art of genius. Not concepts, not descriptive laws, but rules precisely, singular norms which are also orders, imperative statements. When Hegel reproaches the third *Critique* for staying at the level of the 'you must,' he very well evinces the moral order which sustains the aesthetic order. That order proceeds from one freedom to another, it gives itself from one to the other: and as discourse, it does so through a signifying element. Every time we encounter in this text something that resembles a discursive metaphor (nature says, dictates, prescribes, etc.), these are not just any metaphors but analogies of analogy, whose message is that the literal meaning is analogical: nature is properly [*proprement*] *logos* toward which one must always return [*remonter*]. Analogy is always language.

"For example, one reads (at the end of § 46) that 'nature, by the medium of genius, does not prescribe [*vorschreibe*] rules to science but to art . . .' Genius transcribes the prescription and its *Vorschreiben* is written under the dictation of nature whose secretary it freely agrees to be. At the moment it writes, it allows itself literally to be inspired by nature which dictates to it, which tells it in the form of poetic commands what it must write and in turn prescribe; and without genius really understanding what it writes. It does not understand the prescriptions that it transmits; in any case it has neither concept nor knowledge of them. 'The author of a product for which he is indebted to his genius does not know himself how he has come by his ideas; and he has not the power to devise the like at pleasure or in accordance with a plan, and to communicate it to others in precepts [*Vorschriften*] that will enable him to produce [*hervorbringen*] similar products [*Producte*].' Genius prescribes, but in the form of non-conceptual rules which forbid repetition, imitative reproduction" ("Economimesis" 13).

9   Of great interest here is Derrida's reading of disgust, negative pleasure, and the sublime in Kant. See, for example, "Economimesis," 21–25.

10   Music's public character, which potentially impinges on the private and autonomous situation of aesthetic contemplation, is treated by Kant with mild distaste: "The situation here is almost the same as with the enjoyment [*Ergötzung*] produced by an odor that spreads far. Someone who pulls his perfumed handkerchief from his pocket gives all those next to and around him a treat whether they want it or not, and compels them, if they want to breathe, to enjoy [*genießen*] at the same time" (§ 53, *Judgment* 200–201). This is additional evidence for the recession toward an absolute interior that marks the third Critique and informs its parergonal logic. The purest experience of the aesthetic is not a public one; rather, the purest objects of taste are those that render the most private experience, encouraging the freedom and autonomy of the individual as detached from the mass.

Kant also recommends against the singing of hymns at family devotionals for similar reasons. The boisterous devotional exercises of prisoners in the castle at Königsberg, which stood not far from Kant's house, led him to compose a letter of protest to the mayor of the town and perhaps inspired the distasteful unfreedom Kant associates with the public as opposed to private arts. See William Wallace's *Kant*.

11   Kant states that "poetry fortifies the mind: for it lets the mind feel its ability— free, spontaneous, and independent of natural determination—to contemplate and judge phenomenal nature as having [*nach*] aspects that nature does not on its own offer in experience either to sense or to the understanding, and hence poetry lets the mind feel its ability to use nature on behalf of and, as it were, as a schema of the supersensible. Poetry plays with illusion, which it produces at will, and yet without using illusion to deceive us, for poetry tells us itself that its pursuit is mere play, though this play can still be used purposively by the understanding for its business. Oratory [on the other hand], insofar as this is taken to mean the art of persuasion (*ars oratoria*), i.e., of deceiving by means of a beautiful illusion, rather than mere excellence of speech (eloquence and style), is a dialectic that borrows from poetry only as much as the speaker needs

in order to win over people's minds for his own advantage before they judge for themselves, and so make their judgment unfree" (§ 53, *Judgment* 196–97).

In Derrida's comparison, "The orator announces serious business and treats it as if it were a simple play of ideas. The poet merely proposes an entertaining play of the imagination and proceeds as if he were handling the business of the understanding. The orator certainly gives what he had not promised, the play of the imagination, but he also withholds what he had promised to give or to do: namely to occupy the understanding in a fitting manner. The poet does just the contrary; he announces a play and does serious work [*eines Geschäftes würdig*]. The orator promises understanding and gives imagination; the poet promises to play with the imagination while he nurtures the understanding and gives life to concepts. These nursing metaphors are not imposed on Kant by me. It is food [*Nahrung*] that the poet brings by playing at understanding, and what he does thereby is give life [*Leben zu geben*] to concepts: conception occurs through the imagination and the ear, overflowing the finite contract by giving more than it promises" ("Economimesis" 17). Also see Derrida's comparison of rhetoric and poetry on p. 11 of "Economimesis."

12 Derrida continues this line of thought by assessing how "Kant describes this movement of idealizing interiorisation: 'To this is to be added our admiration of nature, which displays itself in its beautiful products as art, not merely by chance, but as it were designedly, in accordance with a regular arrangement and as purposiveness without purpose. This latter, as we never meet with it outside ourselves, we naturally seek in ourselves and, in fact, in that which constitutes the ultimate purpose of our being [*Dasein*], viz. our moral destination [*moralischen Bestimmung*]' [§ 42]. . . .

"Not finding in aesthetic experience, which is here primary, the determined purpose or end from which we are cut off and which is found too far away, invisible or inaccessible, over there, we fold ourselves back toward the purpose of our Dasein. This interior purpose is at our disposal, it is ours, ourselves, it calls us and determines us from within, we are *there* [*da*] so as to respond to a *Bestimmung*, to a vocation of autonomy. The *Da* of our *Dasein* is first determined by this purpose which is present to us, and which we present to ourselves as our own and by which we are present to ourselves as what we are: a free existence or presence [*Dasein*], autonomous, that is to say moral" ("Economimesis," 14).

13 See, in particular, Derrida's reading of the four "sides" of the analytic of aesthetic judgment as a categorical "frame" for the analytic of the beautiful, and of the function of the table or tableau [*Tafel*] in Kant's logic in "The Parergon," 29–30.

14 "*New York Times Magazine*, 2 April 1989, 27.

5. The Historical Image

1 Originally published as *Les mots et les choses* (1966). Kracauer's book on history was for the most part complete with several chapters already in print at the time of his death on 26 November 1966. The later Foucault would, perhaps, have revisited these comments with a deeper irony. Nevertheless what is most striking in bringing Kracauer and Foucault together in this context is their similar critiques of totality, and their presentation of the possibilities of historical knowing as a conflict between historicism and an "analytic of finitude."

2 Cf. Althusser's sections of *Reading Capital*. I am particularly grateful to Phil Rosen for confirming this impression in discussion and in his essay "History, Textuality, Nation: Kracauer, Burch, and Some Problems in the Study of National Cinema." Also see Martin Jay's comments in "The Extraterritorial Life of Siegfried Kracauer." A more likely philosophical precedent is offered by Ernst Bloch's conception of the "(non)synchronous [*(un)gleichzetig*] character of history." See in particular his 1932 essay "Nonsynchronism and Its Obligation to Dialectics." One might also point out here Kracauer's admiration for the Annales historians, especially Marc Bloch.

3 Eric Rentschler notes that similar problems of reception account for a more favorable response in Germany to Kracauer's *Theory of Film* than in America. For a more detailed account of this problem, see Rentschler, "Ten Theses on Kracauer, Spectatorship, and the Seventies."

4 In Kracauer, *Das Ornament der Masse*, 21–39. Tom Levin's superb translation is published in *The Mass Ornament: Weimar Essays* (Cambridge: Harvard University Press, 1995), 47–64. Levin's introduction to this volume is the best overview of Kracauer's work that exists in English.

5 Trans. Barbara Correll and Jack Zipes in *New German Critique* 5 (spring 1975). First published in *Frankfurter Zeitung*, 9 and 10 July 1927. Also see Tom Levin's translation in *The Mass Ornament*, 75–88.

6 I am deeply indebted to Miriam Hansen for drawing my attention to the correspondences between these last two quotes and for fundamentally reorienting my understanding of the concept of mimesis in Kracauer's work.

7 Trans. Barbara Correll and Jack Zipes, *New German Critique* 5 (spring 1975): 59.

8 Cited in Karsten Witte's translation from "Introduction to Siegfried Kracauer's 'The Mass Ornament,' " 63–64.

9 Adorno compellingly articulates this problem in his 1932 text "Die Idee der Naturgeschichte." Also see Susan Buck-Morss's illuminating gloss in *The Origin of Negative Dialectics*, 55. For further explication of the role of Lukács in Kracauer's works, see Jay, "The Extraterritorial Life of Siegfried Kracauer."

10 Hansen, "Early Silent Cinema: Whose Public Sphere?" 180. The interior citations are from Kracauer's essay "Kult der Zerstreuung: Uber die Berliner Lichtspielhauser," in *Das Ornament der Masse*, 311–17, 314. (Also see *The Mass Ornament*

323–28.) Hansen follows this discussion with an interesting critique of this concept in relation to the function of sexual difference in Weimar film theory.

11 Witte, "Introduction to 'The Mass Ornament,'" 63. Martin Jay gives an excellent account of Kracauer's interest in, and sensitivity to, the analysis of visual forms, including architecture and photography.

12 Jay, "The Extraterritorial Life of Siegfried Kracauer," 57. The interior citation is Jay's translation from Kracauer's study *Die Angestellten*.

13 I am grateful to Miriam Hansen for suggesting this line of thought. For an important account of Benjamin's theory of mimesis, especially in relation to his writing on film, see her "Benjamin, Cinema, and Experience: 'The Blue Flower in the Land of Technology.'" I am also indebted to Susan Buck-Morss's account of the *Trauerspiel* book in *The Origin of Negative Dialectics;* see especially 90–95. A full-scale study of Kracauer's understanding of the concept of mimesis would also have to account for his interesting remarks concerning "fragmentation" and "daily life" developed through discussion of Eric Auerbach's *Mimesis* in the last chapter of *Theory of Film.*

14 Benjamin, *Ursprung des deutschen Trauerspiel*, 15, cited in *The Origin of Negative Dialectics,* 91, in Susan Buck-Morss's translation.

15 Also compare the following citation from *History:* "The photographer's approach may be said to be 'photographic' if his formative aspirations support rather than oppose his realistic intentions. This implies that he resembles not so much the expressive artist as the imaginative reader bent on studying and deciphering an elusive text" (55).

16 Buck-Morss, *The Origin of Negative Dialectics,* 102. Adorno's fundamental formulation of this concept appears in his 1931 address "The Actuality of Philosophy."

17 Kracauer, *History,* 50. Kracauer is citing Gay-Lussac's speech to the French House of Peers, 30 July 1839, as reported in Joseph Maria Eder's *History of Photography,* 242.

18 No doubt the reference to Benjamin here will not be missed. Compare, for example, his third thesis on the philosophy of history: "A chronicler who recites events without distinguishing between major and minor ones acts in accordance with the following truth: nothing that has ever happened should be regarded as lost for history. To be sure, only a redeemed mankind receives the fullness of its past—which is to say, only for a redeemed mankind has its past become citable in all its moments" ("Theses on the Philosophy of History" in *Illuminations,* 256).

19 This point also suggests productive comparisons with Benjamin where the decline of aura attributed to photography, which is associated with a certain ambivalent nostalgia, is nonetheless identified with the possibility of knowledge. Cf. Benjamin's discussion on the question of photography in Baudelaire and

Proust in the eleventh section of "On Some Motifs in Baudelaire," in *Illumina-tions,* 188–94.

20   Kracauer, *History,* 101. Despite its surprisingly Benjaminian ring, the interior citation is from Isaiah Berlin's "*History and Theory:* The Concept of Scientific History," 24. Considering the acknowledged place that Benjamin's philosophy of history has in Kracauer's book, I find it quite surprising that Kracauer himself does not draw out here the astonishing parallels of these arguments with Benjamin's theory of dialectical images.

21   Kracauer treats in detail both Focillion's *The Life of Forms in Art* and Kubler's *The Shape of Time: Remarks on the History of Things.*

22   Cf. Kracauer, *History,* 22–25. In presenting these arguments, Kracauer refers explicitly to his essay "Die Gruppe als Ideentraeger," in *Das Ornament der Masse,* 123–56. Also see *The Mass Ornament,* 143–72.

23   Kracauer, *History,* 199. The principal object of Kracauer's criticisms here is Hans-Georg Gadamer's *Truth and Method.* It is also interesting to note that Kracauer exhibits a similar virulence, from the opposite point of view, with respect to Adorno's negative dialectics for its complete elimination of ontology. On p. 201 of *History,* Kracauer lodges the following critique: "His rejection of any onto-logical stipulation in favor of an infinite dialectics which penetrates all concrete things and entities seems inseparable from a certain arbitrariness, an absence of content and direction in these series of material evaluations. The concept of Utopia is then necessarily used by him in a purely formal way, as a borderline concept which at the end invariably emerges like a *deus ex machina.* But Uto-pian thought makes sense only it if assumes the form of a vision or intuition with a definite content of a sort. Therefore the radical immanence of the dialec-tical process will not do; some ontological fixations are needed to imbue it with significance and direction."

24   Cited in Kracauer, *History,* 217, from Kafka's *Parables and Paradoxes,* 179.

6. A Genealogy of Time

1   Foucault, *Dits et écrits,* vol. 1, 32–33; my translation.

2   Objections could be raised to my assertions of a sort of French exceptionalism with respect to the implied philosophy of history of the time-image. Deleuze clearly, though perhaps too concisely, outlines this genealogy in a different way, as is well known. The time-image appears in the context of many differ-ent national cinemas, including Japan (Ozu) and the United States (Welles, the New American Cinema) as well as Europe, and not always in the post–World War II period. Deleuze also suggests something like different waves of cinematic experimentation. The first intimations of the time-image appear immediately after the war in Italian neorealism, are refined in the pure optical and acousti-cal constructions of the French New Wave, and are taken up again in the New

German Cinema. "The timing is," as Deleuze puts it, "something like: around 1948, Italy; about 1958, France; about 1968, Germany" (*Movement-Image* 211). However, as I will argue in the section entitled "Genealogy, Countermemory, Event," only in France is there such a powerful circulation of concepts through the domains of philosophy, film theory, and film practice. I believe the relation between genealogy and time-image can be explored productively in a number of different contexts. But only in France do we find a *philosophical* context that articulates these concepts so clearly while circulating them through the culture at large.

3   The publication of Deleuze's *Nietzsche et la philosophie* in 1961 was the opening volley in this Nietzschean decade. Foucault participated in the 1964 colloquium on Nietzsche organized by Deleuze at Royaumount; together Deleuze and Foucault proposed the publication of a new edition of Nietzsche's collected writings, which appeared in 1967 with an introduction coauthored by the two philosophers. For a succinct critical history of the influence of Nietzsche on modern French thought, see Alan D. Schrift, *Nietzsche's French Legacy: A Genealogy of Poststructuralism.*

4   For a more complete account of these questions, see my *Gilles Deleuze's Time Machine*, especially chapter 5, "Critique, or Truth in Crisis."

5   The prefaces to both the English and the French editions of *Cinema 1* begin with the statement "This is not a history of the cinema." For a discussion of what it means to read Deleuze's two-volume film theory as historical, see András Bálint Kovács's essay "The Film History of Thought." Indeed, I owe my inspiration for considering the two regimes as Hegelian and Nietzschean philosophies of history in images to my discussions with Kovács, who makes the case, quite convincingly, that Deleuze's taxonomy of cinematic signs cannot be defined independently of a conception of film history, or, more deeply, historical thought.

6   It is interesting to compare Deleuze's account of organic narration with Jean Hyppolite's characterization of Hegel's philosophy of history, whose object is a dialectical and supraindividual reality—the life and destiny of a people. See Hyppolite, *Introduction à la philosophie de l'histoire de Hegel* (1948).

7   In a comment that echoes Deleuze, in an interview with *Cahiers du cinéma*, the French political philosopher Alain Badiou characterized the New Wave in a similar way: "Some films which, ideologically, seem only to figure a romantic nihilism without any political consequence (for example, *À bout de souffle*), have a real effect . . . which aims towards other things: errance and delocalization, the fact of asking fresh questions, outside of the mediation of an institutional representation, across a character who is anything but 'settled.' In this sense, these films contributed to the delocalizations of '68." See Badiou, "Penser le surgissement de l'événement: Entretien avec Alain Badiou," 14; my translation.

8   Worringer contrasts the organic and the crystalline as compositional strategies

on the following basis. Each is an a priori will to form that expresses a culture's relation to the world. Organic forms express a harmonious unity where humanity feels at one with the world. Here representations are based on natural forms and are sustained by the belief that natural laws support and lend them truth. Alternatively, crystalline forms represent a will to abstraction. When a culture feels that it is in conflict with the world, that events are chaotic and hostile, it tends to produce pure geometric forms as an attempt to pattern and transcend this chaos. See, for example, Worringer's important studies *Abstraction and Empathy* and *Form in Gothic*. Deleuze's sense of visual history is equally indebted to Heinrich Wöfflin's *Principles of Art History*.

9 Gilles Deleuze and Félix Guattari, *What Is Philosophy?* 37.

10 Foucault, "Sur les façons d'écrire l'histoire," interview with Raymond Bellour, *Les Lettres françaises* 1187 (15–21 June 1967): 6–9. Cited in my translation from *Dit et écrits*, vol. 1, 585.

11 These works include Hyppolite's *Introduction à la philosophie de l'histoire de Hegel* (1948), *Logique et existence: essai sur la Logique de Hegel* (1952), and *Etudes sur Marx et Hegel* (1955). For a brief account of the influence of Hegel, and more specifically Hyppolite, on postwar French philosophy, see Didier Eribon's chapter "La voix de Hegel" in *Michel Foucault* 32–40. The key work in English on this question is Mark Poster's *Existential Marxism in Postwar France: From Sartre to Althusser*. Poster's book is an invaluable account of the influence of Hegel in France through the teachings of Aléxandre Kojève and Jean Hyppolite and the subsequent rereadings and responses in French political and social theory of the 1960s and 1970s. Although my perspective here is to contrast the Hegelian approach to history with a Nietzschean genealogy, one can equally trace this history, as does Poster, as different appropriations of Hegel. Indeed, it is important to mark the very different appearances of Hegel in three contexts: first, in the work of Sartre, Merleau-Ponty, and the early Lacan; second, in the rereading of Hegel by Hyppolite and Althusser, perhaps the greatest mentor figures of the poststructuralist generation; and, finally, in the very different critiques of Hegelian dialectics found in Derrida and Deleuze.

12 Foucault, "L'homme est-il mort?" *Arts et loisirs*, 15 June 1966; translation mine. Reprinted in *Dits et écrits*, 540–45. It should be said that many of the critiques of Sartre's magisterial book were perhaps too quick and unjust. In later years, Foucault found himself more than once in league with Sartre on common political projects. For deeper and more nuanced accounts of the place of Sartre's book in Marxist critical philosophy, see Poster's *Existential Marxism in Postwar France* as well as chapter 4 of Fredric Jameson's *Marxism and Form*.

13 In the little-known but important essay "A quoi reconnaît-on le structuralisme?" Deleuze observes that "if symbolic elements have neither an extrinsic designation nor an intrinsic signification, but only a meaning derived from position, it follows in principle that *meaning always results from a combination of elements which are not themselves meaningful.* As Lévi-Strauss says in his discussion with Paul Ricoeur, meaning is always a result or an effect: not only an effect produced but also an optical effect, an effect of language, of position" (300; my translation). The discussion between Lévi-Strauss and Ricoeur was published in *Esprit* (November 1963). Charles Stivale has recently published a translation of Deleuze's important text as an appendix to his book *The Two-Fold Thought of Deleuze and Guattari.*

14 Foucault, "Foucault répond à Sartre," *La Quinzaine littéraire* 46 (1–15 March 1968); also in *Dits et écrits,* vol. 1, 662–68. For another view of this debate, see Eribon, 187–92.

15 As Schrift describes them, "The conference at Royaumont, presided over by M. Gueroult, took place July 4–8, 1964, and included papers presented by Henri Birault, Karl Löwith, Jean Wahl, Gabriel Marcel, Giorgio Colli and Mazzino Montinari, Edouard Gaède, Herbert W. Reichert, Boris de Schloezer, Danko Grlic, Michel Foucault, Gianni Vattimo, Pierre Klossowski, Jean Beaufret, Gilles Deleuze, and M. Goldbeck. All but the last of these are collected in *Nietzsche: Cahiers du Royaumont,* Philosophie No. VI (Paris: Éditions de Minuit, 1967). The conference at Cérisy-la-Salle, which took place in July, 1972, saw papers presented by Eugen Biser, Eric Blondel, Pierre Boudot, Eric Clemens, Gilles Deleuze, Jeanne Delhomme, Jacques Derrida, Eugen Fink, Léopold Flam, Edouard Gaède, Danko Grlic, Pierre Klossowski, Sarah Kofman, Philippe Lacoue-Labarthe, Karl Löwith, Jean-François Lyotard, Jean Maurel, Jean-Luc Nancy, Norman Palma, Bernard Pautrat, Jean-Michel Rey, Richard Roos, Paul Valadier, Jean-Noël Vuarnet, and Heinz Wismann. The proceedings of this conference were published in two volumes as *Nietzsche aujourd'hui* (Paris: Union Generale D'Éditions, 1973)" (*Nietzsche's French Legacy,* 129).

For an overview in English of the main currents of French Nietzscheanism, see David B. Allison's collection *The New Nietzsche.* Another useful, though certainly less sympathetic, account is Vincent Descombes's *Modern French Philosophy.*

16 See Deleuze, "Lettre à un critique sévère," in *Pourparlers* 14, my translation. Also published as "Letter to a Harsh Critic" in *Negotiations* 5.

17 Translated as "The Discourse on Language" in *The Archaeology of Knowledge,* 235; trans. mod.

18 Foucault, "Jean Hyppolite: 1907–1968," in *Dit et écrits,* vol. 1, 780; my translation. This is the text of Foucault's speech given at the memorial organized by Louis Althusser at the Ecole Normale Supérieur on 19 January 1969, originally published in the *Revue de métaphysique et de morale* (June 1969): 131–36.

19 For a brief account in English of Foucault's influence on contemporary film theory, see "Film and Popular Memory: *Cahiers du Cinéma*/Extracts," *Edin-*

burgh Magazine (1977): 19–36. Also see Guiliana Bruno's essay "Towards a Theorization of Film History."

20 René Prédal describes these films as appearing in two waves. From 1974 to 1976 the first wave includes *Stavisky* (Alain Resnais), *Lacombe Lucien* (Louis Malle), *Souvenirs d'en France* (André Téchiné), *La brigade* (René Gilson), *Que la fête commence* (Bertrand Tavernier), *Section spéciale* (Constantin Costa-Gavras), *Moi, Pierre Rivière* (René Allio), *Je suis Pierre Rivière* (Christine Lipinska), *Le Juge et l'assassin* (Bertrand Tavernier), *L'Affiche rouge* (Frank Cassenti), *Une fille unique* (J. Nahoun), and *La Cecilia* (Jean-Louis Comolli). A second wave occurs in 1979 and 1980 with *La chanson de Roland* (Frank Cassenti), *Ma blonde, entends-tu dans la ville?* (René Gilson), *L'Ombre rouge* (Jean-Louis Comolli), and *Molière* (Ariane Mnouchkine). See Prédal, *50 ans de cinéma français*, 364–68. Undoubtedly the most extraordinary and powerful film to take on the problem of history and memory in this period is Claude Lanzmann's *Shoah* (1985). And experiments continue, a notable example being Hervé le Roux's reexamination of 1968 in *Reprise* (1997).

21 In Foucault, *Language, Counter-memory, Practice: Selected Essays and Interviews.* Originally published in *Critique* 282 (November 1970): 885–908. Page numbers in italics indicate that I have revised the translation and invite the reader to consider the French version as published in *Dit et écrits,* vol. 2, 75–99.

22 Also in *Language, Counter-memory, Practice: Selected Essays and Interviews.* Originally published in *Hommage à Jean Hyppolite* (Paris: PUF, 1971). Page numbers in italics indicate that I have revised the translation and invite the reader to consider the French version as published in *Dit et écrits,* vol. 2, 136–56.

23 This is in fact the argument of the last chapter of *The Movement-Image.* Unfolding logically through Peirce's categories of Firstness (quality), Secondness (cause), and Thirdness (relation) — or perception and affection-images, to action-images, and finally to mental-images — in the first fifty years of cinema, the movement-image discovers every logical permutation available to it until it achieves its final synthesis. "Inventing the mental image or the relation-image," Deleuze writes, "Hitchcock makes use of it to close the set of action-images, and also of perception and affection-images. Hence his conception of the frame. And the mental image not only frames the others, but transforms them by penetrating them. For this reason, one might say that Hitchcock accomplishes and brings to completion the whole of the cinema by pushing the movement-image to its limit. Including the spectator in the film, and the film in the mental image, Hitchcock brings the cinema to completion" (*Movement-Image* 204).

24 Nietzsche, "On the Uses and Disadvantages of History for Life," in *Untimely Meditations* 60.

25 The conceptualization of time according to Deleuze's original reading of Nietzsche's concept of eternal recurrence is the great project of *Difference and Repetition*. On the difference between Cronos and Aïon see the 23d series of *The Logic of Sense*, 162–68. I discuss this redefinition of time more completely in *Gilles Deleuze's Time Machine*, especially chapter 5.

26 "In 1970, this film was called *Victory*. In 1974 it's called *Here and Elsewhere*, and elsewhere, and. . . ."

27 Deleuze and Guattari, *What Is Philosophy?* 157–58. On the question of history and the Event in relation to direct images of time, also see "The Memory of Resistance," the concluding chapter of my *Gilles Deleuze's Time Machine*.

28 See Deleuze, *Difference and Repetition*, 276.

7. An Uncertain Utopia—Digital Culture

1 The products showcased in these ads include software (voice and handwriting recognition, smart agent or automated information retrieval on the Internet, real-time language translation), smart cards (universal debit cards as well as medical documentation), cellular and mobile communications (handheld personal digital assistants, mobile fax, wrist telephones, global positioning systems and virtual reality maps for automobiles), and networked communications and vending.

2 It is also important to think about this advertising campaign in the context of the "hacker crackdown" of 1989–1990. The hacker crackdown was a nationwide police effort comprising multiple operations carried out primarily by the Chicago Computer Fraud and Abuse Task Force, the Secret Service, and the Arizona State Attorney General's office. This was an effort to curb "crimes" of computer intrusion, credit card theft, and telephone code abuse. Its targets were largely computer bulletin board systems dedicated to exchanging information about hacking (defined rightly or wrongly as illegal computer intrusion) and "phreaking" (theft of phone service). The heavy-handedness of these operations, which resulted in some embarrassing setbacks when the prosecuted cases entered the court system, was one of the motivating factors for the founding of the Electronic Frontier Foundation. Before and after the crackdown, AT&T, and the regional Bell systems spun off in the antitrust action of 1983, had been the target of intense hacker disdain for several reasons: their perceived resistance to digital technologies and packet-switched networks; their limitation of access and restriction of knowledge of telecom networks; and of course their size, stodgy bureaucratic and elitist image, and policy of secrecy. As of 1993, AT&T was perhaps the most technologically uncool company on the planet, so much so, in fact, that its corporate logo was universally reviled in the hacker community as the "Death Star." (This refers, of course, to the evil empire's doomsday weapon in the Star Wars trilogy.) The best account of these operations and the history of the hacker underground through the early nineties is Bruce Sterling's *Hacker Crackdown! Law and Disorder on the Electronic Frontier.*

Therefore, the 1993–1994 ad campaign is clearly an effort to restore an image of AT&T as technologically "cool" as opposed to the subcultural images of a hidebound and secretive behemoth, slow to change or innovate. These objectives are clearly articulated in the preface that accompanies the videotape of the television ads made for corporate distribution. The tape begins with a reverse tracking shot down a virtual corporate hallway generated from the clean, geometric lines of computer imaging. The walls are lined with moving images reproduced from the ads. (Curious here that the movement of the virtual camera is backward, not into the future, but rather a space of continual recession.) A male voice-over flatly states the campaign's objectives: to target the eighteen to thirty-four year olds who represent AT&T's future customers into the next century; to convince them that AT&T is an innovative company, uniquely qualified to help them expand their personal and professional capabilities with leading-edge technologies; and to associate AT&T with the lifestyles, fashions, sensibilities, and an electronic media orientation that appeals to this demographic while convincing them of the human benefits they can expect to enjoy in the very near future thanks to AT&T technologies. I should also mention that this campaign was quickly and mercilessly parodied in a number of contexts, the best known of which was MTV's "You wish!" ads. See note 23 hereafter.

3   "Audiovisual culture" is a name I coined for cybernetic societies of control in an earlier version of this chapter, "Audiovisual Culture and Interdisciplinary Knowledge." In this way, I wanted to emphasize how a new semiotic environment is being put in place by digital technologies in contrast to a previous culture of the book. I prefer now the more general term "digital culture," one of whose aspects is a reconfiguration of the audiovisual regime according to a conceptualization of the figural. The figural, however, defines only the representational aspects of digital culture, and indeed every historical epoch may be defined by its own particular audiovisual regime, that is, its configuration of the expressible in relation to the visible as a way of organizing knowledge in relation to power.

4   See, for example, Fredric Jameson's thought-provoking account in *Postmodernism, or The Cultural Logic of Late Capitalism.* Among the more urgently needed projects is a study of the ideology and culture of the *Wired* generation from the point of view of the political economy of Silicon Valley (regardless of the geographic locations of the subjects that subscribe to this mentality) that has the philosophical breadth of Jameson's important book. For very different, though equally compelling, perspectives on this question, see Arthur Kroker and Michael Weinstein's "Theory of the Virtual Class," in *Data Trash,* Vivian

Sobchack's "'Teenage Mutant Ninja Hackers," Langdon Winner's "Silicon Valley Mystery House," and two important books by Mark Poster, *The Mode of Information: Poststructuralism and Social Context* and *The Second Media Age*. Also see note 16 hereafter.

5   See his essay "Postscript on Control Societies," in *Negotiations,* 177–82. I will return to Deleuze's characterization of control societies in the section entitled "Machinic and Collective Arrangements."

6   Science fiction passing as social policy is one of the more disturbing aspects of popular reporting on technology in the United States today. This is undoubtedly due to the cultural rise of "futurist" writers in the wake of the renewed popularity of works by, among others, Alvin and Heidi Toffler. Among the more hallucinatory examples of this kind of writing is *Wired*'s account of the next twenty-five years of prosperity, "The Long Boom," penned by Peter Schwartz and Peter Leyden, which has been followed by a number of articles on the "new economy." For a critical reply, see Doug Henwood's "The Long Boom," *Left Business Observer* 78 (1997). Alternatively, while I prefer more Marxist cultural and economic analyses, one of the great ironies one finds in rereading *The Third Wave* today is that in some respects, Toffler got it right. "Late capitalism" has turned out to be a transitional period to "cybernetic capitalism," a period of painful institutional crisis preceding the elaboration and setting in place of new markets and commodities, forms of exchange, and mechanisms of power.

7   Deleuze, "Les intercesseurs," in *Pourparlers* 165; my translation. Also in *Negotiations* 121.

8   On the concept of remediation, see Jay David Bolter and Richard Grusin's essay "Remediation." The complex and sometimes contradictory debate on the history and consequences of hypermedia and the fate of writing now comprises an extensive body of critical literature. Among the key works in this debate are Michael Heim's *Electric Language: A Philosophical Study of Word Processing,* Jay David Bolter's *Writing Space: The Computer, Hypertext, and the History of Writing,* George P. Landow's *Hypertext and Literary Study: The Convergence of Contemporary Critical Theory and Technology,* and Richard Lanham's *The Electronic Word: Democracy, Technology, and the Arts.* For a critical review of this literature, see John Palatella's essay "Formatting Patrimony."

9   On the philosophical consequence of the passage from analog to digital representation see Timothy Binkley's essays "Refiguring Culture" and "Camera Fantasia." In her important essay, "The Scene of the Screen: Envisioning Cinematic and Electronic Presence," Vivian Sobchack also explores these issues, but from a phenomenological perspective.

10   The paradoxical history of photography's claims to truthfulness, as well as the philosophical consequences of the aesthetic and cultural shift to digital imag-

ing, are addressed in William J. Mitchell's book *The Reconfigured Eye,* especially chapter 3, "Intention and Artifice," and chapter 9, "How to Do Things with Pictures."

11   The phrase "cybernetic capitalism" was coined by Kevin Robins and Frank Webster in their influential essay. See also their book *Information Technology: A Luddite Analysis.* One of the best essays on the culture of cybernetic capitalism in Langdon Winner's "Silicon Valley Mystery House." Also see the collections *Culture on the Brink,* ed. Gretchen Bender and Timothy Druckrey, and *Resisting the Virtual Life,* ed. James Brook and Iain Boal.

12   On the social consequences of the commodification of data images and social control through "dataveillance," see Oscar Gandy's *The Panoptic Sort: A Political Economy of Personal Information,* as well as David Lyon's *The Electronic Eye: The Rise of Surveillance Society.* On hacker ethics, see Stephen Levy's classic account, *Hackers: Heroes of the Computer Revolution,* especially chapter 1.

13   An interesting international policy struggle is now taking place between the free market initiatives of the United States and the more privacy-conscious countries of the European Economic Union. See, for example, Simon Davies's article "Europe to U.S.: No Privacy, No Trade," *Wired* 6.05 (May 1998); also at www.wired.com/wired/archive/6.05/europe.html. These and other issues are also becoming of increasing concern to international human rights organizations. Human Rights Watch devoted an entire section of its 1998 report to a discussion of freedom of expression on the Internet," at www.hrw.org.

14   The transformation of the concept of desire as agencement is the great lesson of *Anti-Oedipus* and *A Thousand Plateaus.* Deleuze provides a beautifully succinct overview of the concept in a televised interview with Claire Parnet. See "D comme Désir" in the *Abécédaire de Gilles Deleuze.* Charles Stivale presents a free translation in English at: www.langlab.wayne.edu/romance/FreD_G/ABC1. html. His complete translation will appear as a book from Semiotext(e).

15   See, for example, Lévy's book *Cyberculture* 129–43.

16   Paradoxically, the virtual communities with the most staying power tend to be ones that reassert themselves culturally through periodic social meetings face-to-face. This is particularly true in hacking and phreaking subcultures whose sociability is marked not only on-line but also in monthly *2600* meetings and hacker conventions such as Defcon and HOPE (Hackers on Planet Earth).

On the mutability and volatility of on-line personae, especially in relation to gender categories, see the important work of Amy Bruckman, Elizabeth Reid, and Allucquère Rosanne Stone. Sherry Turkle, for one, has argued in her books *Life on the Screen* and *The Second Self* that the emergence of these personae is representative of a new form of "postmodern" subjectivity, although the philosophical *locus classicus* for discussions of "cybernetic" subjectivity remains Donna Haraway's essay "A Manifesto for Cyborgs." For a darker look at the ethical consequences of computer-mediated communications, see Julian Dibble's classic essay on "A Rape in Cyberspace."

17 Rheingold, *The Virtual Community: Homesteading on the Electronic Frontier.*

18 I develop this argument in greater depth in "The Memory of Resistance," the last chapter of *Gilles Deleuze's Time Machine.*

19 For a popular overview of the invention of the Internet, see Katie Hafner and Matthew Lyon's *Where Wizards Stay Up Late: The Origins of the Internet.*

20 Žižek, "Multiculturalism, or The Cultural Logic of Multinational Capitalism" 29. I would like to thank Michael Westlake for bringing Žižek's interesting argument to my attention.

21 See Edwards, *The Closed World: Computers and the Politics of Discourse in Cold War America.*

22 See, for example, John Perry Barlow's "A Declaration of Independence for Cyberspace."

23 Yet another caution is in order here, since even the most canny cultural *détournement* is subject to corporate recontextualization and commodification. As I have already mentioned, MTV responded almost immediately to the AT&T ads with its own savvy parodies. With low-tech mise-en-scène, flat space, and color field backgrounds, MTV's art school parody humorously undercut AT&T's appeal to a televisual and technological utopia. Nevertheless this utopia, no matter how false, is discredited here only to say that there is no future except for a present with reduced expectations. This knowing wit is also corporate competition. Plug into MTV! Our technology is here and now. MTV's countercampaign was thus actually a form of corporate competition and a savvy exploitation of popular skepticism on the part of its popular audience, alienated by the repetitiveness and ubiquity of the AT&T campaign.

24 See, for example, Mark Dery's *Culture Jamming;* also available on-line at http://gopher.well.sf.ca.us:70/0/cyberpunk/cultjam.txt. Also see Andrew Ross, "Hacking Away at the Counter-Culture," in *Technoculture.*

BIBLIOGRAPHY

Adorno, T. W. "Die Aktualität der Philosophie." *Gesammmelte Schriften* I, Frankfurt am Main: Suhrkamp Verlag, 1973, 325–44. Trans. as "The Actuality of Philosophy." *Telos* 31 (spring 1977): 120–33.

———. "Die Idee der Naturgeschichte." In *Philosophische Frühschriften. Gesammmelte Schriften* I, Frankfurt am Main: Suhrkamp Verlag, 1973, 344–65.

Allison, David B., ed. *The New Nietzsche: Contemporary Styles of Interpretation.* New York: Dell Publishing, 1977.

Althusser, Louis, et al. *Reading Capital.* Trans. Ben Brewster. London: Verso Editions, 1979.

Auerbach, Eric. *Mimesis: The Representation of Reality in Western Literature.* Trans. Willard R. Trask. Princeton: Princeton UP, 1953.

Badiou, Alain. "Penser le surgissement de l'événement." *Cahiers du cinéma* (numéro hors série 68, 1998).

Barlow, John Perry. "A Declaration of Independence for Cyberspace." February 1996. http://www.eff.org/pub/Publications/John_Perry_Barlow/barlow_0296.declaration.

Barthes, Roland. *Camera Lucida: Reflections on Photography.* Trans. Richard Howard. New York: Hill and Wang, 1981.

———. "From Work to Text." In *Image/Music/Text,* Trans. and ed. Stephen Heath, 155–64. New York: Hill and Wang, 1977.

———. "The Photographic Message." In *Image/Music/Text,* 15–31.

———. *S/Z.* Trans. Richard Howard. New York: Hill and Wang, 1974.

———. "The Third Meaning." In *Image/Music/Text,* 52–68.

Bellour, Raymond. *L'Entre-images, Photo, Cinéma, Vidéo.* Paris: La Différance, 1990.

———. *L'Entre-images, 2, Mots, Images.* Paris: POL, 1999.

———. "The Unattainable Text." *Screen* 16, no. 3 (autumn 1975): 19–28.

Bender, Gretchen, and Timothy Druckrey, eds. *Culture on the Brink: Ideologies of Technology.* Seattle: Bay Press, 1994.

Benjamin, Walter. "The Doctrine of the Similar." Trans. Knut Tranowski. *New German Critique* 17 (winter 1979): 65–69.

———. *Illuminationen.* Franfurt am Main: Suhrkamp, 1977. Trans. Harry Zohn as *Illuminations.* Ed. Hannah Arendt. Glasgow: Fontana, 1977.

———. *Ursprung des deutschen Trauerspiel.* Frankfurt am Main: Suhrkamp, 1974. Trans. John Osborne as *The Origin of German Tragic Drama.* London: NLB, 1977.

Benveniste, Emile. *Problèmes de linguistique générale.* Vol. 2. Paris: Gallimard, 1974.

Berlin, Isaiah. "*History and Theory:* The Concept of Scientific History." *History and Theory* 1, no. 1 (1960): 1–31.

Binkley, Timothy. "Camera Fantasia." *Millennium Film Journal* 20–21 (fall–winter 1988–1989): 7–43.

———. "Refiguring Culture." In *Future Visions: New Technologies of the Screen,* ed. Philip Hayward and Tana Wollen, 92–122. London: British Film Institute, 1993.

Bloch, Ernst. "Nonsynchronism and Its Obligation to Dialectics." Trans. Mark Ritter. *New German Critique* 11 (spring 1977): 22–37.

Bolter, Jay David. *Writing Space: The Computer, Hypertext, and the History of Writing.* Hillsdale: Lawrence Erlsbaum Associates, 1991.

Bolter, Jay David, and Richard Grusin. "Remediation." *Configurations* 3 (1997): 311–58.

Brand, Stewart. *The Media Lab.* New York: Penguin, 1987.

Brook, James, and Iain A. Boal, eds. *Resisting the Virtual Life.* San Francisco: City Lights, 1995.

Brunette, Peter, and David Wills. *Screen/Play.* Princeton: Princeton UP, 1989.

Bruno, Guiliana. "Towards a Theorization of Film History." *iris* 2, no. 2 (1984): 41–55.

Buck-Morss, Susan. *The Origin of Negative Dialectics.* New York: Free Press, 1977.

Carroll, David. *Paraesthetics: Foucault, Lyotard, Derrida.* New York: Methuen, 1987.

Cassirer, Ernst. *The Philosophy of the Enlightenment.* Princeton: Princeton UP, 1951.

Caygill, Howard. *Art of Judgement.* Oxford: Basil Blackwell, 1989.

Davies, Simon. "Europe to U.S.: No Privacy, No Trade." *Wired* 6.05 (May 1998): 135–36.

Deleuze, Gilles. *L'Abécédaire de Gilles Deleuze.* Video. Paris: Vidéo Editions Montparnasse, 1996.

———. "A quoi reconnaît-on le structuralisme?" In *La Philosophie au XXeme siècle,* vol. 4, ed. François Chatelet. Paris: Hachette (Marabout), 1978. Trans. Melissa McMahon and Charles Stivale as "How Do We Recognize Structuralism?" In *The Two-Fold Thought of Deleuze and Guattari,* 251–82.

———. *Cinema 1: The Movement-Image.* Trans. Hugh Tomlinson and Barbara Habberjam. Minneapolis: U of Minnesota P, 1986.

———. *Cinema 2: The Time-Image.* Trans. Hugh Tomlinson and Robert Galeta. Minneapolis: U of Minnesota P, 1989.

———. *Difference and Repetition.* Trans. Paul Patton. New York: Columbia UP, 1994.

———. *Foucault.* Paris: Éditions de Minuit, 1986. Trans. and ed. Seán Hand. Minneapolis: U of Minnesota P, 1988.

———. *The Logic of Sense.* Trans. Mark Lester with Charles Stivale. Ed. Constantin V. Boundas. New York: Columbia UP, 1990. Originally published as *Logique du sens.* Paris: Éditions de Minuit, 1969.

———. *Negotiations: 1972–1990.* Trans. Martin Joughin. New York: Columbia UP, 1995. Originally published as *Pourparlers.* Paris: Éditions de Minuit, 1990.

———. *Nietzsche et la philosophie.*

Paris: PUF, 1962. *Nietzsche and Philosophy.* Trans. Hugh Tomlinson. New York: Columbia UP, 1983.

Deleuze, Gilles, and Félix Guattari. *Anti-Oedipe.* Paris: Éditions de Minuit, 1972. Trans. Robert Hurley et al. Minneapolis: U of Minnesota P, 1983.

———. *A Thousand Plateaus.* Trans. Brian Massumi. Minneapolis: U of Minnesota P, 1987.

———. *What is Philosophy?* Trans. Hugh Tomlinson and Graham Burchell. New York: Columbia UP, 1994.

Derrida, Jacques. "Economimesis." In *Mimesis des articulations,* Sylviane Agacinski et al., 57–93. Paris: Aubier-Flammarion, 1975. Trans. R. Klein. *Diacritics* 11 (1981): 3–25.

———. "Freud and the Scene of Writing." In *Writing and Difference,* Trans. Alan Bass, 196–231. Chicago: U of Chicago P, 1978.

———. *La verité en peinture.* Paris: Flammarion, 1978. Trans. Geoff Bennington. *The Truth in Painting.* Chicago: U of Chicago P, 1987.

———. *Of Grammatology.* Trans. Gayatri Chakravorty Spivak. Baltimore: Johns Hopkins UP, 1976.

———. "The Parergon." Trans. Craig Owens. *October* 9 (summer 1979): 3–40.

Dery, Mark. *Culture Jamming.* Westfield, N.J.: Open Magazine. Also http://gopher.well.sf.ca.us:70/0/cyberpunk/cultjam.txt.

———, ed. *Flame Wars: The Discourse of Cyberculture.* Durham: Duke UP, 1994.

Descombes, Vincent. *Modern French Philosophy.* Trans. L. Scott-Fox and J. M. Harding. Cambridge: Cambridge UP, 1980.

Dibble, Julian. "A Rape in Cyberspace." In *Flame Wars: The Discourse of Cyberculture,* ed. Mark Dery, 237–62. Durham: Duke UP, 1994.

Duhême, Jacqueline. *L'oiseau philosohie.* Paris: Éditions du Seuil, 1997.

Eagleton, Terry. *The Ideology of the Aesthetic.* Cambridge: Basil Blackwell, 1990.

Eder, Joseph Maria. *History of Photography.* New York: Dover, 1945.

Edwards, N. Paul. *The Closed World: Computers and the Politics of Discourse in Cold War America.* Cambridge: MIT Press, 1996.

Eisenstein, Sergei M. "Perspectives." In *Film Essays and a Lecture,* ed. Jay Leyda, 35–47. New York: Praeger, 1970.

———. *Selected Works,* vol. 1, *Writings, 1922–34.* Ed. and trans. Richard Howard. London: BFI Publishing, 1988.

Eribon, Didier. *Michel Foucault.* Paris: Flammarion, 1991.

"Film and Popular Memory: *Cahiers du Cinéma*/Extracts," *Edinburgh Magazine* 2 (1977): 19–36.

Focillion, Henri. *The Life of Forms in Art.* Trans. Charles Beecher Hogan and George Kubler. New Haven: Yale UP, 1963.

Foucault, Michel. *The Archaeology of Knowledge.* Trans. A. M. Sheridan Smith. New York: Harper and Row, 1972.

———. *The Birth of the Clinic.* Trans.

A. M. Sheridan Smith. New York:
Vintage Books, 1975.

———. *Discipline and Punish*. Trans.
Alan Sheridan. New York: Vintage,
1979.

———. *Dits et écrits*. Ed. Daniel Defert
and François Ewald. 4 vols. Paris:
Gallimard, 1994.

———. *Language, Counter-memory,
Practice: Selected Essays and Inter-
views*. Ed. Donald F. Bouchard.
Ithaca: Cornell UP, 1977.

———. *Les mots et les choses*. Paris:
Gallimard, 1966. *The Order of Things*.
New York: Vintage Books, 1973.

———. *This Is Not a Pipe*. Trans. James
Harkness. Berkeley: U of California P, 1983.

Freud, Sigmund. "A Child Is being
Beaten." In *Collected Papers*, vol. 2,
trans. Joan Riviere, 171–202. London:
Hogarth Press, 1971.

———. *The Interpretation of Dreams*.
In *The Standard Edition of the Complete Psychological Works of Sigmund
Freud*, trans. and ed. James Strachey,
vols. 4–5. London: Hogarth Press,
1953.

———. "The Unconscious." In *The
Standard Edition of the Complete
Psychological Works of Sigmund
Freud*, vol. 14, 159–216.

Gadamer, Hans-Georg. *Truth and
Method*. New York: Crossroad, 1984.

Gandy, Oscar H., Jr. "Operating the
Panoptic Sort." In *The Panoptic Sort:
A Political Economy of Personal Information*. Boulder: Westview Press,
1993.

Goodman, Nelson. *Languages of Art:
An Approach to a Theory of Symbols*.
Indianapolis: Hackett, 1976.

Guillory, John. *Cultural Capital: The
Problem of Literary Canon Formation*.
Chicago: U of Chicago P, 1993.

Hafner, Katie, and Matthew Lyon.
*Where Wizards Stay Up Late: The
Origins of the Internet*. New York:
Simon and Schuster, 1996.

Hansen, Miriam. "Benjamin, Cinema,
and Experience: 'The Blue Flower
in the Land of Technology.' " *New
German Critique* 40 (winter 1987):
179–224.

———. "Early Silent Cinema: Whose
Public Sphere?" *New German Critique* 29 (spring–summer 1983):
147–84.

Haraway, Donna. "A Cyborg Manifesto:
Science, Technology, and Socialist-
Feminism in the Late Twentieth
Century." In *Simians, Cyborgs, and
Women: The Reinvention of Nature*,
149–81. New York: Routledge, 1991.

Hegel, G. W. F. *Phänomenologie des
Geistes*. In *Sämtliche Werke*, vol. 3.
Leipzig: Verlag von Felix Meiner,
1928.

Heim, Michael. *Electric Language: A
Philosophical Study of Word Processing*. New Haven: Yale UP, 1987.

Henwood, Doug. "The Long Boom."
Left Business Observer 78 (1997): 1–2.

Human Rights Watch. "Freedom of
Expression on the Internet." 1998.
http://www.hrw.org/hrw/advocacy/
internet/fe-wr98.htm.

Hyppolite, Jean. *Etudes sur Marx et
Hegel*. Paris: Marcel Rivière, 1955.

———. *Genèse et structure de la Phéno-*

ménologie de l'esprit de Hegel. Paris: Éditions Montaigne, 1946.

———. Introduction à la philosophie de l'histoire de Hegel. 1948. Paris: Editions du Seuil, 1983.

———. Logique et existence: Essai sur la logique de Hegel. Paris: PUP, 1953.

Jakobson, Roman. "Closing Statement: Linguistics and Poetics." In Style in Language, ed. Thomas A. Sebeok, 350–77. Cambridge: MIT Press, 1964.

Jameson, Fredric. Marxism and Form. Princeton: Princeton UP, 1971.

———. Postmodernism, or The Cultural Logic of Late Capital. Durham: Duke UP, 1991.

Jay, Martin. Downcast Eyes: The Denigration of Vision in Twentieth-Century Thought. Berkeley: U of California P, 1993.

———. "The Extraterritorial Life of Siegfried Kracauer." Salmagundi 31–32 (fall 1975–winter 1976): 49–106.

Kafka, Franz. Parables and Paradoxes. New York: Schocken Paperbacks, 1966.

Kant, Immanuel. Anthropology from a Pragmatic Point of View. Trans. Victor Lyle Dowdell. Rev. and ed. Hans H. Rudnick with an introd. by Frederick P. Van De Pitte. Carbondale: Southern Illinois University Press, 1978.

———. Kritik der Urteilskraft. Frankfurt am Main: Suhrkamp Taschenbuch Verlag, 1974. Trans. Werner S. Pluhar. Critique of Judgment. Indianapolis: Hackett Publishing, 1987.

Klee, Félix, ed. P. Klee par lui-même et par son fils F. Klee. Paris: Les libraires associés, 1963.

Klee, Paul. Das bildnerische Denken. Ed. Jürg Spiller. Bâle-Stuttgart: Benno Schwabe, 1956.

Kojève, Aléxandre. Introduction à la lecture de Hegel: Leçons sur la Phénoménologie d l'esprit. Ed. Raymond Queneau. Paris: Gallimard, 1947.

Kovács, András Bálint. "The Film History of Thought." In The Brain Is a Screen: Gilles Deleuze and the Philosophy of Cinema, ed. Gregory Flaxmann, 153–70. Minneapolis: U of Minnesota P, 1999.

Kracauer, Siegfried. Das Ornament der Masse. Frankfurt am Main: Suhrkamp Verlag, 1963. The Mass Ornament: Weimar Essays. Trans. with introduction by Thomas Y. Levin. Cambridge: Harvard UP, 1995.

———. Die Angestellten. Frankfurt am Main: Frankfurter Societäts-Druckerei, 1930.

———. History: The Last Things before the Last. New York: Oxford UP, 1969.

———. "The Mass Ornament." Trans. Barbara Correll and Jack Zipes. New German Critique 2 no. 5 (spring 1975): 67–76.

———. Theory of Film: The Redemption of Physical Reality. New York: Oxford University Press, 1965.

Kristeva, Julia. Semeiotikē: Recherches pour une sémanalyse. Paris: Seuil, 1969.

Kroker, Arthur, and Michael Weinstein. Data Trash. New York: St. Martin's Press, 1994.

Kubler, George. The Shape of Time: Remarks on the History of Things. New Haven: Yale UP, 1962.

Kuntzel, Thierry. "The Film-Work."

Trans. Lawrence Crawford, Kimball Lockhart, and Claudia Tysdal. *Enclitic* 2, no. 1 (spring 1978): 38–61.

———. "The Film-Work, 2." Trans. Nancy Huston. *Camera Obscura* 5 (spring 1980): 6–69.

Lacan, Jacques. *Écrits: A Selection.* Trans. Alan Sheridan. New York: W. W. Norton, 1977.

Landow, George P. *Hypertext and Literary Study: The Convergence of Contemporary Critical Theory and Technology.* Baltimore: Johns Hopkins UP, 1992.

Lanham, Richard. *The Electronic Word: Democracy, Technology, and the Arts.* Chicago: U of Chicago P, 1993.

Lessing, Gotthold Ephraim. *Laocoön: An Essay on the Limits of Painting and Poetry.* Trans. with an introduction by Edward Allen McCormick. Baltimore: Johns Hopkins UP, 1962.

Lévi-Strauss, Claude. *The Savage Mind.* London: Wiedenfeld and Nicolson, 1966. *La pensée sauvage.* Paris: Plon, 1962.

Lévy, Pierre. *Cyberculture.* Paris: Editions Odile Jacob, 1997.

Levy, Stephen. *Hackers: Heroes of the Computer Revolution.* New York: Dell, 1994.

Lukács, Georg. *History and Class Consciousness.* Trans. Rodney Livingstone. Cambridge: MIT P, 1971.

———. *Theory of the Novel.* Trans. Ann Bostock. Cambridge: MIT P, 1971.

Lyon, David. *The Electronic Eye: The Rise of Surveillance Society.* Minneapolis: U of Minnesota P, 1994.

Lyotard, Jean-François. *Discours, figure.* Paris: Klincksieck, 1971.

———. "The Dream-Work Does Not Think." Trans. Mary Lydon. *Oxford Literary Review* 6, no. 1 (1983): 3–34.

———. *Driftworks.* Ed. Roger McKeon. New York: Semiotext(e), 1984.

———. "Fiscourse, Digure: The Utopia behind the Scenes of Phantasy." Trans. Mary Lydon. *Theatre Journal* 35, no. 3 (October 1983): 333–57.

———. *Leçons sur l'Analytique du sublime.* Paris: Galilée, 1991.

———. *L'inhumain: Causeries sur le temps.* Paris: Galilée, 1988.

———. *The Postmodern Condition: A Report on Knowledge.* Trans. Geoff Bennington and Brian Massumi. Minneapolis: U of Minnesota P, 1984.

———. "Presenting the Unpresentable: The Sublime." *Artforum* 20, no. 8 (April 1982): 64–69.

———. "The Sublime and the Avant-Garde." *Artforum* 22, no. 8 (April 1984): 36–43.

Mandel, Ernst. *Late Capitalism.* Trans. Joris De Bres. London: Verso, 1980.

Merleau-Ponty, Maurice. *Sense and Non-Sense.* Trans. Hubert L. Dreyfus and Patricia Allen Dreyfus. Northwestern UP, 1964.

Metz, Christian. *Film Language.* Trans. Michael Taylor. Chicago: U of Chicago P, 1974.

———. *Language and Cinema.* Trans. Donna-Jean Umiker-Sebeok. The Hague: Mouton, 1974.

Mitchell, William J. *The Reconfigured Eye: Visual Truth in the Post-photographic Era.* Cambridge: MIT P, 1994.

Nietzsche, Friedrich. *Untimely Medi-*

tations. Trans. R. J. Hollingdale. Cambridge: Cambridge UP, 1983.

Palatella, John. "Formatting Patrimony: The Rhetoric of Hypertext." *Afterimage* 23, no. 1 (1995): 13.

Peters, F. E. *Greek Philosophical Terms.* New York: New York UP, 1967.

Pittmann, Robert W. "We're Talking the Wrong Language to 'TV Babies.'" *New York Times,* 24 January 1990, A23.

Polan, Dana. " 'Desire Shifts the Difference': Figural Poetics and Figural Politics in the Film Theory of Marie-Claire Ropars-Wuilleumier." *Camera Obscura* 12 (summer 1984): 67–85.

————. "Powers of Vision, Visions of Power." *Camera Obscura* 18 (September 1988): 106–19.

Poster, Mark. *Existential Marxism in Postwar France: From Sartre to Althusser.* Princeton: Princeton UP, 1975.

————. *The Mode of Information: Poststructuralism and Social Context.* London: Blackwell, 1990.

————. *The Second Media Age.* Cambridge: Polity Press, 1995.

Prédal, René. *50 ans de cinéma français.* Paris: Nathan, 1996.

Prigogine, Ilya, and Isabelle Stengers. *Order Out of Chaos.* New York: Bantam, 1984.

Reid, Elizabeth. "Cultural Formations in Text-Based Virtual Realities." Thesis, University of Melbourne, 1994.

Reif, Rita. "Dede Brooks Makes Her Bid." *New York Times Magazine,* 2 April 1989, 27.

Rentschler, Eric. "Ten Theses on Kracauer, Spectatorship, and the Seventies." Paper presented at the conference of the Society for Cinema Studies, New Orleans, Louisiana, 4–6 April 1986.

Rheingold, Howard. *The Virtual Community: Homesteading on the Electronic Frontier.* Reading: Addison-Wesley, 1993.

Robins, Kevin, and Frank Webster. "Cybernetic Capitalism." In *The Political Economy of Information,* ed. Vincent Mosco and Janet Wasko, 44–75. Madison: U of Wisconsin P, 1988.

————. *Information Technology: A Luddite Analysis.* Norwood: Ablex, 1986.

Rodowick, D. N. "Audiovisual Culture and Interdisciplinary Knowledge." *New Literary History* 26 (1995): 111–21. Also www.rochester.edu/College/FS/DigiCult/.

————. *The Crisis of Political Modernism: Criticism and Ideology in Contemporary Film Theory.* 2d ed. Berkeley: U of California P, 1994.

————. *The Difficulty of Difference: Psychoanalysis, Sexual Difference, and Film Theory.* New York: Routledge, 1991.

————. *Gilles Deleuze's Time Machine.* Durham: Duke UP, 1997.

Ropars-Wuilleumier, Marie-Claire. "The Graphic in Filmic Writing: *À bout de soufflé,* or The Erratic Alphabet." *Enclitic* 5.2–6.1 (spring 1982): 147–61. Also published as "L'Instance graphique dans l'écriture du film: *A bout de soufle,* ou l'alphabet erratique," *Littérature* 46 (1982): 59–81.

————. "Overall Perspectives." The

Enclitic International Conference on the Textual Analysis of Film. 16 May 1981.

———. "The Overture of *October*." Trans. Kimball Lockhart and Larry Crawford. *Enclitic* 2, no. 2 (fall 1978): 50–72.

———. "The Overture of *October*, Part II." Trans. Kimball Lockhart and Larry Crawford. *Enclitic* 3, no. 1 (spring 1979): 35–47.

———. *Le texte divisé.* Paris: PUF, 1981.

Rorty, Richard. *Philosophy and the Mirror of Nature.* Princeton: Princeton UP, 1979.

Rosen, Phil. "History, Textuality, Nation: Kracauer, Burch, and Some Problems in the Study of National Cinema." *iris* 2, no. 2 (1984): 69–84.

Ross, Andrew. "Hacking Away at the Counter-Culture." In *Technoculture*, ed. Constance Penley and Andrew Ross, 107–34. Minneapolis: U of Minnesota P, 1991.

Saussure, Ferdinand de. *Cours de linguistique générale.* Paris: Payot, 1982.

Schwartz, Peter, and Peter Leyden. "The Long Boom." *Wired* 5.07 (July 1997): 115–29. Also www.wired.com/wired/archive/5.07/longboom.html.

Schrift, Alan D. *Nietzsche's French Legacy: A Genealogy of Poststructuralism.* New York: Routledge, 1995.

Sobchack, Vivian. "The Scene of the Screen: Envisioning Cinematic and Electronic 'Presence.'" In *Materialities of Communication*, ed. Hans Ulrich Gumbrecht and K. Ludwig Pfeiffer, 83–106. Stanford: Stanford UP, 1994.

———. "Teenage Mutant Ninja Hackers." In *Flame Wars: The Discourse of Cyberculture*, ed. Mark Dery, 11–28. Durham: Duke UP, 1994.

Sollers, Philippe. "Niveaux semantiques d'un texte moderne." In *Théorie d'ensemble*, 317–25. Paris: Seuil, 1968.

Sterling, Bruce. *Hacker Crackdown! Law and Disorder on the Electronic Frontier.* New York: Bantam Books, 1992.

Stivale, Charles. *The Two-Fold Thought of Deleuze and Guattari: Intersections and Animations.* New York: Guilford Press, 1998.

Stone, Allucquère Rosanne. *The War between Desire and Technology at the Close of the Mechanical Age.* Cambridge: MIT P, 1995.

———. "Will the Real Body Please Stand Up?" In *Cyberspace: First Steps*, ed. Michael Benedikt, 81–118. Cambridge: MIT P, 1991.

Toffler, Alvin. *The Third Wave.* New York: William Morrow, 1980.

Turkle, Sherry. *Life on the Screen: Identity in the Age of the Internet.* New York: Simon and Schuster, 1995.

———. *The Second Self: Computers and the Human Spirit.* New York: Simon and Schuster, 1984.

Walker, John. "Through the Looking Glass." In *The Art of Human-Computer Interface Design*, ed. Brenda Laurel, 430–47. Reading: Addison-Wesley Publishing, 1990.

Wallace, William. *Kant.* Philadelphia: Lippincott, n.d.

Wellbery, David. *Lessing's "Laocoön":*

Semiotics and Aesthetics in the Age of Reason. Cambridge: Cambridge UP, 1984.

Wicke, Jennifer. "The Perfume of Information." *Yale Journal of Criticism* 1, no. 1 (1987): 145–60.

Williams, Raymond. *Keywords.* New York: Oxford University Press, 1976.

Winner, Langdon. "Silicon Valley Mystery House." In *Variations on a Theme Park: The New American City and the End of Public Space,* ed. Michael Sorkin, 31–60. New York: Hill and Wang, 1992.

Witte, Karsten. "Introduction to Siegfried Kracauer's 'The Mass Ornament.'" Trans. Barbara Correll and Jack Zipes. *New German Critique* 5 (spring 1975): 59–66.

Wölfflin, Heinrich. *Principles of Art History.* Trans. M. D. Hottinger. New York: Dover Publications, 1932.

Originally published as *Kunstgeschichtliche Grundbegriffe: Das Problem der Stilentwicklung in der neueren Kunst.* Basel: Schwabe, 1963.

Worringer, Wilhelm. *Abstraction and Empathy.* Trans. Michael Bullock. New York: International Universities Press, 1953.

———. *Form in Gothic.* Ed. Herbert Read. New York: Schocken Books, 1964.

Žižek, Slavoj. "Cyberspace, or The Unbearable Closure of Being." In *Endless Night: Cinema and Psychoanalysis, Parallel Histories,* ed. Janet Bergstrom, 96–125. Berkeley: U of California P, 1999.

———. "Multiculturalism, or, The Cultural Logic of Multinational Capitalism." *New Left Review* (1997): 28–51.

INDEX

D. N. RODOWICK is Professor of Film Studies at King's College, London.

Library of Congress Cataloging-in-Publication Data
Rodowick, David Norman.
Reading the figural, or Philosophy after the new media / D.N. Rodowick.
p. cm. — (Post-contemporary interventions)
Includes bibliographical references and index.
ISBN 0-8223-2711-2 (cloth : alk. paper) — ISBN 0-8223-2722-8 (pbk. : alk. paper)
1. Mass media—Philosophy.   2. Visual communication.   3. Semiotics.
4. Aesthetics.   I. Title: Reading the figural.   II. Title: Philosophy after the
new media.   III. Title.   IV. Series.
P91 .R626   2001   302.23′01—dc21   2001023111